SCOTT BURTON: COLLECTED WRITINGS ON ART & PERFORMANCE, 1965–1975

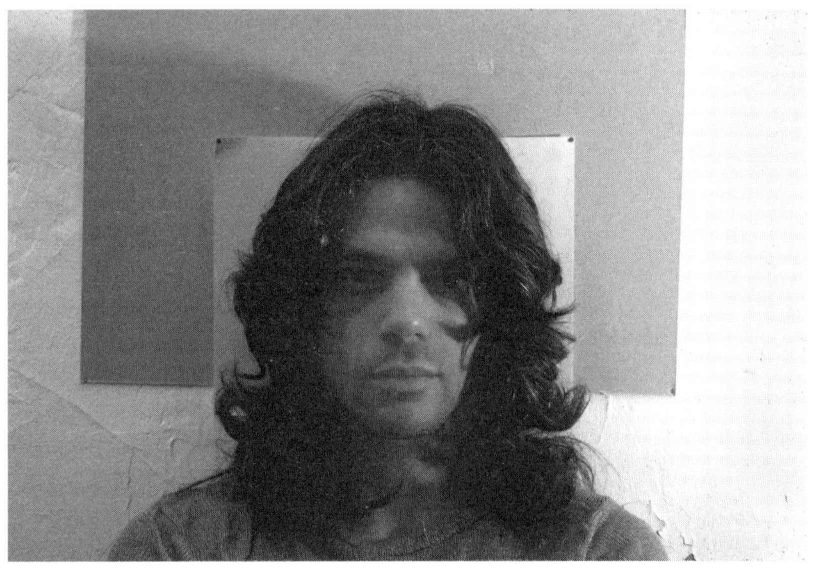

Photo of Scott Burton, c.1973. Scott Burton Papers V.10, Museum of Modern Art Archives, New York.

SCOTT BURTON

COLLECTED WRITINGS ON ART & PERFORMANCE, 1965–1975

EDITED BY DAVID J. GETSY

SOBERSCOVE PRESS
CHICAGO

Soberscove Press
1055 N Wolcott, 2F
Chicago, IL 60622 USA
www.soberscovepress.com

Library of Congress Control Number: 2012945896
Burton, Scott, 1939–1989
Scott Burton: collected writings on art and performance, 1965–1975 / edited by David J. Getsy.

First Printing, 2012
Design by Rita Lascaro
ISBN-13: 978-0-9824090-4-6

CONTENTS

CREDITS

Tony Smith and Minimalist Sculpture (1967). Scott Burton Papers, [II.12], The Museum of Modern Art Archives, NY. © 2012 Estate of Scott Burton/Artist Rights Society (ARS).

Tony Smith: Old Master at the New Frontier (1966). Copyright © 1966, ARTnews, LLC.

"Notes on the New," in Harald Szeemann, ed., *Live in Your Head: When Attitudes Become Form* (Bern: Kunsthalle Bern, 1969). Copyright © 1969 Kunsthalle Bern.

Time on Their Hands (1969). Copyright © 1969, ARTnews, LLC.

David Weinrib: See-Through Sculpture (1967). Copyright © 1967, ARTnews, LLC.

Ralph Humphrey: A Different Stripe (1968). Copyright © 1968, ARTnews, LLC.

Al Held: Big H (1968). Copyright © 1968, ARTnews, LLC.

Scott Burton, "Adja Yunkers: The Eye's Edge," Studio International 175.899 (April 1968). Courtesy The Studio Trust. www.studiointernational.com

Doug Ohlson: In The Wind (1968). Copyright © 1968, ARTnews, LLC.

Leon Berkowitz: Color It Berkowitz (1969). Copyright © 1969, ARTnews, LLC.

"Generation of Light, 1945–70," in Thomas Hess and John Ashbery, eds., *Light in Art* (New York: Collier Books, 1971). Copyright © 1969, ARTnews, LLC.

Robert Beauchamp: Paint the Devil (1966). Copyright © 1966, ARTnews, LLC.

"Letter to the Editors," *Artforum* 5.5 (January 1967). © *Artforum*, January, 1967.

Herman Rose: Telling and Showing (1967). Copyright © 1967, ARTnews, LLC.

George McNeil and the Figure (1967). Copyright © 1967, ARTnews, LLC.

The Realist Revival. Reprinted, with permission from the publisher, from Scott Burton, *The Realist Revival* (New York: The American Federation of Arts, 1972).

"Three Street Works," *0 to 9* 6 / supplement (1969). Courtesy Vito Acconci and Bernadette Mayer.

Literalist Theater (1970). Scott Burton Papers, [II.27]. The Museum of Modern Archives, NY. © 2012 Estate of Scott Burton/Artist Rights Society (ARS).

The Group Behavior Tableaux, early texts (1971–72). Scott Burton Papers, [II.43]. The Museum of Modern Archives, NY. © 2012 Estate of Scott Burton/Artist Rights Society (ARS).

Lecture on Self (1973). Scott Burton Papers, [II.52]. The Museum of Modern Archives, NY. © 2012 Estate of Scott Burton/Artist Rights Society (ARS).

The Primacy of Sensibility: Scott Burton writing on art and performance, 1965–1975

David J. Getsy

Scott Burton is often narrowly associated with the art of the 1980s, the decade in which his functional and intentionally self-effacing sculpture was widely exhibited and discussed. However, Burton was an active participant in the art world of the 1960s and 1970s—as an art critic, as an editor for *ARTnews* and *Art in America*, as a curator, and as a performance artist. He only turned to sculpture as his primary practice around 1975, after becoming established as an artist with his *Behavior Tableaux* performances, which were shown throughout the 1970s at major venues including the Whitney, the Guggenheim, and Documenta VI. Burton's identification with the burgeoning field of performance art in the 1970s, too, transformed his earlier reputation; up to that point, he had been known principally as a critic.

This book brings together Burton's writings on art and performance from these years, tracing his development as an art critic and including his early artist statements. This period, from 1965 to 1975, was foundational for Burton's later artistic practice and was remarkably varied in the commitments he pursued. After he started making art in 1969 amidst his active engagement with art writing, Burton became a unique and opinionated example of the artist-critic that characterized the contentious period and its heated debates.

Despite the fact that Burton produced a substantial body of art writing—including important texts such as the introduction to the groundbreaking exhibition of Postminimal art *Live in Your Head: When Attitudes Become Form* in 1969—his criticism has rarely been discussed. This is perhaps due to its eclecticism: Burton championed positions that others held as mutually exclusive and antagonistic. He advocated for reductive abstract art at the same time as he did figuration; he wrote extended evaluations of artists as different as Tony Smith and Alex Katz; and he argued for the urgency of considering time-based and ephemeral artistic practices in the same years that he curated exhibitions of realist painting. Burton also loved the underdogs, and he often chose to write about artists whose work needed articulate spokespersons to differentiate them from dominant tendencies. This was especially the case with Burton's critical relationship to Minimalism. He immersed himself in the ideas surrounding Minimalism and came out on the other side with an appreciation of its emphasis on the viewer but also with a suspicion of its rarefied and homogenizing account of that viewer. By contrast, he came to advocate for artists who used reductive formal vocabularies quite differently than the "methodical cerebrations of a Judd or a Noland."[1] Indeed, when Burton emerged as an artist he became exemplary of "Postminimalism," the term coined by Robert Pincus-Witten to describe the time- and process-based reactions to Minimalism that emerged in the late 1960s.[2]

I began to be interested in Burton's writing as part of my own research on his early performance art. I was struck by the moments of perspicacity and prescience in the texts and by the unexpected collisions he offered. As I came to realize, most important in these writings is the central role he gave to the theatrical, the temporal, the affective, and the performative. One can find in Burton a critic who argued for the cross-fertilization

---

1. "Ralph Humphrey: A Different Stripe," p. 101.

2. Pincus-Witten would write two essays on Burton's work in the 1970s: Robert Pincus-Witten, "Scott Burton: Conceptual Performance as Sculpture," *Arts Magazine* 51, no. 1 (September 1976): 112–17 and Robert Pincus-Witten, "Camp Meetin': The Furniture Pieces of Scott Burton," *Arts Magazine* 53, no. 1 (September 1978): 103–05. The former was reprinted in Robert Pincus-Witten, *Postminimalism* (New York: Out of London Press, 1977) and both essays were included in the expansion of that book as Robert Pincus-Witten, *Postminimalism into Maximalism: American Art, 1966–1986* (Ann Arbor, Michigan: UMI Research Press, 1987).

of sculpture and performance as a means of understanding how art could be social, personal, and accessible.

Taken together, these texts do reveal Burton's early formulation of a desire to make public and demotic art, his critique of the art world's hermeticism and elitism, and his critical grasp of the implications and exclusions of mainstream narratives of 1960s art. He pursued his writing with humor and purpose, hoping to establish alternative positions from the dominating and normative critical positions. Distinct in the texts is Burton's increasing concern with art's appeal to affects, empathies, and subjective responses. His own Postminimalism involved finding a place for particularity and difference contra the blanked universalism that the Minimalist invocation of the viewer implied. Accessibility was a consistent theme of his artistic and critical practice, up through his development of public art. In these early years, he came to see realism, figuration, and the literalist address to the viewer's co-presence as key terms for moving art away from elitism and as incitements for individual and public engagements.

At the same time, these texts are valuable beyond the ways in which they inform Burton's own art. He was an adroit commentator on art theory, often making wild and perverse connections across party lines. Art criticism became urgent in the 1960s because of its participants' awareness that they were formulating a new canon, and many writers were narrow in their advocacy. Burton, however, remained consistent in his ethics and interests but promiscuous in the styles and positions he defended. Consequently, his voice is distinct from his contemporaries, and readers from many different positions will recognize their own priorities in Burton's texts. This openness is what he intended, so those concerned with the status of figuration or with reductive geometric art will both find Burton making insightful observations. Many of the artists about whom Burton wrote will be unfamiliar to all but the most specialized of readers, but each of the essays contains discussions of larger themes for the art of the 1960s and 1970s that are relevant to an understanding of this contentious period of artmaking. These are joined by Burton's contributions to the theorization of performance art in the early 1970s—texts that provide important commentary on the status of performance as well as Burton's own varied practices.

Burton always saw himself as a bit of an outsider. Born in Alabama in 1939 and raised by a single mother there and, later in his teen years, in Washington, D.C., he understood his entry into the New York art world as one of the infiltrator. His attachment to the vernacular and the rustic that would emerge in some of his earliest sculptures was an expression of his critical position toward the self-congratulatory culture of New York as cultural center. He did, however, receive a focused education in art, most importantly from the Washington-based abstract painter Leon Berkowitz and his wife Ida Fox, both of whom were important influences on the teenage Burton. In addition to his own teaching, Berkowitz was also instrumental in arranging Burton's study with Hans Hofmann in Hofmann's summer school in Provincetown in the late 1950s. It was there that Burton also found his first sustained engagement with gay culture, and his sexuality grew to become a central theme of much of his work in the 1970s.[3] Referring to the small town's historic role as a haven both for artistic and for gay and lesbian communities, Burton recalled, "Hofmann was a very important teacher, and I was one of his last students. I learned something from Hofmann about art, but I learned a great deal more from Provincetown about life—and about art."[4] For his undergraduate education, he moved through a few colleges starting in 1958

3. I discuss the relation of Burton's sexuality to his artistic priorities at length in the chapter on Burton from the book I am currently completing.

4. Audio recording of March 1980 interview with Burton by Edward de Celle, Edward Brooks de Celle Papers, Archives of American Art, Smithsonian Institution.

(Goddard College, George Washington University, and Harvard University) before moving to New York in 1959, where he would complete his BA magna cum laude at Columbia University in 1962. It was in New York that he became romantically involved with the figurative painter John Button (around 1961), who proved to be a decisive influence during their almost decade-long relationship throughout the 1960s.

Burton's ambition in this decade was to be a writer, and he stopped painting during his undergraduate years. He went on to receive a master's degree in English literature from New York University in 1963, and his first related job was as a reader for the notable New York literary agency Sterling Lord from 1964 to 1965. Theater became his main focus. He wrote a play based on the Ganymede myth titled "The Eagle and the Lamb," and his "Saint George" was produced at the Shakespeare Memorial Theater in Stratford, Connecticut, in 1964, with the support of Lincoln Kirstein. Button, older than Burton by a decade, was instrumental. He introduced his younger partner to the gay social networks that ran throughout the New York artistic and literary scene, and it was in this milieu that Burton spent most of his twenties. It was there that Burton came into contact with and often was befriended by the likes of Kirstein, Jerome Robbins, Frank O'Hara, Edwin Denby, Edward Albee, and his fellow Columbia student Terrence McNally.[5] (He also became friends with other figurative artists such as Sylvia Sleigh and Philip Pearlstein.) These same circles introduced Burton to the New York School poets, and Burton's earliest professional entrées came from gay men associated with theater, poetry, and criticism.[6] These years were formative for Burton's

5. See Scott Burton interview with Lewis Kachur, Oral History Project, Archives of American Art, Smithsonian Institution, Washington, D.C., Interview I: May 22, 1987.

6. On this milieu, see, for instance, Maggie Nelson, *Women, the New York School, and Other True Abstractions* (Iowa City: University of Iowa Press, 2007) and Gavin Butt, *Between You and Me: Queer Disclosures in the New York Art World, 1948-1963* (Durham and London: Yale University Press, 2005)

attitudes on art, and his engagement with both figurative art (as in the work of Fairfield Porter, Pearlstein, or Alex Katz) and the more lyrical strain of Abstract Expressionist criticism (exemplified by O'Hara) can be understood to have come from this social network. It was only after his break-up with Button in the late 1960s that Burton made a decisive social break that manifested itself, in part, as an embrace of conceptual art. This artistic education of Burton's set him apart from the largely heterosexual group of Minimalist artists that he came to see as dominating the late 1960s, and his sense of both outsiderness and purpose was fueled by it.

Burton was largely unsuccessful as a playwright. His most important theatrical contribution of the 1960s was to write the libretto for an experimental ballet created to accompany an Aaron Copland composition for the New York City Ballet in 1965. The ballet, *Shadow'd Ground*, was based on Copland's *Dance Panels* (composed some years earlier in 1959 and revised in 1962). It premiered on January 21, 1965, and took the unorthodox format of having four screens behind and above the dancers onto which were projected contextual and narrative images. This experiment did not meet with critical approval.[7] Nevertheless, this was the first manifestation of Burton's interest in tableaux as a means of storytelling, for Burton's libretto was conveyed through the projections of staged photographs of a man and a woman acting out the story. This use of successive still images or tableaux would return in his performance art of the 1970s.

Soon after *Shadow'd Ground*, Burton started writing art criticism. He published his first substantive essay in *Art and Literature* in 1965—the same year that journal republished such heavyweight contributions as Clement Greenberg's "Modernist Painting" and Maurice Merleau-Ponty's "Cézanne's

---

7. Allen Hughes, "Notes on New Ballets," *New York Times* (31 January 1965): X7.

Doubt."[8] Also in 1965, he began writing capsule reviews for *ARTnews*, a magazine at that time associated with both Abstract Expressionism and the New York School poets, many of whom worked as reviewers. As Carter Ratcliff recalled,

> All the poets I was interested in were writing for *ARTnews* or had written for it at some point. Frank O'Hara had written for the magazine. Barbara Guest, James Schuyler. Ted Berrigan, Peter Schjeldahl a little later. Jill Johnston wrote for them at a certain point. And Scott Burton, who wasn't a poet but was very much a part of that world. Bill Berkson. Gerrit Henry. Kenward Elmslie. So many on that list of editorial associates were poets. [. . .] The *ARTnews* review was almost a genre of poetic writing.[9]

Burton joined *ARTnews* as an editorial associate in November 1965, and began writing the short and often unsigned capsule reviews that characterized the magazine's attempt to cover every exhibition in New York. He would start writing regular feature articles the next year and eventually became an assistant editor at the magazine in 1972. Two years later, he became senior editor at *Art in America*, a position he held until 1976. While working at *ARTnews*, Burton also taught English at the School of Visual Arts for five years (from 1967 to 1972), even co-editing a textbook of writings on art for SVA in 1969.[10]

Burton wrote his first major feature article for *ARTnews* in 1966 on Tony Smith. (He had, earlier that year, written an

8. Both in *Art and Literature* 4 (Spring 1965). In addition to new pieces like Burton's, *Art and Literature* (under its editor John Ashbery) sometimes republished important writings such as the 1945 and 1960 essays by Merleau-Ponty and Greenberg, respectively.

9. Carter Ratcliff in Amy Newman, *Challenging Art: Artforum 1962-1974* (New York: Soho Press, 2003), 41.

10. Dorothy Wolfberg, Scott Burton, and John Tarburton, eds., *Exploring the Arts: An Anthology of Basic Readings* (New York: Visual Arts Press, 1969).

essay on his friend Robert Beauchamp for the magazine, but the Smith article was the cover story for the December 1966 issue.) It was an important project for Burton, and it required an extended period of research and interviews. Though it came by way of an assignment from Thomas Hess, the magazine's editor, it grew to be central to Burton's thought.[11] Previously, his interests primarily had followed the figurative art identified with his partner Button, but the Smith essay compelled Burton to engage with reductive abstraction. In many ways, Burton's intellectual independence from Button began through the work on Smith, and one can see early formulations of Burton's critical commitments emerging from within his obeisance to the expectations of an *ARTnews* feature article for Hess. After moving through the required biographical and contextual material, Burton turned to a defense of Smith. For Burton, Smith's reductive formal vocabulary and classical monumentality conveyed "eruptive emotional content."[12] He became excited by what he saw in Smith's work as a direct appeal to the viewer's emotions through physical relations and a sense of scale.

Burton understood Smith's avoidance of overt representation and his disavowal of the autographic gestures that underwrote most other expressive abstraction as expanding, rather than limiting, the ways in which the viewer could subjectively relate to the works. He contrasted this to the "Primary Structurists," his term for those artists who would become associated with Minimalism following the pivotal exhibition *Primary Structures* held earlier that year at the Jewish Museum in New York. Discussing Smith's *Die* (1962), the six-foot cube that would become iconic of reductive formal tendencies in the decade, Burton argued:

11. "[T]he first piece of writing [was] on Tony Smith, who I totally fell in love with and who was a big influence in some way on me ever since. I think Smith is one of the great American artists." Scott Burton interview with Lewis Kachur, Oral History Project, Archives of American Art, Smithsonian Institution, Washington, D.C., Interview I: May 22, 1987.

12. "Tony Smith: Old Master at the New Frontier," p. 42.

> *Die*, his famous black, 6-foot steel cube, looks close to the "new esthetic." Andre, Judd, Morris, and others have all made works as simple in form. But theirs seem to be, among other things, reducing the definition of sculpture to simply "that which man makes with the intention of filling real space." Smith's cube is far from such an esthetic of intention or concept, and is as interesting to look at as to think about. It has an ambiguous scale, a referential color and a loaded title (which Smith explains as both the imperative form of the verb and the noun meaning matrix or mold). Visually, the work fully equals the intensity of its title. *Die*, with a minimum of form, indelibly gives form to—shapes—its environment. What is around it, outdoors as well as in, begins to "lead up" to it, as to a climax. *Die* is not the elimination or antithesis of expression, but the culmination of expression—like a scream so high it can no longer be heard.[13]

Die, he continued, "demands and provokes affective response." He saw the possibility for multiple, particular emotional reactions in viewers incited by the confrontational simplicity of Smith's works, and this realization would characterize Burton's defense of abstract painting and sculpture, as well as his own development of reductive sculptural objects. Disparaging the bland and ironic stance he saw in the work of the Judd, Morris, and Andre, Burton instead began to see how the physical relationality that underwrote minimal forms of 1960s sculpture could be the pathway to particularized, emotive experiences for the viewer.

Burton considered his Tony Smith article only a partial success, and in the following months he expanded his ideas

13. "Tony Smith: Old Master at the New Frontier," p. 42–43.

into a lecture for the Walker Art Center in October of 1967. In this remarkable piece of writing, previously unpublished, Burton bared his convictions and expanded his criticism of Minimalism. Demonstrating a solid grasp of the major themes in the sculpture of the 1960s, Burton positioned Smith in a wide field of his peers and took aim, in particular, at the work of Judd, Andre, and Morris. The rhetoric of Minimalism emphasized the activation of the viewer's encounter, but Burton claimed that Judd's work, for instance, "seems to mock us" and exhibited a "parody of rationality."[14] Though Burton saw value in all of these other artists' positions, he nevertheless considered them to lack urgency and to evince a pedantic and condescending stance toward the viewer:

> [A] great deal of 'reductive' art has real intensity. But it is always didactic; we are being taught; we must think [. . . .] This is *not* the most important thing about looking at a Tony Smith. His art is expressive of feelings, ideas, attitudes that are about more than sculpture, more than art.[15]

Affect, rather than concept, is what Burton valued and what he saw as the promise of Smith's monumental sculpture.

Contained in Burton's writings on Tony Smith are two of the main themes of Burton's subsequent criticism and artistic production: affective response and temporality. Smith's sculpture demanded both, and Burton committed to developing these terms around the work of artists he advocated.

Smith's "art is allusive in a way Minimal art is not," Burton remarked.[16] Allusion, the indirect evocation or reference, became a keyword for his writings on abstraction.

---

14. "Tony Smith and Minimalist Sculpture," p. 50.
15. "Tony Smith and Minimalist Sculpture," p. 53.
16. "Tony Smith and Minimalist Sculpture," p. 57.

Burton argued against what he saw as pretentions to neutrality, regularity, and objectivity in many artists' justifications for geometric and reductive formal vocabularies. Instead, he believed that simplified form opened up the possibility for individualized and particularized engagements, both emotional and intellectual. That is, abstract art's avoidance of representation had the potential to make space for the viewer's own affective responses and identifications. He was critical of accounts of 1960s abstraction that claimed neutrality, seeing in them a compulsory universalism that suppressed—rather than facilitated—individual or alternative engagements by viewers. This focus on a personal and individual relationship between viewer and artwork would become the foundation for his subsequent furniture sculptures, which create an intimate and direct bodily relation between viewers and objects that is unforeclosed and open (in contrast to what he saw as the generic, impersonally cerebral experience of spatial activation that became a common theme of writings on Minimalism). Such recognition of the need for difference and particularity in the viewers' responses also contributed to the aims of other Postminimalist artists such as Eva Hesse and Jackie Winsor. At the formal level, Hesse and Winsor both rejected the homogenous regularity of Minimalist seriality, creating the conditions for difference and uniqueness within their playing out of repetition and geometry. That is, the aim was to create works that displayed both seriality and variation.

Burton, too, wanted to make space for particularity and for alternatives. He understood that activations of the viewers' experiences will be necessarily as multiple and divergent as the number of viewers themselves. He upheld allusion as a means to sanction viewers' personal histories and emotional responses as well as the differences and variety they produced. He insisted on the ways in which the individual's response could never be wholly subsumed into the generic or universal. I would argue that it was Burton's own daily experience of difference as an out gay man that contributed to his suspicion of universality and normativity. Indeed, compared to the proclamations of a Judd or an Andre, Burton's appeals to emotions and personalized engagements stand out. In keeping with his belief in openness, however, Burton would not prioritize any one responsive position—even that of his own personal history. His aim, by contrast, was to defend art that allowed for allusion and affect as a means of promoting particularity and possibility.

Burton's article on the painter Ralph Humphrey contained one of his most important statements on the issue of allusion in abstraction. In it, he praised a number of artists such as Agnes Martin, Ronald Bladen, and Doug Ohlson. He argued that their work, as Tony Smith's, evoked emotional and affective engagements through extremely simplified formal vocabularies. He wrote,

> they share qualities of feeling, of emotional reference expressed in a vocabulary in no way illustrational. They are "abstract allusionists," sometimes dramatic and grand, like Smith or Held, sometimes quiet and contemplative, like Martin, but all dealing essentially in affect rather than idea. They are image-makers, not art-makers, allowing full expression to the subjective or passional impulse which has intermittently shown itself in the haunting strangeness of certain Stellas and Robert Morris's, but which is fundamentally counter to the methodical cerebrations of, for example, Judd or Noland.[17]

Again, it was this appeal to "affect rather than idea" that was so important to Burton.

---

17. "Ralph Humphrey: A Different Stripe," p. 101.

The second key theme emerging from Burton's engagement with the work of Smith was the importance of the temporal duration of the viewer's experience. During the summer in which he was expanding his article on Smith into the more opinionated lecture for the Walker Art Center, Michael Fried's game-changing essay "Art and Objecthood" was published in *Artforum*.[18] Burton seized upon Fried's essay and its central term—"theatricality"—and adapted it to his defense of Smith.

"Art and Objecthood" had the effect of consolidating a group identity for Minimalism through its critique, despite the fact that the aims of the artists associated with the "movement" were divergent. Such was the case with Smith, whom Fried not only equated with Judd and Morris, but also singled out in his attack. Without a doubt, this spurred Burton to further articulate Smith's difference from the others as he had in his earlier article. More importantly, however, he found in Fried not an ally but another opponent. Fried's famous argument against Minimalism was that it was "theatrical," and that theater was antithetical to art and to modernism.[19] Fried wrote, "The literalist espousal of objecthood amounts to nothing other than a plea for a new genre of theater, and theater is now the negation of art."[20] Given Burton's decade-long association with the theater, such a claim could do nothing but enrage him. As he wrote in 1969, "The main inaccuracy of the 'formalist' criticism which calls much recent art 'theatrical' is in the conservative assumption that the adjective is pejorative."[21] In opposition to Fried and to the Minimalists, Burton espoused theater as a means to differentiate Smith from both positions (even going so far as to conclude by comparing Smith

18. Michael Fried, "Art and Objecthood," *Artforum* 5, no. 10 (June 1967): 12–23

19. On the contours of Fried's use of "theatricality," see especially James Meyer, "The Writing of 'Art and Objecthood'," in *Refracting Vision: Essays on the Writings of Michael Fried*, ed. Jill Beaulieu, Mary Roberts, and Toni Ross (Sydney: Power Institute, 2000), 61–96.

20. Fried, "Art and Objecthood," 15.

21. "Time on Their Hands," p. 79.

to Eugene O'Neill). With work like Smith's, he argued, the viewer's encounter was spatially activated and became highly particularized precisely because of the works' simple yet dramatic unfolding over time.

Burton developed his interest in temporality throughout this period, and by 1973 he would concisely assert that an expanded definition of theater was "simply art in time."[22] For Burton, as with Fried, the temporal dimension of theater was its core trait, and this it fundamentally shared with all sculptural encounters.[23] Experiences occurred in time, necessarily having beginnings, sequences, and endings. "Even in the most radical play ever written, *Waiting for Godot*, there are lines or moments more charged, more revealing than others," he reminded.[24] It was the differentiation of moments within a temporal experience that Burton believed was the potential of theater and the key to expressivity. The "psychological structure of theater" was "inescapably one of intensification, climax, and release."[25] In championing its temporality and emotive potential, Burton was not only using theater to look beyond modernism, he was also deploying it to argue against the elitism and preciosity he saw in artists such as Judd and Andre. Since he believed that the Minimalist aspirations to uninflected, non-ordered experiences "mocked" viewers with their willful blankness, he saw the narrative and expressive potential in Smith's work to have great potential as a factor of—not despite—his reductive and geometric structures.

Temporality became an important concern for Burton, and it characterized both his art-critical priorities and his own

---

22. "Sculpture as Theater: The *Lecture on Self*," p. 229.
23. On Fried's opposition to duration and endlessness in "Art and Objecthood," see Pamela Lee, *Chronophobia: On Time in the Art of the 1960s* (MIT Press: Cambridge, Massachusetts, 2004), 37–51.
24. "Tony Smith and Minimalist Sculpture," p. 60.
25. "Tony Smith and Minimalist Sculpture," p. 60.

development of performance art. It even can be evidenced as a criterion and value in his 1967 essay on Button's figurative paintings, which he said compelled duration in the viewer's experience: "A Button reveals itself gradually, not through multiplicity of incident but through depth of concentration—which takes *time* to filter to the surface."[26] He said something similar about time's representation by light in Edward Hopper's paintings in "Generations of Light," but Burton's most important, if concise, statement on temporality was his 1969 essay "Time on Their Hands." (*ARTnews* often assigned its own titles to the articles.) In it, he used an engagement with temporality and duration as the organizing theme through which he discussed what would soon be called Postminimalism.

Burton's interest in temporality in "Time on Their Hands" focused on the ways in which any activation of time or duration served to acknowledge the viewer. As in his writings on Smith, Burton took the concept of theatricality and turned it into a positive value. For Burton, duration and the passage of time served to establish a comparative relation and a commonality between viewer and work of art, connecting them. Richard Serra was a key example:

> Serra is as concerned with the results of (human) activities on materials as he is with the properties of those materials; naturally, the two are mutually determinant but Serra's production (including series involving folding, sawing, hanging and balancing also) is as assertively in our time as a Donald Judd–box is in our space, by virtue of its emphasis on both its past (its identity as a result) and its future (its potentialities).[27]

---

26. "John Button," p. 164.
27. "Time on Their Hands," p. 82.

Burton saw the acknowledgment of the common ground of time's passage as a means to bridge the separation between artwork and viewer or, more bluntly, between art and life. Burton praised Serra's works such as *Splashing* for their impermanence. The "impermanent" was, for Burton, a condition that was analogous to the allusiveness he argued for in the work of Tony Smith or abstract painters such as Humphrey or Ohlson. The foregrounding of the work of art's lifespan—not just its creation, but its foreseeable disintegration or demise—established a parallel to the viewer's own mortal existence. For Burton, the acknowledgement of time's effects on the work of art humanized it and opened the door to the kind of intimate and personal identifications that he sought to make room for with his criticism. It also eroded the hierarchical distinction between art and life, making art and artworks more like the quotidian world of actions and objects. (This would be a driving force in his development of barely noticeable, but functional and useful public art.) He resoundingly concluded the essay by asserting (with due acknowledgment of the possible impermanence of the value he stressed): "This is the ultimate (at least, the current ultimate) in the idea of art as the 'imitation of life'; not to aspire to an impossible permanence is at once audacious and humble."[28]

Burton's "Time on Their Hands" was technically a review essay on two major exhibitions in New York (*Nine Young Americans* at the Guggenheim and *Anti-Illusion: Procedures/Materials* at the Whitney), both of which helped to establish the more process-based and variable-form work that would signal the emergence of Postminimalism's deformation of Minimalism's rigid geometries. The essay, however, did not really address the exhibitions so much as step above them to discuss these general tendencies. In many ways, the essay is

---

28. "Time on Their Hands," p. 85.

better understood as a refinement and expansion of the ideas Burton had put forth in the preceding months in his essay for the important exhibition originated by the Kunsthalle Bern, *Live in Your Head: When Attitudes Become Form,* which opened in the spring of 1969. Burton was given—by the curator Harald Szeemann—the unenviable position of writing about indeterminate, impermanent, process-oriented, and often site-specific work not only in advance of the exhibition (and ahead of the creation of many of its ephemeral works!) but also from across the Atlantic. Burton's essay "Notes on the New" took the form of a discussion of many of the American artists in the exhibition, based on his familiarity with them from the New York scene. Burton's own priorities were rapidly shifting toward the Postminimal; for him, Minimal art objects were very clearly high art objects, but these new works demanded a new perspective based in time, performance, and lived engagement. As he wrote, "Art has been veritably *invaded* by life, if life means flux, change, chance, time, unpredictability."[29]

Burton argued that the direct correspondence—if not equivalence—between the everyday and art was the most important new direction in contemporary art. It could be seen in process-based and anti-form work. His essay was almost utopic in its proclamations about the move beyond modernism and its dictates. Discussing the breakdown of distinctions between painting and sculpture, art and idea, the visual and the verbal, and the skilled and the untrained, Burton predicted the rise of performance from an engagement with duration and temporality. For him, performance and its direct relation to everyday life were the payoff of the art of the 1960s. "Literalism has been extended to modes of temporal existence," as he said in his subsequent article.[30] Burton saw the distinction between art and life fading through the

29."When Attitudes Become Form: Notes on the New," p. 76.
30."Time on Their Hands," p. 79.

incorporation of temporality and impermanence, and it was performance that he held up as exemplary of this shift.

Burton understood that the most direct acknowledgement of the shared passage of time between viewer and artwork occurred, most obviously, in live performance and theater. It is no coincidence, then, that these same months saw Burton's first performance art pieces. At the end of the 1960s, he and Button had split, and Burton developed his own circle of friends, including Eduardo Costa (his then neighbor), Jane Kaufman, Marjorie Strider, John Perreault, Mac McGinnes (then working at the important Fischbach Gallery), and Steve Gianakos. It was within this new, younger milieu that Burton was spurred to turn his interest in theater into the practice of performance.[31]

He was one of the central participants in the *Street Works* events that were organized by Strider, Perreault, and Hannah Weiner and held under the auspices of the Architectural League in New York over the course of 1969. Each *Street Work* event involved a group of heterogeneous performances by disparate artists executed within a set time period and within a defined number of blocks in Manhattan. For these, Burton expanded on this practice to create what he would term *Self-Works*. In this category, he included *Disguise* for *Street Works II* (in April 1969) and *Ear-Piece* for *Street Works III* (in May 1969) as well as other works that involved acting on his own body, such as in *Dream* when he drugged himself to sleep at the opening party for the Architectural League's *Street Works IV* held at the American Federation of Arts in October 1969.

Burton discussed these performances in his lecture at the University of Iowa ("Literalist Theater"), his performance text for *Lecture on Self*, and his "Three Street Works" from 1969. This last text is exemplary in that it is composed entirely of

31. A useful memoir of this period of Burton's work can be found in John Perreault, "Scott Burton's Escape from Language," in *Scott Burton*, ed. Ana María Torres (Valencia: Institut Valencià d'art Modern, 2004), 36–42.

quotations from published reviews of the *Street Works* events. This is an important textual move that exemplified Burton's early attitudes toward performance. In what could be considered a practice of critical mimesis, Burton's *Street Works* events all involved a blurring of art and life, reframing (or putting in quotation marks) everyday experience. It was almost as if he were attempting to address the question with which he concluded his essay "Notes on the New," borrowed from Duchamp:

> No afunctional act can really be anything but symbolic, but it is compelling to see, at least, the continuing dilation of art's limits, to watch the quotation marks get further and further apart. In 1913, Marcel Duchamp wrote, "Can one make works which are not works of 'art'?[32]

Just as he saw temporality and theater as means to break down the hierarchical distinction between art and non-art, art and life, and art and the quotidian, his performances involved either subtle or extreme actions that reframed his experience of the everyday. Whether in the invisibility of his moving through *Street Works II* dressed as a woman or the hyper-visibility of his chemically induced unconsciousness among his friends and colleagues in *Dream*, Burton explored the ways in which performance-as-art was crucial to the performer. That is, even if it went unnoticed by the audience (as in *Ear-Piece* or *Disguise*), Burton's performance practice put quotation marks around "life" for him. He expanded this idea of performance's effect on the performer in his "Literalist Theater" lecture, transforming the idea of the *Self-Works* into a series of instructions that could be executed by his students and, indeed, anyone. These particular *Self-Works* he encouraged them to do involved "just pretending, doing ordinary

32. "When Attitudes Become Form: Notes on the New," p. 78.

actions, but just pretending to in a sense, doing them gratuitously" in order to "imitate ordinary life."[33] If the year before he had argued that someone like Serra's acknowledgement of time and contingency established a parallel relation with the viewer's experience of time, then with "Literalist Theater" he advocated for an artistic practice in which the work of art could only be experienced by doing it—by being both artist and the art. This experience, importantly, would necessarily vary from individual to individual, making each instantiation of the work personal, singular and intimate.

During that same summer Burton would develop a completely different mode of performance art that involved highly structured artificial situations of viewing. At Iowa, he began experimenting with a wide range of performance works intended for the stage, not the street, such as *Ten Tableaux*.[34] In 1972, this mode of practice eventually became the *Behavior Tableaux* that I discuss below. Even as he moved from quotations of the quotidian to staged pieces involving other performers, the idea of critical mimesis persisted as a recurring theme in Burton's work. It would manifest itself in his own parodic reframing of himself in his quotation of the genre of the artist's talk in *Lecture on Self* and, perhaps more deeply, redouble his long-running engagement with realism.

Concurrent with his attempt to define the "Abstract Allusionists" and his engagement with Postminimal, performative, and conceptual practices, Burton remained committed to the belief that realism and figuration were not just valid options in contemporary art; they were important. By "realism," Burton often meant an engagement with—as well as a representation of—the actual and the observable. His burgeoning belief that art should be demotic and accessible fueled both his interest in pictorial realism and in conceptual performance, both of

33. "Literalist Theater," p. 219–20.

34. See also Scott Burton, "[Furniture Works 1970-71]," *TriQuarterly* 32 (Winter 1975): n.p.

which embraced (albeit in different ways) the everyday. That is, Burton did not see a contradiction between representational art and what he heralded in "Notes on the New" as "a new naturalism or realism born of extended collaborations between the artists and nature, chance, material, event, the viewer."[35] Nor was there a mutual exclusivity with abstraction. He addressed both Hopper and de Kooning in the same terms in "Generation of Light," and he would write in 1967 that "'Abstract' and 'illusionist' are not antonyms."[36] In doing this, he took a cue from Duchamp, whose work was central to Burton's thinking.[37] Duchamp had once stated,

> Art is produced by a succession of individuals expressing themselves; it is not a question of progress. Progress is merely an enormous pretension on our part. [. . .] And 'abstract' or 'naturalistic' is merely a fashionable form of talking—today. It is no problem: an abstract painting may not look at all 'abstract' in 50 years.[38]

In such a shared attitude, Burton recognized his aims for individuality and the breaking down of hierarchical distinctions.

---

35. "When Attitudes Become Form: Notes on the New," p. 76–77.

36. "George McNeil and the Figure," p. 187.

37. For instance, Burton designed a special cover for the September 1973 *ARTnews* featuring the Marcel Duchamp retrospective. It is one of the only *ARTnews* covers in which a specific artist/designer for the cover is noted in the credits. Eduardo Costa described the importance of this work for Burton: "Scott liked very much a cover he made for *ARTnews* in the mid-seventies. The cover was a great abstract of Marcel Duchamp portraits, four consecutive photographs of his own head, which Scott distributed simply on the page. The portraits were Duchamp with the star haircut, Duchamp with the hair full of foamy soap in the shape of two small horns, Duchamp as Rrose Selavy, Duchamp at 85 (taken when he was 58). Scott thought of these as very early examples of art photography, and was happy to have been able to lay them out as the cover of an art magazine." Eduardo Costa, "Scott Burton and Photography" (2004), essay published on his website titled *The Non-Art Photographs of Scott Burton*, http://www.scottburton.com.ar, accessed 10 October 2011.

38. Marcel Duchamp, "The Great Trouble with Art in This Country [1946]," in *Salt Seller: The Writings of Marcel Duchamp*, ed. Michel Sanouillet and Elmer Peterson (Oxford and New York: Oxford University Press, 1973), 123.

Burton wrote about a range of representational art, from precise verisimilitude to gestural and abstracting treatments of the human form. As he had with abstraction and conceptual art, Burton attended closely to the formal dynamics of these varied modes and repeatedly asked about the effects of decisions on the individual viewer's experience and associations. In his writings on representational art, he often urged that there should be no hierarchical parsing of the abstract versus the figurative. In his essay on Alex Katz, for instance, he thought that the painter was exemplary of a move "forward to an open situation in which the formal and the expressive elements of art will once again be understood to be synonymous in figurative as well as in abstract styles."[39]

Burton's two main statements on representational art were the exhibitions of realist painting he curated in 1969 (*Direct Representation*) and 1972 (*The Realist Revival*). In both, he put forth artists such as Yvonne Jacquette, Sylvia Plimack Mangold, and Philip Pearlstein as exemplary of this tendency. He even went so far as to suggest, in 1969, that because of the dominance of sculpture in the forms of Minimalism and Postminimalism, painting had little choice but to return to representation:

> Straight figuration is, I think the only major mode now available to painting adequate for the expression of the fullest individuality. Besides a reinvigorated fidelity to the surface of the perceived world, the new representationalists share an historical situation in which, briefly, three-dimensional work has absorbed the premises of most earlier modernists styles and taken them to extremes where painting cannot follow.[40]

39. "Alex Katz," p. 194.
40. "Direct Representation: Five Younger Realists," p. 195.

Both his 1969 and 1972 texts offer manifesto-like defenses of this "risky embrace of illusionist precision," as he called it.[41] The latter text even calls realism the "evolution of modernism rather than a retreat from it."[42] It should be remembered that Burton's relationship with Button had brought him into contact with the networks of representational artists and he counted such artists as Pearlstein, Katz, Sleigh, and others as personal friends. Button had painted him as Ganymede, and Pearlstein did an astonishing portrait of him.[43] Sleigh famously included Burton, along with the other art critics Lawrence Alloway and Carter Ratcliff, in her important painting *The Turkish Bath* (1973). All of this is evidence of Burton's sustained engagement with the ideas and key players of figurative painting during these years.

Burton's advocacy of realism was, in addition, a function of his distaste for narrowly normative and canonical values. He saw the elitism of the art world as a kind of club that enforced a singular developmental narrative at the expense of all divergent positions. Identifying with the outsider and the underdog, Burton would often attack mainstream positions for their suppression of differences and alternatives. In a memoir of Burton, Robert Rosenblum wrote:

> He never stopped reading, looking, and learning with the zeal of a new graduate student. From this, he acquired plenty of ammunition for the frequent announcements of his latest enthusiasms and hates, which usually went against the grain of all shared beliefs. In the 1970s, for instance, he would claim that his friend Philip Pearlstein's neorealist

---

41. "Direct Representation: Five Younger Realists," p. 196.

42. "The Realist Revival," p. 202.

43. Burton discussed sitting for Pearlstein in Scott Burton, "Introduction," in *Philip Pearlstein* (New York: Hirsch & Adler Modern, 1985), n.p.

> canvases of nude models, objectively recorded with scrupulous detail, were far more avant-garde than any of the minimal art (including his own) we were cheering. [. . .] His seemingly perverse opinions were not pronounced for the sake of camp, but because Scott had genuinely been smitten by new enthusiasms and new challenges to inherited prejudices.[44]

The refusal of "inherited prejudices" and the suppression of difference were, after all, the driving forces behind Burton's attempts to personalize the impersonal tactics of Minimalism—to allow space for the individual, the non-standard, and the marginal.

Burton's own artistic practice also fed off his interest in realism. Not only was the critical mimesis of the *Self-Works* related to his advocacy of representational art, but it can also be seen as fundamental to his work of the 1970s. His *Bronze Chair* (conceived in 1972, but executed in 1975) was a functional bronze-cast of an abandoned Queen Anne revival-style chair. One of the very first of his sculptures, it was usable as furniture (hence literally a chair) at the same time that it was (through the associations of bronze with figurative sculpture) a realist sculptural rendering of a chair. In this way, *Bronze Chair* combined all of Burton's interests. It exhibited literality and theatricality just like any Minimalist object while, at the same time, being representational and realist. The *Bronze Chair* asks to be used, and it incites actual bodily contact. To sit in the *Chair* is to bring one's body into the sculpture's arms, turning away from it, and backing on to it. Such an experience of the realist sculpture as usable furniture, he learned, was fundamentally more direct and more accessible in its solicitation of and literal bodily engagement with the viewer/sitter.

44. Robert Rosenblum, "Scott Burton," in *Loss within Loss: Artists in the Age of AIDS*, ed. Edmund White (Madison: University of Wisconsin Press, 2001), 240.

He subsequently pursued making more such "pragmatic sculpture," as he called his functional furniture art, to expand on the *Bronze Chair*'s fusion of literality, representation, and implicit figuration.

Beyond his belief in the potential of illusionistic or representational image-making, Burton was particularly interested in the human figure. For him, the critical mimesis of the *Self-Works* and the *Bronze Chair* were, significantly, also figurative in their incorporation of the body of the performer or the viewer/sitter (as well as the *Bronze Chair*'s blatantly anthropomorphic associations as a bronze statue). He saw the presence of the live body of the performer in relation to the representation of the human form in figurative art. In his brief survey of performance art in his *Lecture on Self*, he stated that performance was "however transformed, an art essentially of the human figure."[45] Both figuration and performance, he believed, opened avenues of identification and empathy for the viewer. Crystalized through his opposition to the impersonal coldness of Minimal sculpture, Burton came to see any incorporation of the human body (whether live or represented) as a means for art to become more accessible and to directly engage the viewer. Consequently, figuration (like realism) became an expansive and inclusive category for Burton, as he attempted to bridge modes of artistic practice that had previously been opposed in mainstream narratives of modernism's progress.

The fusion of his ideas led him to develop the performances he would call *Behavior Tableaux*. As he explained about his own work in the text for his *Lecture on Self*, these works would "herald a large-scale art of the human figure."[46] Unlike his *Self-Works* and his *Lecture on Self*, Burton stepped back from using his own body and instead created elaborate

45. "Sculpture as Theater: The *Lecture on Self*," p. 232.
46. "Sculpture as Theater: The *Lecture on Self*," p. 238.

living pictures (tableaux vivants) with groups of performers he would direct and rehearse. At the University of Iowa and Finch College, Burton showed different types of such performance works (many of which are detailed in the text for *Lecture on Self*), but settled on a practice (starting with his 1972 *Group Behavior Tableaux*) that used slowly moving tableaux vivants to address the bodily and social relations between people. On a stage, these works would contain individual scenes separated by blackouts in which a group of performers would move extremely slowly to adopt poses that illustrated various social relations to each other. Burton's interest in these works was to address the codes whereby the body spoke to and exercised power over others. He further hoped to evoke each viewer's own particularized history of the acquisition and experience of this spatial, bodily communication. As he explained in *Lecture on Self*:

> The achievement of this piece is to have found the exact location where human psychology and visual art meet: in the non-verbal language of the body. [The *Behavior Tableaux*'s] placement, posture, and gesture and its observations and violations of personal-space and body-surrounding territories reveal the unconscious attitudes literally shaping and deploying [body language].[47]

These were complex performances, and each manifestation explored different sets of meanings.[48] His aim with them was to bring art, via live figuration, back into dialogue with viewers' daily experience by activating their personal histories of power in social relations—here figured through the staging of

47. "Sculpture as Theater: The *Lecture on Self*," p. 241.

48. Again, I discuss the *Behavior Tableaux* in more detail in my analysis in my forthcoming chapter on Burton in the 1970s.

body language and its coercions. Like his earlier advocacy of Smith and the Abstract Allusionists, Burton hoped that these performances could be understandable and affective for audiences from outside the specialized language of the New York art world despite their reductive and unorthodox formats. The works' development extends beyond the chronological frame of this book, through to 1980, but I have included here some early texts that describe his initial formulations. Taken with the detailed discussion of his work that Burton incorporated into the *Lecture on Self*, these early texts help to show how these performances emerged out of Burton's commitments to performance, duration, realism, painting, and figuration. As with his other work and his criticism, they derived from his unique conjunction of these often disparate concerns.

One of the most remarkable texts included in this volume is the lecture script for Burton's performance *Lecture on Self*, to which I have given the title "Sculpture as Theater," appropriated from the opening line of the text. As I explain in the editor's notes to the text, Burton engaged in an extended quotation of himself by presenting a lecture lasting over an hour on his own work at Oberlin College in 1973. Speaking in the third person, he offered an assessment of the state of performance art and detailed descriptions of his work. In essence, he put himself in quotation marks and offered a figurative performance of "the artist." This should be understood as an extension of his *Self-Works* from 1969, as his selective resumé "Odd Years" indicates. This text, reconstructed in its entirety, serves as one of the most important statements of Burton's attitude toward performance and provides a key documentation of his ephemeral works. It was this unpublished manuscript (and "Tony Smith and Minimalist Sculpture") that first made me realize how important it was to undertake work on this collection.

Elizabeth Baker, the former editor of *Art in America*, recalled that "As a critic [Burton's] enthusiasms were passionate, his dislikes were categorical. He wrote as he would later cut granite, with high style, great clarity of form, and a very sharp edge."[49] Burton's perspective was unique among his peers, both artists and critics alike. The texts contained here help to show the development of the attitudes that would lead him to make public, functional art as well as provide a rogue commentary on the art of the late 1960s and early 1970s. There is no doubt that these texts move in very different directions, but they nevertheless cumulatively demonstrate Burton's perspicacious attention to the effects of formal and conceptual decisions. More than that, they show a writer and an artist who engaged a critical stance against conformity, arguing for the distinctly personal, eclectic, and individual potential of many different modes of making art.

As Burton started to gain recognition as a public artist in the early 1980s, he came to downplay much of his earlier work. Burton did not want the heterogeneous practice he had pursued in the 1970s to distract from the critical stance he was pursuing by making his demotic, albeit nearly anonymous, public art. This self-abnegation was the point, however, as it allowed his public art to find a place in the everyday, even if its users did not know it was art at all. This is not to say that Burton did not have a sense of purpose (or ego). Rather, he opted for relative simplicity as the tactic of his work in the 1980s, in order to develop an accessible mode of artistic practice.

The texts in this collection reveal how many of the issues in his 1980s practice have their origins in his participation in the debates of the late 1960s. Burton disregarded his own work as a critic, and his lack of recognition in this arena is due in part to this. Speaking to Lewis Kachur in 1987, Burton stated "There's nothing of mine from that period that I would wish

49. Elizabeth Baker quoted in Roberta Smith, "Scott Burton, Sculptor Whose Art Verged on Furniture, Is Dead at 50," *New York Times*, 1 January 1990.

to reprint—nothing at all. So I'm a failed critic." About his work from this period, he said in the same interview, "It's not a thing I'd put into a retrospective—this whole period of the late 1960s to early 1970s."[50] Clearly, I disagree. Such statements from the end of the 1980s arose from Burton's relentless self-critical stance, which was heightened as he saw his social and professional worlds devastated by AIDS. A sense of urgency about his projects, about their completion, and about his agenda to make a new kind of public, accessible art pervaded the interviews he gave in these years. Burton died of AIDS-related complications in 1989, and I take Burton's selective self-editing as a retrospective attempt to clarify and to control the message he wanted his work and his legacy to make. Despite such dismissals of his own early work and criticism, he kept vast amounts of material from these years and donated it to the Museum of Modern Art archives. All of the work and criticism he would disavow he nevertheless made sure was preserved. Because of this—and because of my belief in the importance and distinctiveness of Burton's early work—I have been emboldened to assemble what he (perhaps too modestly) said he did not want, a collection of his writings.

The present volume collects the majority, but not all, of Burton's writings. Excluded from this book are the many capsule reviews (ranging from a single line to perhaps a paragraph) from *ARTnews* in the early years, as well as scattered very short reviews.[51] By and large, I have focused on

---

50. Scott Burton interview with Lewis Kachur, Oral History Project, Archives of American Art, Smithsonian Institution, Washington, D.C., Interview I: May 22, 1987.

51. A standout among Burton's many such capsule reviews was his three-sentence account of Robert Smithson's 1968 exhibition at Dwan Gallery, in which he remarked that the artist's *Nonsites* were "geological samples in handsome Minimal containers from places (sites) which Smithson has chosen to visit, plus documents (maps, photographs, and verbal descriptions) of the site and, therefore, of the visit itself. The many differences between the sites and the *Nonsites* ultimately become, in Smithson's compulsively dialectical mind, the very distinction between art and nature. Smithson is brilliant because he makes art out of what art cannot be." Scott Burton, "Robert Smithson's 'Nonsites'," *Art Scene* (April 1968): 22.

more extended texts. Even though some of these, too, were assigned by an editor, they nevertheless show the development of Burton's perspective. There are a small number of *ARTnews* articles I have not included because they seemed too perfunctory.[52] Similarly, I have not included texts that I considered to be largely repetitive.[53] Burton was a prolific critic, and it is possible that there are additional published writings out there, but I have done my best to include (or cite in this Introduction) all of the essays and articles I have found in my research in the archives. After the early 1970s, Burton largely stopped writing art criticism, but he did write some important historical essays in the 1980s to which I would point the reader, despite the fact that they fall out of the chronological range of this volume.[54]

I chose to end the collection in 1975 because the year seemed to mark a decisive change in his work. That year, he had his first one-person exhibition (at Artists Space), where he showed his *Bronze Chair*. By this time, he had stopped writing criticism and devoted himself to being an artist. I include "Odd Years" (1975) because it is retrospective of his work to that point. Overall, the decade from 1965 to 1975 reflects a coherent phase of Burton's production, even as it foreshadows later developments. His work shifts a great deal in the mid-1970s, and he became more forthright about the importance of sexuality as part of his practice after 1974 (first hinted at in his "Make a Political Statement"). The archives and published interviews of the late 1970s and 1980s are rich. It was tempting to consider including his writings and statements of

---

52. "Two for May: Dunn, Hendler," *ARTnews* 66.3 (May 1967): 55, 71–72; and "Cool and Concrete from the 'Thirties," *ARTnews* 66.2 (April 1967): 34, 69–71.

53. As with his short essay on Robert Beauchamp for the exhibition pamphlet for the painter's one person exhibition at the Utah Museum of Fine Arts, Salt Lake City, in 1968.

54. Most important are his "Furniture Journal: Gerrit Rietveld," *Art in America* 68.9 (November 1980): 102–108; and "My Brancusi," exhibition brochure for Burton's exhibition *Artist's Choice: Burton on Brancusi* at the Museum of Modern Art, April 7 to June 28, 1989, revised and republished posthumously as Scott Burton, "My Brancusi," *Art in America* 78.3 (March 1990): 148.

the 1980s, but I felt that this volume would speak louder by revealing the forgotten Burton of the late 1960s and 1970s, which the work of the 1980s often overshadows.

In organizing the book, I have separated the texts into four broad groupings that follow a more-or-less chronological development of Burton's writing and art in this decade. As would be expected from Burton's stance, many of the essays could easily be put into different sections. Nevertheless, I think these general themes can aid readers in following the main threads of Burton's thinking in these years. Within each section, writings are organized chronologically, with the exception of Burton's 1967 essay on his partner John Button, to which I give precedence in the "Realisms" section in light of Button's formative influence on Burton. From the archival materials, I have selected writings that provide concise accounts of Burton's art activities during these years. He was a prodigious note-taker, and it would be infeasible to include them all. Instead, I have relied on the synthetic statement made with the *Lecture on Self* and augmented it with a few short writings, published and unpublished, in which he characterized his own performances. These are meant to stand in for the active process of conceptualizing his own practice through writing in which Burton was engaged in these years.

A small amount of the archival materials have been published previously in partial form in the catalogue to the retrospective at the Institut Valencià d'art Modern (2004). Unfortunately, the research for that exhibition was undertaken before Burton's bequest had been processed by the archivists at the Museum of Modern Art, New York. Consequently, that publication did not benefit from the meticulous research and organization of Burton's voluminous materials by MoMA, and it contains historical errors and flawed transcriptions. For instance, that catalogue reprints only the first two pages of the *Lecture on Self*. (At one point, Burton had begun to type out the manuscript he had written by hand, but accomplished only two pages even though the handwritten text runs continuously for many pages more.) Hence there are substantial discrepancies with those few texts it shares with this volume because I have endeavored to provide accurate and comprehensive versions of Burton's important unpublished manuscripts. For consistency's sake, some minor changes have been made across the texts (such as the capitalization of such terms as "Primary Structurists" that Burton sometimes capitalized and sometimes did not.) Editorial notes (*E.N.*) are included at the heads of some texts to indicate more specific editorial approaches and to provide background to the texts.

I first encountered Burton's work as an undergraduate at Oberlin College, where the Allen Memorial Art Museum had in its collection a 1979 replica of the *Bronze Chair* that Burton made for his friend, the dealer Donald Droll. This strange and unexpected sculpture has stuck with me for two decades, shadowing my scholarly work on a range of different topics and periods. Once Burton's archives were opened by MoMA, I decided to investigate Burton's early work which was, then and now, still difficult to learn about from the published record. In the archives I encountered a perceptive and independent critic as well as a wide-ranging artist with convictions about facilitating marginal perspectives. Burton proposed unlikely alliances between the artists about whom he wrote, and he tried to make room for difference and individuality in the viewer's affective responses. Such a form of criticism, he wrote in 1968, demands "the primacy of sensibility over formal techniques,"[55] and it is in his committed appeal to sensibility that these texts seem to me not just current but useful—the trait, after all, he valued most in his work.

55. "Ralph Humphrey: A Different Stripe," p. 102.

I.
BEYOND MINIMALISM

Tony Smith: Old Master at the New Frontier (1966)

"Old Master at the New Frontier," *ARTnews* 65.8 (December 1966): 52–55, 68–70.

E.N.: *Burton's essay on Tony Smith was his first major feature for* ARTnews. *In it, he was developing his critical priorities while also attempting to satisfy the editor, Thomas Hess, in hopes of further assignments. Burton recalled in 1987 that Hess's assignment of Smith to him was catalytic: "[T]he first piece of writing [was] on Tony Smith, who I totally fell in love with and who was a big influence in some way on me ever since. I think Smith is one of the great American artists." (Archives of American Art Oral History Interview, May 22, 1987, 60) Burton, however, considered this essay "inadequate." Indeed, there is a reticence not evident in the unpublished lecture on Smith's work given in Minneapolis the following year.*

When art history is written as quickly as it is these days, it has to be rewritten often. We must now revise our accounts of modern American sculpture to include Tony Smith. Only two of his pieces have ever been seen publicly, one, *The Elevens*, at Samuel J. Wagstaff's 1964 "Black, White and Grey" show at the Wadsworth Atheneum, Hartford, and the other, *Free Ride*, at Kynaston McShine's "Primary Structures" at the Jewish Museum last spring. Now there are *two* major exhibitions of Smith's work at the same time, one at the Wadsworth Atheneum [Nov 8–Dec 31], another in Philadelphia at the Institute of Contemporary Art, University of Pennsylvania [Nov 21–Jan 6]. (A group of smaller works by Smith is scheduled to be shown next March in New York at the Fischbach Gallery.) So we must adjust our charts and graphs oncc more.

For a while, it looked as if the polarities of American sculpture had been set by our two Old Masters, Nakian and David Smith, with the only organized New Frontier being offered by Judd, Morris, et al., and artists like Hague, Agostini, Sugarman, or di Suvero running strong but without benefit of party. It is to be hoped that the public appearance of Tony Smith will not result merely in political realignments, but will instead remind us that any artist's work must, first and last, be comprehended on its own terms. Smith's is perfectly suited to do so, for it matches easily the heroic scale of Nakian, the formal authority of David Smith, the advanced rigorousness of the Primary Structurists, or the originality of any contemporary sculptor. Yet all this absolutely independently.

Obviously, it is not the achievement of a *Wunderkind.* Tony Smith has been as long and as closely involved in the inside development of postwar–American art as anyone could be, first as an architect and *amicus curiae*, counting such painters as Pollock, Still and Newman as close friends and (one supposes) mutually influencing minds. Also, Smith has been painting—but not showing—for over thirty years. He began by studying nights at the Art Students League with Vytlacil and George Grosz, between 1931 and 1935, while working in the daytime in his father's (and his father's before him) New Jersey iron-works, where water supplies were manufactured. Even today, "A. P. Smith" can be read like a signature on fire hydrants around New York. When questioned about his sources, Smith said, "Ah, if you really want to see where I come from, you should go over to the factory." The factory is no longer in the family, but Anthony Peter Smith's grandson and namesake has transformed the memories of the plates and dies and forges of his industrial ancestry into some of today's most radical sculpture. (One is reminded of David Smith's similar preoccupation with our pre-electronic era, but there the resemblance ends.)

Tony Smith as a sculptor only seems to have sprung full-grown from the brow of Hephaestus. Blake's "botany" was accurate, as usual, when he said that the growth of a flower is the product of centuries of labor. As a young industrial worker; an *hors-concours* painter; an architectural student (of Moholy-Nagy, Archipenko, and Kepes at the New Bauhaus in Chicago, 1937–38) and, in reaction, an architectural apprentice to Frank Lloyd Wright for two years after that; then, for two decades (1940–60) as a practicing architect, building about 14 houses; as, since 1946, a teacher of crucial importance to a younger generation; as a responsive colleague of major painters—Tony Smith's "centuries of labor" have produced, in less than a decade, a body of work equal to that any single-minded lifetime pursuit could produce.

Between 1953 and '55, while living in Germany, Smith did a few small, tentative sculptures—studies or sketches—which he has barely looked at since then. (He says about them, "It's not so much that I take more time with [sculpture] now . . . it's just that then I was thinking about other things.") And, before that, he had planned one or two pieces of sculpture as components of houses he was designing. Then, in 1957, when he was back and teaching design at Pratt Institute, he made a demonstration model out of acoustical tiles and electrician's tape (because they happened to be handy) of a phenomenon in solid geometry his class was studying. It was a tetrahedral angle, which has, as Smith explains, "in a word, the least number of spokes possible in a three-dimensional configuration." While putting it together, he noticed that it was developing a resemblance (now lost) to African sculpture, to a carved throne. So, the associative imagination taking over, geometry became art. Though *Throne* exists as yet only in the battered original model, the experience was a turning-point for Smith, for constructing this piece first gave him the idea of using steel plate to make sculpture. The decision catapulted him into a multiplying series of works, some of which are still under construction (at this writing, not more than a month away from his exhibitions) though they may have existed for several years as models or in plan. So far, only a few—*Die, Black Box, Free Ride*—are in steel; the rest are in plywood painted with autobody undercoating. (Practically all his sculptures are black.)

They are made at Smith's Orange, NJ, studio with the help of his permanent assistant, Arthur File. The studio is in a garage behind Smith's enormous old brick house. This house is a recent acquisition; there is also one a few minutes' drive away in South Orange, where he lives with his wife and three young daughters, and where he was born (in 1912). In almost every room of both houses is a work of art or personal memento to provoke a story or revelation from Smith about the early history of the New York artists' world. But as fascinating as his life is, it is his sculpture, the 18 pieces divided between Philadelphia and Hartford, that is of immediate—and ultimate—concern.

The initial impression of his work (and I am talking on that basis; with greater familiarity, it will undoubtedly change for us, only proving its density and vitality) is likely to be one of great emotional power, his radical sculptural means only gradually asserting themselves. Soon, of course, the two draw together, until you cannot think of them separately. Smith's expressive content often seems to deal with the absolutes of human experience—and this conveyed strictly in physical terms. (That is why it is no more than a critical convenience to segregate these elements for discussion.) *The Elevens* is two black "walls," each 8 by 8 by 2 feet; they stand parallel to each other, 4 feet apart, thus making the whole an 8-foot cube with an open central shaft. Looking at and walking through it can be terrifying, like Mycenaean tomb—architecture. It is not necessary to be aware of the title's specific reference, for the scale and ineluctable "passageway" of *The Elevens* speak with finality of human limits and of life's unavoidable direction.

The Marriage has a similar central aperture, but because it is a portal and not a corridor, and because of the work's (relatively) less severe structure, *The Marriage* is not so oppressive, though it is as monumental as anything of Smith's. The piece can only be described as poetic (if hardly lyrical)—the locus of a ritual ceremony. It is tempting to imagine the "bride and groom" of *The Marriage* as the private and the public: intense personal feeling, even obsession, has been realized to be a constant of human life, something we all undergo. Here the two connect in a Pascalian equation.

The Marriage's unsymmetrical component, its arm extending out across the ground, opposes the verticality of the gateway and tempers the possible reference to a classic propylaea or triumphal arch with a surprising, almost playful freedom. Noticeably playful is *Willy*, with its eccentric, splayed volumes, rhyming planes and near-anthropomorphism. The only other piece of Smith's close to *Willy* is the behemoth-like *Grace Hoper* (in Bennington, Vermont, and not to be seen in either museum show) Indeed, in both, the punning humor which verges on the monstrous is not un-Joycean. (*Willy's* title is from Beckett's *Happy Days*; Smith's self-proclaimed Irishness is a theme running through his work.)

But his comic sense does not seem to me related to Dadaist absurdity. *Cigarette*, a gigantic, twisting rod, is one of his most formalist pieces, gaining little from its resemblance to a crushed-out super-cigarette. And *Wall*, which is simply that: an 18 by 8 by 2 foot wall, derives its interest not from the ploy of turning something "real" and ordinary into art, but rather, at least in part, from the strict, self-evident accuracy of its translation of the metaphoric (wall as barrier, frustration, repression) into the concrete. In other words, Smith works not out of gratuity, but out of inevitability.

He does not parody the inevitable by using a "systemic" method of repetition. Though he thinks of and describes his sculpture in terms of modules, he is not infatuated with conceptual anti-process. The basic unit of *The Marriage*, for example, was a 2 by 4 by 8 foot box, but when the four components were assembled, he felt that the resulting aperture was too narrow. So he removed the lintel and replaced it with one 10 feet long, thus sacrificing methodic consistency to the demands of sensibility or intuition. Repetitive structure in his work is usually not striking, though it is possible to figure out in, say, *Spitball* its combination of tetrahedrons, octahedrons, equilateral triangles, etc. In some works, such as *The Keys to. Given!* (like *Grace Hoper*, a *Finnegans Wake* title), which is three solid L's joined three-dimensionally at their tops, and thus the same when resting on any of its three bases, the principle of repetition is limited and not unfamiliar because not infinitely extensible. One more L, at most, could be added. And even then, the feet of the L's would probably have to be redirected. This is another aspect of working out of, or arriving at, the inevitable—when nothing can be added and nothing taken away.

Positing the inevitable is an attribute of classicism, and formally, as well, Smith is classical (though without Idealism.) First of all, his sculpture can be rightly seen only by walking around it. It is volumetric, not planar. (This, and not the exigencies of plywood or steel-plate construction, is why the edges are often bevelled; the contiguity of individual planes is thus emphasized.) Planar sculpture of one century is usually essentially pictorial, relief-like even if free-standing, but none of Smith's work can be seen sufficiently when seen frontally. There is no front, no back to it (except perhaps in *The Marriage*). *Amaryllis*, for example, in both the large and the small versions, offers a superb demonstration of space-filling energy, quite in keeping with its erect sexuality; its abstract *contrapposto* leads us around and around to gather the fullness of its two fixed but shifting masses. Its "deep" space, unlike pictorial or quasi-pictorial space, is continuous with our own, despite its internalization of the pedestal. For such continuity or "actuality," large size is essential to Smith's intention. It is obvious in works big enough and open enough to pass under or through, works like *Cigarette*, *Spitball*, or the 10 and 2/3-foot cubic *We Lost*, which is otherwise remote in its mute, hermetic symmetry. But even in smaller and more compact pieces, like *Free Ride* or *Playground*, there is no slackening of sculptural energy; their space is organized to interlock firmly with our own.

Wall is unique in its formal paradox. When you look directly at either of its long sides, it looks like pictorial sculpture carried to the extreme, because all you see is a single plane. But you have only to walk one-fourth of the way around it, to one of its two narrow sides, for the piece to reassert itself in all its solidity. And its 2-foot width seems exactly the right proportion to establish *Wall's* allusion to two-dimensionality but maintain safely its volume; it is more than just a free-standing plane.

Moreover, though *Free Ride*, *Cigarette* and even the more massive *Spitball* may be looked at as drawing-in-space, their angular arabesques describing linear forces, this means simply that Smith is assured enough about his ability to control volume to allow himself the freedom of incising an indeterminate void with a precise gesture. The authority is breathtaking; I know of no other modern sculptor who can combine volume, monumentality and geometry like Tony Smith.

An unclassical discontinuity in some of his sculptures—notably the large versions of *Amaryllis* or *Snake*—is perhaps in their abrupt dissimilarity from different angles. Sometimes the whole is not clear from any one side. But this discreteness reinforces rather than negates Smith's classical affiliations by reminding us that standing in one place is not enough. Emphasizing our physical relationship to the work avoids both the monolithic and "domestic" varieties of sculpture, neither of which is truly joined with the viewer's own body-space.

(By calling Tony Smith classical, I do not mean to suggest that he is some latter-day Pythagorean playing with ideal form and appealing to rationalism; the eruptive emotional content of his work makes him almost a card-carrying Romantic.)

Such insistence on continuity and totality of space and form has been rare in large-scale modern sculpture until recently. It is being revived by the Primary Structurists, but I have been at pains to stress Smith's classicism and expressiveness because I feel that he is not to be wholly situated within their ranks. There are, to be sure, affinities: he shares with the younger artists a move away from previous geometric sculpture, up to and including David Smith; he sometimes orders his sculptures from the factory (though he always avoids the machine-made finish); he is equally uninterested in the mystique of technology. But Smith is not only more "impure" formally and emotionally than the Primary Structurists, and more pro-classical, he is also, when he chooses, openly relational—though his work never generates its tensions from a complex interplay of details, and its relations are usually simple and explicit.

He does not always choose the relational. *Die*, his famous black, 6-foot steel cube, looks close to the "new esthetic." Andre, Judd, Morris and others have all made works as simple in form. But theirs seem to be, among other things, reducing the definition of sculpture to simply "that which man makes with the intention of filling real space." Smith's cube is far from such an esthetic of intention or concept, and is as interesting to look at as to think about. It has an ambiguous scale, a referential color and a loaded title (which Smith explains as both the imperative form of the verb and the noun meaning matrix or mold). Visually, the work fully equals the intensity of its title. *Die*, with a minimum of form, indelibly gives form to—shapes—its environment. What is around it, outdoors as well as in, begins to "lead up" to it, as to a climax. *Die* is not the elimination or antithesis of expression, but the culmination of expression—like a scream so high it can no longer be heard.

Donald Judd, in reviewing the Wadsworth Atheneum's "Black, White, and Gray" show, wrote that the new sculpture, in its opposition to "hierarchical values," suggests "the equal existence of things." Perhaps *Die* shares this attitude in its implication that, as in the catatonic state, all communication is equally urgent and equally futile. But the level is psychological, not esthetic or metaphysical. *Die* has such a presence, is so Expressionist in its aggression—in the way it acts on its surroundings, including people—that it seems far from the kind of art that declines to speak. It demands and provokes affective response, like the art called for by Kafka when he dreamed of works that would serve as "an axe for the frozen sea within us." *Die* is different from Smith's other sculptures only in the degree of apparency of its action; none of them are ever self-enclosed, tautological, object-like.

Too, *Die* lacks the irony of appropriating for its effect a "bland, neutral-looking form" (as Barbara Rose described primary structures or "ABC art").

Like the Primary Structurists, Smith does not commit what is known in literary criticism as the "fallacy of imitative form," but the simpler and more holistic his form, the stronger is the emotional tension. An absolute correspondence between form and content is implied.

Perhaps the most exact context for Tony Smith is not in sculpture at all, but in painting. (Except in its general architectonic quality, his sculpture does not look like sublimated architecture—or vice versa; he makes professional distinctions.) The common elements in the styles of Pollock, Newman, Still, Rothko, which need no summary here, seem to me more relevant to Smith's style than anything else in modern sculpture. With Newman especially, a parallel might be drawn: in their spareness of means, their fullness of emotional purpose, their fleeting similarity but fundamental dissimilarity to Neo-Plastic art, their ambivalent paternity of the younger generation. Tony Smith and Barnett Newman seem remarkably alike. To Smith's sheer volume, as to Newman's sheer color, an imagination of radical scale and eloquent simplicity is joined.

We will be sorting out for years the complex esthetic implications of such achievement, but what is immediately clear about Tony Smith's appearance is the addition of a major artist to the ranks of modern sculpture.

Tony Smith and Minimalist Sculpture (1967)

Unpublished text of lecture given at Walker Art Center, Minneapolis, October 10, 1967. Scott Burton Papers [II.12]. The Museum of Modern Art Archives, NY

E.N.: *In this prescient text written in the immediate wake of the pivotal summer 1967 issue of* Artforum *(which contained important texts such as Michael Fried's "Art and Objecthood" and Robert Morris's "Notes on Sculpture III"), Burton concisely summarizes the recent history of post-war sculpture and the presumptions of Minimalism. In this text, one can see Burton's nascent critique of Minimalism's coldness, elitism, and inhumanity—a position that would lead to the development of his usable furniture sculpture seen as exemplary of Postminimalism. More so than the tamer text he published in* ARTnews *the year before (from which it does admittedly repeat some arguments), Burton in this lecture criticizes the Minimalists while nevertheless perspicaciously evaluating and occasionally complimenting some of their tactics. Burton included slide cues in the margins of his manuscript, which are indicated in brackets in bold throughout the text.*

There are several similarities between Tony Smith and that group of younger artists whom we have been encouraged to think of as defining the major new direction in sculpture. I mean the Minimalists, the Primary Structurists, the makers of "specific objects," the "reductive" or "rejective" sculptors, namely Robert Morris, Donald Judd, Sol LeWitt, Ronald Bladen, John McCracken, Carl Andre, Robert Smithson, Larry Bell, Dan Flavin, and others. However, between Smith and these other artists who have come to prominence in the 1960s, there are also several important differences.

One of the most important things he has in common with them is an historical situation. These are all sculptors of the sixties and are very different from those of the fifties. Sculpture in the last decade was generally welded [**HERBERT FERBER**], though sometimes carved. Much was made of the work's material, and its "integrity." This sculpture always looked hand-made—not just man-made, but deliberately hand-made. In this way, it emphasized the artist's process of creating, as it also did in its frequent use of found objects. [**RICHARD STANKIEWICZ**] Whether the found object was a typewriter or a tree trunk, its relocation in a new context underlined the idea of art as the product of an *act*. Sculpture of the fifties was typically irregular in contour, surface, and color, or patina. It was usually *open* in form, often linear, or created of twisted, separated planes. Active interchange between void and solid was sought. The vocabulary was one of organic forms, referring to the human body; it was an anthropomorphic sculpture. [**ROBERT HAGUE**] It was gestural, using bodily movements, expressionistically, for emotional reference. [**ROBERT MALLARY**] It had, in general, an anguished and/or aggressive tone. Like its big brother, Abstract Expressionist painting, it was an art of *crisis*, of pathos. These qualities are found, more or less, in the work also of [Ibram] Lassaw, [Seymour] Lipton, [Philip] Pavia, [Theodore] Roszak, [Peter] Grippe, [Peter] Agostini, [Robert] Hague, and [Richard] Stankiewicz. The more polished and elegant work of artists like [Richard] Lippold, [Isamu] Noguchi, [Louise] Nevelson, or [José] de Rivera was unsupported by the serious artistic community. By the end of the fifties, the two Americans with the most intellectual prestige were [Reuben] Nakian and David Smith. They were thought of as establishing the polarities of our sculpture. [**REUBEN NAKIAN**] The style of Nakian, with its shredded surfaces, anxious bravado, and erratic form, seemed to be the ultimate expression in sculpture of the Abstract Expressionist sensibility. Postponing comparisons with David Smith for a moment, one can see very quickly how opposed is the Minimalist sensibility to the style which culminates in Nakian.

The sculpture of the sixties is—most obviously—geometric. It is made precisely, it bears no traces of the hand. It is always regular in color and surface. It is regularized in form, often standardized, modular. If it incorporates found objects—bricks, tubing, etc.—it does so matter-of-factly instead of transforming them: Flavin, for example. [**DAN FLAVIN**] It is not an anthropomorphic sculpture; it avoids not only the biomorphic form but also the latent human image. It is static instead of gestural. Two parts of a Judd don't thrust against each other. [**DONALD JUDD TWO-PART WITH WEDGE, TWO VIEWS**] It's not emotionally expressive but mute, and not aggressive, as we normally use that word. Sculpture of the sixties is almost always *closed* in form, not open but sealed off, volumetric rather than linear, dealing in large simple masses. [**MCCRACKEN PYRAMID**] The cube is a typical shape. It is removed from the maker's psyche; it does not dramatize his creative act. This style is in almost symmetrical contrast, point by point, to the preceding style (except in the case of David Smith's late work, that of the late fifties and sixties). [**DAVID SMITH CUBI**]

Primary Structurist sculpture has a more complex relation to David Smith than to the Abstract Expressionist sculptors; it is close to him in a fundamental way but is also very far removed. The closeness is one of spirit: both embrace the look of modern life. Their motifs are industrial, mechanical, technological. In fact, all abstract geometric art, whether of 1917 or 1967, inevitably has something in common. Meyer Schapiro, writing in 1937, long before David Smith or Tony Smith or Primary Structures, points out the "the forms of pure abstract art, which seem to be entirely without trace of representation [. . . are] influenced in their material aspect, as textures and shapes, and in their expressive qualities of precision, impersonal finish, and neatness (and even in subtler informalities of design), by the current conceptions and norms of the machine."[1] What Professor Schapiro called "technology as a norm in art" affects equally the styles of David Smith and [Piet] Mondrian, of Tony Smith and [Kazimir] Malevich, of Futurist, of Constructivist, and Minimalist. The vision of the industrial landscape has impressed us all. But different ways of transmitting a vision alter its meaning drastically. Thus, David Smith's sculpture and more recent geometric sculpture, including that of Tony Smith, are also deeply dissimilar.

For David Smith, technology meant the industrial forge, the factory, the metal-working plant. He wrote that his sculpture means to "duplicate as nearly as possible the production equipment used in making a locomotive."[2] He was moved by those utilitarian places in which men *make* things, by the way complex functioning objects are put together, the way wholes are constructed from parts. This preoccupation is expressed physically in his sculpture by its *relational* quality—how one part affects plastically another part. Like an automobile in Detroit, a David Smith *Cubi* is the result of a series of additions. The whole is built up hierarchically from the arrangement of smaller units, some outstanding, some subordinate. *Organization* is the central carrier of meaning, as it is in the theory of mass production, where the role of man is diminished but still essential. Faced with the [David] Smith sculpture, the viewer becomes involved in completing it; he has to make the visual effort to add it all together, to compare this part with that part, and finally to hold all the parts in his sight and mind in order to grasp firmly the whole, to arrive at the finished product. This effort is furthermore a rational act because it is a means to a known end. There is a goal in sight; whether it is the completion of an automobile or the full experience of a work of art, the parts fit together efficiently. A good David Smith looks logical. We test

1. Meyer Schapiro, "Nature of Abstract Art" [1937], in *Modern Art: 19th & 20th Centuries, Selected Papers, Vol. II* (New York: George Braziller, 1978), 205–06.

2. David Smith, "David Smith, Sculptor," *Everyday Art Quarterly 23* (1952): 20.

the relation of its parts and they make sense. Relationalism, by the way, is a quality of almost all art ever created; it is just that in David Smith, and modern geometric art before him, we are made extremely *aware* of the active interplay between parts, whereas in earlier arts they usually remain implicit. We look beyond them. But in the newer sculpture, there are often no parts to relate to each other. [**RONALD BLADEN**] We are confronted with simple, unitary forms which cannot be broken down into dominating and secondary elements.

In the background of all this is a very different experience of technology than David Smith's. Today, we sense that instruments do not need men to operate them. They are fully automated and their workings are invisible. David Smith's idea of a machine was a locomotive; ours is a computer bank. David Smith's material was steel; today plastics and fiberglass are typical. In our idea, the human presence is irrelevant. Is that not precisely the effect conveyed by Minimalist sculpture? It is alien, utterly withdrawn. Your participation is not invited. The sculptors I am speaking of decidedly do not draw the same optimistic conclusions from the "current conceptions and norms of the machine" that Marshall McLuhan does, by the way. They give us a catatonic feeling of total otherness, rather than a tribal oneness. Theirs is not a relational mentality, either of part to part of whole to viewer. When there *are* parts to compare to each other, their relation is always completely obvious. [**DONALD JUDD WALL PIECE WITH VERTICAL BLUE BARS**] It is usually one of equality—all parts exactly alike, interchangeable; nothing accented. Donald Judd writes, "In the new work the shape, image, color and surface are single and not partial and scattered. There aren't any neutral or moderate areas or parts, any connections or transitional areas."[3] Nothing is left for us to figure out, to discover. It is extremely disturbing.

3. Donald Judd, "Specific Objects," *Arts Yearbook 8* (1965): 78.

Sometimes this work even seems to mock us. If the unequal weighting of parts in a David Smith involves us in a rational act, the aim of which is possessing the whole, then the *equal* weighting in a Donald Judd, it seems to me, involves a *parody* of rationality. It is, as we say about farce, so logical that it's absurd. Reason is used to subvert reason.

[ROBERT MORRIS STAIRCASE] Robert Morris is the only one of the group who makes explicitly humorous works, like this staircase with footprints in it, but a Dadaist irony pervades the whole esthetic. This undercurrent is foreign to any previous geometric art. Think of Mondrian who wrote of the fixed and timeless laws of art, of dynamic equilibrium, and the search for the true content of reality. There is nothing transcendent or Purist like that in the geometric art of today.

To get back to the visible formal differences between David Smith and the newer sculptors, we may note some things that Smith, even at his severest and most geometrical, has in common with Nakian and the expressionist sculptors but not with the Primary Structurists. [ANOTHER SMITH, ANTHROPOMORPHIC] Even in the late series, David Smith was anthropomorphic; though there are no organic forms, a subliminal human image—a head on a torso supported by legs—asserts itself. The body is still providing the subject matter. Also, surface irregularities remained important to him, thus the stainless steel of the *Cubis* is not left alone but burnished and scoured with steel wool to produce variations of texture as unpredictable as those of a Nakian. Finally and most importantly, David Smith's work, like most of the sculpture of the fifties and especially like Nakian, is *frontal*. It is pictorial. There is one point from which we view the work to best advantage. That is the front; side or back views are less compelling and subordinate. (Volumes go back and forth. Central axis.) The sculpture becomes like a relief, even though it stands in the open, and ultimately like a picture. It exists in a shallow space, making us more aware of its planes than of the volumes behind them. It seems to be removed from us—indeed, in another space. That's why American sculpture in the fifties reintroduced something previous modern sculpture had tended to eliminate—the base.

Tony Smith and the Minimalists almost never put their work on bases. [**ROBERT MORRIS NON-BASE CIRCULAR PIECE**] It's in the room. It is not frontal or pictorial. The implications of this I will take up later, but for now I think it is clear that these artists are as far from David Smith as they are from Nakian or Ferber or Lassaw, even though they embrace, as David Smith did, "technology as a norm in art."

Tony Smith understands technology intimately. His background, as you know, is in engineering and architecture. He comes from a family of industrial manufacturers. The designs on blueprints, the forms in engineering drawings, interested him far beyond their immediate purpose. He has said that his speculations with plane and solid geometry and crystal forms were what led him to making models for sculpture. And his first serious piece, *Throne*, conceived in 1956, started, in his words, "with an idea that had nothing to do with sculpture. It was made in order to demonstrate an economical joint—one with four spokes meeting at the center of a tetrahedron."[4] In its tenor, Tony Smith's art is like that of the Primary Structurists—a mechanical imagery which dictates, in Robert Morris's summary description, "symmetry, lack of traces of process, abstractness, non-hierarchical distribution of parts, non-anthropomorphic orientations, general wholeness."[5] Seen in terms of esthetic evolution, of historical context, Tony Smith has much in common with Morris, Bladen, McCracken, Judd, Andre, and the others. However, to emphasize this, I have not only over-simplified, but have distorted Tony Smith's *oeuvre*.

4. In Samuel Wagstaff, Jr., "Talking with Tony Smith," *Artforum* 5.4 (December 1966): 17.

5. Robert Morris, "Notes on Sculpture III: Notes and Nonsequiturs," *Artforum* 5.10 (June 1967): 26.

He is not quite like that. In fact, the ways in which he is different from the Minimalists are as important and perhaps more interesting than the ways in which he is like them.

First of all, in the question of motivation, Smith's art does not originate, as does that of the Structurists, in stylistic rebellion. A large part of their energy is derived from the *rejection* and *negation* of their predecessors. They *try* to be radical. It is a point-by-point inversion, an exact opposite, almost, of earlier sculpture. Where A was black, B shall be white. The same thing is true in sixties painting. But this about-face in sensibility does not motivate Tony Smith. His art is the culmination of life-long preoccupations, and the shift in taste accounts only for the *reception* of his work, not for its very *genesis*. The history of sculptural style is not at all irrelevant to an understanding of Smith's art, but it is not *essential* to it in the way it is to the Minimalist movement. In several revealing ways, Smith's output differs from those of Judd, Morris, and the others.

Smith is not consistent. [**TONY SMITH FREE RIDE**] I have said that sixties sculpture is not gestural. Smith has done gestural pieces, like *Free Ride* and notably *Cigarette*. Sixties sculpture is not relational. Smith has relational works, in which he builds up the whole from an interplay of parts. Sixties sculpture is not anthropomorphic. [**TONY SMITH WILLY**] Smith can even be that; in at least one piece, *Willy*, the human body is inevitably recalled in its clumsy, crawling, sprawling disposition. Sixties sculpture is mute, inexpressive. Sometimes, Smith is not only expressive but nearly expressionist, intimating a violence and "crisis-content" similar to that of Abstract Expressionism. Sixties sculpture deals in closed forms, allowing the interpenetration of solid and void. [**SOL LEWITT**] By the way, this seems untrue. There are LeWitt's unfaced scaffoldings, Larry Bell's glass cubes, Morris's grills or wire mesh constructions, Judd's hanging wall-boxes with transparent sides. [**JUDD PINK BOX;**

BELL GLASS BOX] These forms are not closed, are they? Yes they are in that only the *eye* can pass through them. They have air in them, but the air is *caged*. Certain Tony Smiths, on the other hand, are literally open in that not only the eye, but the whole body can pass through them. And the voids play a role in the design as important as the role of the volumes. This is untrue of Primary Structures, whose makers are notably consistent. Tony Smith is so heterogeneous, so unprogrammatic, that he now plans to do inflated, pneumatic sculpture—organic in form and, as he says, "Surrealist in effect!" Indeed, he thinks of his geometric works as rather Surrealist. When *Life* magazine called them "dinosaurs," he was very pleased. His own descriptions are "presences of a sort," "seeds or germs that could spread growth or disease," "probably malignant."

How different from Carl Andre, for example, who describes his works as "atheistic, materialistic, and communistic [...] without transcendent form, without spiritual or intellectual quality."[6] In other words, deliberately lifeless. The only thing the Minimalists consider it proper to talk about is the esthetics of sculpture—what it is, what it should be. They are prescriptive, in their work as well as in their writing. Carl Andre is wrong; his work has nothing if not an "intellectual quality." An essential part, perhaps the most essential part, of looking at his work is *thinking*. This is not at all a passionless act, but the way; a great deal of "reductive" art has real intensity. But it is always didactic; we are being taught; we must *think*—about the *concept* of the works, about the esthetic behind it or expressed in it.

This is *not* the most important thing about looking at a Tony Smith. His art is expressive of feelings, ideas, attitudes that are about more than sculpture, more than art. If some of his work looks alien or withdrawn, the effect comes from an

6. Quoted in David Bourdon, "The Razed Sites of Carl Andre" [1966], reprinted in Gregory Battcock, ed., *Minimal Art: A Critical Anthology* (New York: E. P. Dutton & Co., 1968), 107.

experiential and not a conceptual source. That is, the remoteness is the *point* of the work, its very reference, and not a by-product or side-effect

To illustrate: Robert Morris once made a piece which was a grey or white triangle place in the corner of a room. It hid the point where the three planes of the walls and floors met, thus made a four-sided figure—a cube sliced diagonally in half. You couldn't tell from looking at it whether it was solid or hollow. You really didn't need to know; the point of it was that here was a new part of space for sculpture to occupy. Why should sculpture be in the middle of the room? Why not in a forgotten, invisible place like the corner? As brilliantly inventive as this piece was, what I have just told you about it has exhausted it. It is not unfortunate that I have no slide of it. It is a sculpture whose effect can be duplicated in words. It is animated exclusively by its concept, which can be transmitted verbally. Its actual physical existence becomes secondary. [**MORRIS 4 BOXES MIRROR**] (Morris 4 boxes mirrored in fact deprecates its own physical characteristics. Mirror makes surface arbitrary, whatever is before it.)

Let's take a very different work, a "plank" by John McCracken. It has an immediate physical impact. A typical one is eight feet tall, one foot wide, and one inch thick. It is bright shiny red or chartreuse or yellow. And it just leans against the wall. It has a knock-out color, a marvelous smooth finish, and a startling shape. But what is the *main* thing we notice about it? It is leaning against a wall. Have you ever seen a piece of sculpture before which simply leans against a wall? You've seen sculpture which rests on the ground (most does), sculpture which is affixed to a wall, even sculpture on the ceiling (in Calder or a Baroque church), but here is a leaning piece, one whose relation to the space it is in is unfixed—is, in fact, *arbitrary*. It could lean at any number of other angles—steeply or low—close to the wall or far out from it. The sculptor has relinquished his control over his work. Compare McCracken's plank to another work, innovational in its time, Calder's mobile. The Calder seems also to be arbitrary, to depend for its arrangement on something uncontrollable—gusts of air. However, the Calder's randomness is limited; its variety exists within a fixed system. There are only so many ways the pendants can rearrange themselves. But the McCracken is totally unfixed. It could even be displayed flat on the floor. The piece's relation to the space around it is arbitrary. This amounts to a *deprecation* of the actual physical existence of the work of art, no less than in the Morris corner piece, though less *obviously* because of the color, surface, and startling proportions. McCracken's is a brilliant idea, but it is an *idea*. His other plans may have different colors, and different heights and widths, but their point is the same—a new way for sculpture to occupy space. And it is a point, a concept, which can be communicated in words like any intellectual construct.

Now look at a Tony Smith, which has a minimum of visual interest, a severely reduced physical existence. [**TONY SMITH THE WALL**] *The Wall* bears a strong resemblance to Minimalist work; it can even be described accurately and completely in words. It is 18 feet long, eight feet high, and two feet thick. It is flat black. You can imagine it easily enough without actually seeing it. But you cannot *experience* it without seeing it.

The Wall has a vivid psychological impact which results from a series of dialectical tensions. To begin with, it is a wall. What is a wall? An element of architecture whose function is to hold up the roof, to bear weight. This piece bears no weight, though; it recalls function but denies function. It is a purposeful form without a purpose. But what about, say, a garden wall? It doesn't support a roof, but it functions to define and separate areas—to keep you *out* or keep you *in*. This wall does neither, you can walk around it. When you are on the other side, are you out or in? This wall separates, but only visually.

Thus another dialectic begins to operate, like that of function and non-function [or] the difference between looking and walking—that is, between two-dimensional and three-dimensional modes of perception. You can't see through Smith's wall but you can move around it and see the other side. Optical and kinesthetic experience are played against each other. And there is an extension of this two-and three-dimensional dialectic: If we stand directly in front of one of its long sides—you can't speak here of front and back—what do you see? A flat, two-dimensional plane. In other words, a painting, something like the ultimate [Ad] Reinhardt, perhaps. But move a few steps to the right or left and you see one of the narrow sides. Three-dimensional existence is restored. So, what is this object, a plane or a volume? Another dialectic, another unanswered question. We become puzzled by this work. Then remember the fact that it is too high for anybody to look over—eight feet. That is deliberate. What we are confronted with, in fact, is the very prototype of a baffling situation. Think of the expressions "like knocking your head against a wall," "his back to the wall," "like looking at a blank wall," "a wall of indifference."

Smith's piece *is* about the esthetics of sculpture, especially the distinction between two- and three-dimensionality, but it doesn't stop there. Formal analysis is insufficient. Looking at this work recalls barriers, frustrations, anxiety, repression. Its formal characteristics are a *means* to the metaphoric enactment of a kind of psychological experience. It is almost a symbolic work. It refers outside itself, and cannot be reduced to its own esthetic instigation, its own concept. You will have noticed that some of the words I have used to describe *The Wall* are also used to describe the Minimalists' sculpture—puzzling, frustrating, blank, baffling. But those qualities fade when you are more familiar with Primary Structures. They actually become quite lucid. Smith is obscure and mute only when he wants to be, as with *The Wall*. In other Smiths, the character of the experience can be very different. But when he chooses the qualities of futility and frustration, they do not diminish but *grow* with increased familiarity.

His art is *allusive* in a way Minimal work is not. It is mysterious in a way Minimal work is not. This can be seen by comparing two six-sided figures: Smith's *Die* and Donald Judd's grey box. [**DIE**] Smith's is a cube, black, and completely enclosed. Judd's is rectangular, a no-color grey, and its top is depressed, not flush.[7] It is four or five feet high. Anyone can see over it. No one misses the depressed top. Already I've said "top." *Die* has no top, is the same on every side, by definition. It is neither overpoweringly higher nor assuredly lower than the viewer. Its size is ambiguous in relation to the viewer in a way the Judd's size is not. Is *Die* hollow? We can't tell by looking; it is sealed. The Judd is obviously hollow; he's told us so by dropping the top so we can see that the four sides are material of a certain thickness. Judd takes pains to be specific. His box reveals explicitly the data about itself. (Judd also did a box with its top slightly raised though level—same thing.) *Die*, on the other hand, doesn't answer any questions. It is highly evocative. It starts to make us think of tombs—death is one of Smith's constant themes. It remains enigmatic and mysterious, especially outdoors. [**DIE OUTDOORS**] Who would think that two six-sided figures could be so different?

From these comparisons, a paradox appears. It is that in Minimalist sculpture, which appears to refer to nothing beyond itself, the actual, physical work is of secondary importance, whereas in Tony Smith's work, which always refers beyond itself, the actual, physical work is of primary importance. The effect of a Tony Smith can never be reconstituted in words, while the effect of a Morris or McCracken or Andre or Judd often can be.

7. The work Burton refers to is the Judd sculpture numbered DSS 79, exhibited at Leo Castelli Gallery in 1966.

Related to this is something else very important. I have said that a Tony Smith or a Primary Structure is not frontal or pictorial, as is a David Smith or a Nakian. The new sculpture is one of volume and mass, rather than plane and line. We are aware that it is in a space continuous with our own, is in our space, and we in its. It is not literally removed, by being set up on a base, and is not psychologically removed by having one position—the front—from which it looks best, like a picture or relief. The new sculpture, furthermore, *lets us know* that it is in our space, like this recent Morris which stretches across the open floor and makes us step over it or walk around it. [**MORRIS FLOOR BAR**] Tony Smith's *Marriage* or *Cigarette* we actually walk through. This is art of which we take direct physical cognizance. We walk around it. All sculpture exists in our own physical space, of course, but what is new is to be made so aware of it. Much new sculpture has an obstructionary quality. In that sense, it *can* be quite aggressive. It seems odd that a style featuring closed-off forms would emphasize its spatial continuity with the viewer, but it does just that because it is volumetric.

According to [Clement] Greenberg, "the essence of Modernism lies, as I see it, in the use of the characteristic methods of a discipline to criticize the discipline itself, not in order to subvert it, but in order to entrench it more firmly in its area of competence," and "Each art had to determine . . . the effects peculiar and exclusive to itself."[8] Thus painting had to declare explicitly its own flatness, demonstrating the principle of *plus ça change, plus c'est la même chose.*

What is the one thing sculpture has, then, that nothing else has? Its three-dimensionality, its existence in real space. But that's not quite true. Everything physical exists in real space—in the arts, obviously architecture and theatre do. Also

8. Clement Greenberg, "Modernist Painting" [1960], reprinted in John O'Brian, ed., *Clement Greenberg: The Collected Essays and Criticism* (Chicago: University of Chicago Press, 1993), 4:85 and 4:86.

painting and literature do, and painting has recognized that. Shaped canvases, often with extra thick stretchers, make you aware of it. You are even made aware of it by the arrangement of words on a page. There have been several significant experiments from [Stéphane] Mallarmé through [Guillaume] Apollinaire to [e. e.] cummings and others which reinforce the physicality of the poem. But especially do architecture and theatre share the condition of sculpture.

There have, of course, been many criticisms of geometric structure-art, especially Smith's, that it is really displaced architecture. And more recently and more sophisticatedly from Greenberg and [Michael] Fried, that this kind of sculpture fails because it is theatrical—not in the sense that [Auguste] Rodin is theatrical, demonstrating a high moment of human action, but in the sense that it depends too much on its environment. "Literalist sensibility," I quote Fried, "is theatrical because it is concerned with the actual circumstances in which the beholder encounters literalist work."[9] I suggest that this concern with actual circumstances is an essential condition of any sculpture. It is obvious in the case of a Greek pedimental sculpture or Michelangelo's Medici tomb figures, but is nonetheless true of sculpture not intended to collaborate with architecture, with works meant to exist independently. Sculpture is at once the most tangible and the most fragile—the solidest and the least secure—of all the arts. Fried fails to see, I think, that the new artists' concern with the "actual circumstances"—the way they emphasize the environment by reducing the physical complexity of the work itself—is an attempt to restore, to revitalize one of the few things that sculpture can call its own. We have seen that three-dimensionality is not something that sculpture has all by itself. It competes not only with certain other arts in this respect but

9. Michael Fried, "Art and Objecthood," *Artforum* 5.10 (Summer 1967): 15.

with the whole of the material world in a way these other arts do not. Fried is accurate in his perception but shaky in his judgment. One admires Morris and Judd and others for that very thing—for making us aware once again that sculpture exists in *our* space, in our world.

The question becomes not what *makes* it art, but what *keeps* it art? Fried's complaint is Judd's boast—the work becomes one more object in a world of objects. Now this is the exact opposite of theatrical—the very idea of theatre presupposes the unequal existence of things, presupposes valuation. Some things—passions, thoughts, actions, character changes, some very movements—are more significant than others in any theater. Even in the most radical play ever written *Waiting for Godot*, there are lines or moments more charged, more revealing than others. The psychological structure of theater is inescapably one of intensification, climax, and release. So, what I am saying is that in a very important way Primary Structures are anti-theatrical in that their forms are anti-hierarchical. They do not mime the climactic or anti-climactic (Tony Smith excepted as we will see) form of drama or performance. But, also, that in a very important way Fried is right that Primary Structures *are* theatrical, but *I* think that this is one of the best things about the work—it *reconnects* sculpture to something sculpture had lost: *its* existence in a real environment. In fact that is almost the *only* characteristic of some Primary Structures.

This is true of Tony Smith *and* the Minimalists, but they do it in very different ways: a Robert Morris does it by looking the same from all sides, and a Tony Smith does it by looking different from different sides. Take Morris's rhomboid and Smith's *New Piece*. [NEW PIECE] The Morris is a grey pyramid with the top sliced off level. All four of its sides slope at the same angle. Thus it looks just the same from any point—completely unlike the Nakian or David Smith, which have discernible fronts, sides, and backs. The Morris insists on in-the-roundness by being the same from all angles. *New Piece* does too but in just the opposite way—by being *different* from all angles. From one it appears massive, bottom-heavy, stable. From another it leans sharply, precariously, without quite threatening to fall over. From yet another angle it is positively menacing; it slices out at you, rearing up and looming over you. *New Piece* changes its character very definitely from different vantage points. Who is to say which is the front? It is, in fact, multiply frontal. Its contours and distribution of volume are radically transformed as you walk around it. In the Morris, they are not. This is exactly what Morris *wants*; he calls it "gestalt" art—work about which all visual information is instantly available.[10] That's why he eliminates parts. *New Piece* has no parts either, but it does not yield itself up instantly—it has activity and surprise.

Amaryllis is a notable example of this. [**AMARYLLIS TWO VIEWS**] Its two halves—which are exactly alike, by the way—make it look now rising, now falling, quietly recumbent or ponderously hooking off into space. It has a kind of contrapposto which leads one around it again and again for a fuller perception of its shifting volumes. The Structurists want volume but without that liveliness. Perhaps that is what has led Donald Judd to do wall pieces. [**JUDD WALL PIECE (ORANGE)**] There is no possibility of the profile changing as you walk around it because you can't walk around it.

Carl Andre prevents his work from any possible metamorphosis in another way. Like the small slate or metal tiles which lie flat on the floor arranged in a square, his bricks give themselves up wholly at the first glance. Everything to be known about the work can be known immediately. It is, at it were, "at your feet." Andre has ingeniously staked out another way for sculpture to occupy space, like Morris's corner-sculpture

10. In Robert Morris, "Notes on Sculpture, Part 2," *Artforum* 5.2 (1966): 20–23.

or McCracken's plank. Here it is the floor. Not since Greek and Roman mosaics has the floor been a suitable place for art, and even then only for decorative art, which Andre's is not. The ground is, or was, what sculpture rises up from. Now we have supine sculpture. It's very novel, and yet it's very familiar. What else in art is flat and rectangular? A painting. One of the basic attributes of a painting is that it is all there at once. So is the "gestalt" sculpture of Morris and Judd and Andre. Therefore another paradox presents itself: here is an anti-pictorial sculpture which strives toward the condition of painting. Tony Smith is the only one of the newer geometric sculptors whose work changes very much from different angles. Though the Minimalists also restore the volumetricity of traditional sculpture, they use radical means to do it—the unitary or "gestalt" form— and end up in something resembling a contradiction: mass which is to be apprehended with the instantaneity of a painting.

Tony Smith is, on the other hand, in some way profoundly conservative, just as [Paul] Cézanne was. Cézanne wanted to redo [Nicolas] Poussin and wound up altering the course of painting. Tony Smith might be said to want to redo the Laocoön or Michelangelo or Bernini, but his impulse toward traditional plasticity looks today very innovational. [BERNINI TWO VIEWS] In this Bernini, the *Rape of Persephone*, for example, our sense of its three-dimensionality, its in-the-roundness, is continually reinforced by its changing aspects of profile and weight. The tradition lasted from Hellenism through Canova. [CANOVA TWO VIEWS] See how different this *Cupid and Psyche* is from two sides. Then think of the first modern sculptor, Rodin. His only real attempt at group composition is the *Burghers of Calais*, and that is already weak. It is not equally satisfactory from all sides, even though an attempt is made with the turning figures. From one point the *Burghers* is quite like watching a play from behind the scenes. With Rodin, sculpture loses its in-the-roundness just as, after [Édouard] Manet, painting begins to shed its illusionism. [Constantin] Brancusi's sculpture, though it is conceived truly three-dimensionally, is usually too small and intimate to connect with the viewer's body-space, and it is set on pedestals. When Brancusi did his largest piece, though, the *Endless Column*, he anticipated astonishingly the Primary Structure. [Alberto] Giacometti's attenuated figures hardly affect our sense of corporeality.

Tony Smith is the first artist in a very long time to bring that full, almost exuberant, physical awareness to sculpture. Primary Structures aim at it, but they do not encourage one to walk around them—at least more than once—because they offer a repetitive experience. So in the end, one thinks about them in the round as little as one does a David Smith or a Nakian. On the other hand, we are made eager by a Tony Smith like *New Piece*, *Amaryllis*, or *Cigarette* to know all the facets of its form and personality. For this, Smith employs very traditional means, multiple plasticity, and yet there is also something deeply *un*traditional in his treatment of volume. Compare *Amaryllis* with these two views of Giovanni da Bologna's *Rape of the Sabines*. [**GIOVANNI DA BOLOGNA**] The *Rape* is indeed different from changing angles, but one view leads into another. Each prepares for the next. As violent as the work is, it is not at all violent in that fundamental way. Its transitions are smooth and fairly even. From one view we can predict the next. Its movement is continuous. The same cannot be said of *Amaryllis*. Nothing prepares us for its drastic transformations from different angles. It has not transitions, but wrenching juxtapositions.

In Tony Smith there is a very modern *discontinuity* of experience. It is the same discontinuity we find in the space of a Cubist collage, the abrupt rhythmic changes of [Igor] Stravinsky, the chapter-by-chapter stylistic changes of [James] Joyce's *Ulysses*, the dislocation of meaning in a William Burroughs collage-novel, or the narrative elisions of a [Jean-Luc] Godard film. It is a typically modern psychological structure, not to be found in the Giovanni da Bologna, which behaves consistently, but rather an inconsistent, discontinuous structure. In those Tony Smiths which change so radically, we are confronted with the fragmentation of experience.

This is not the case with the Primary Structurists, as is shown in the way they use modules. [**JUDD WALL PIECE (GREEN)**] Donald Judd's vertical wall-piece consists of seven identical units. Why seven? Why not eight? Would that change the character of the work very much? The work is in fact capable of indefinite extension, it is "open-ended." Or this Andre spiral piece. Each bar is in the very same position relative to its neighbors. Logically, it could go on and on, higher and higher. Work like this seems permanently incomplete. Where it stops is arbitrary, no less arbitrary than the spatial positioning of the McCracken plank. It is gratuitous whether there are twelve units or twenty or fifty. It's so logical it's absurd. Andre often uses systems—same number in each, simple as ABC. [**ANDRE GALLERY SHOT**]

But Tony Smith does not parody rationality in this way when *he* uses modules. Sometimes we are not aware that his work is modular. *Spitball* is constructed entirely from a number of tetrahedral units—four-sided figures—but the eye does not grasp their sameness, subsumed as they are into a massive whole. Sometimes Smith begins with modular units and then abandons them. [**MARRIAGE**] *The Marriage* was originally four boxes, two by four by eight feet, but when assembled, the result had, as he says, "a pinched look," so he made the lintel, the top box, two feet longer to open the work out. As I said, he is not consistent. [**KEYS TO. GIVEN!, TWO VIEWS**] In a work like *The Keys to. Given!*, which *is* consistent in its modules—they are three L's—the work is too complex for us to grasp its modularity without an effort. And even when we do grasp it, we can see that no more units could be added. It is not unfinished or unfinishable, but symmetrical three-dimensionally, and complete.

The Primary Structurists use repeated identical units in a deliberately simple way. Such work, as Donald Judd wrote, "in its opposition to hierarchical values suggests the equal existence of things."[11] Their music would be that of Erik Satie—one phrase repeated eight hundred or a thousand times. Satie's statement, "Experience is one of the forms of paralysis," applies to this style, which shrinks experience by reducing its variety to a minimum, or when it retains parts, turns them into modules. This is not anti-human, by the way; some say of this style that it is estranged and mute but others say that it is tranquil and meditative. It is certainly elegant, often beautiful in fresh ways.

In either case, the structure of experience is different with Tony Smith, whose work offers not only the plasticity but the drama of traditional sculpture, the emotional hierarchy of conflict, intensification, climax, and release. [**CIGARETTE, VIEW A**] This view of *Cigarette* shows it. See how it starts off heavy and thick, narrows at the top, suddenly bloats, and then curves down, quietly thinning. It is dramatic in its transitions, like the Giovanni da Bologna was. And yet unlike that work, Smith's varies unpredictably from different angles. And this means that he has not one climax or drama in his work, but many—as many as there are angles to view it from. [**CIGARETTE, VIEW B**] There is the opposite side of *Cigarette* with a whole other drama. It begins at the ground very heavily, then immediately shrinks to its narrowest, expands as it climbs, then turns and

11. This is not a direct quote but rather a paraphrase based on Burton's 1966 article on Tony Smith. He is referring to Donald Judd's March 1964 *Arts Magazine* review of the exhibition *Black, White and Gray* at the Wadsworth Atheneum (reprinted in *Donald Judd: Complete Writings 1959–1975,* Halifax: Press of the Nova Scotia College of Art and Design and New York: New York University Press, 1975) in which Judd states "Western art has always asserted very hierarchical values. [Robert] Morris's work and that of others in this show, in different ways, seem to deny this kind of assertion." (117)

makes a smooth, unmarred descent. And from another side, or from underneath its arch, there are still other distributions of energy. From each position the force is unequally distributed, in an un-Minimalist way, yet all positions are equally compelling.

I have said that Smith is not formally consistent in the way the Minimalist sculptors are. *Cigarette* is an example. It is linear and gestural, a giant arabesque in space. It is not unlike a [Jackson] Pollock line, in fact, in the way it is flung, in the way it swells and slows and twists, narrows and shoots ahead. Another linear piece of Smith's is *Free Ride*, though it is also evidence of his preoccupations with the cube, for it describes a cube's three axes. But it does trace, rather snakily, a line in space. *Spitball* also traces a gesture—up, down, and back—but the thickness and closeness of its columns make it also a ground-hugging mass. [**NIGHT**] *Night* is a right-angled gesture with four segments. [**ELEVENS ARE UP**] There are several cubic pieces—obviously *Die*, but also *The Elevens are Up*, which is two walls eight by eight by two feet standing parallel six feet apart, thus making an eight-foot cube. *The Keys to. Given!* would also fit into a cube. Less obviously related to the cube is *New Piece*, which does look as if it might once have been square. There are works based on the pyramid, like *Willy* or *Spitball.*

And then there is another motif which is not taken from geometric figures. It is the architectural motif, as in *The Wall. The Marriage* is part of this group. Its gate form brings to mind Greek propylaea or a Roman triumphal arch—something solemn and ritual, something which figures in a ceremony. The Roman arch is for civic celebration, but a marriage is a ceremony of privateness, and I think this piece tells us something central about Tony Smith's art. He unifies the public and the private. His sculpture is civic in that it is large, monumental, un-intimate in scale, in the viewer's own space so that he can often pass through it; and his sculpture is also intensely private, a medium for the expression of his own feelings. It has drama, crisis. It often speaks of tragedy or death. It is not an accident that his sculptures are black.

Here is *The Elevens are Up* in a closer view. [ELEVENS] Though it is quite innovational, formally—a sculpture in parts which don't touch—the only thing like passing into and through it I can think of is entering a Mycenaean tomb, the high, straight walls impelling you inexorably on. Fortunately, one can come out on the other side of the Smith! And look at *We Lost.* [WE LOST] It is in a ten-foot cube, but is like two arches connected by two ground bars, a little like *The Marriage* twice. It is a desolate little house, a kind of tragic gazebo.

Smith's best work gives us abstract images of the absolutes of human experience. He reminds me very much of another Irish-American artist, Eugene O'Neill. It is more than the similarity of their social backgrounds and difficult personal histories. It is more than the similar shape of their careers. Smith's houses and paintings, like O'Neill's early plays, as interesting as they may be, turn into apprentice work when compared to what is achieved in the middle and later years. No, the real similarity is one of temperament. From both we have enormous, monumental structures, pessimistic and somber, but grand, and sometimes humorous in some wild, extreme way. Both men deal in extremes, formal as well as emotional. O'Neill pushed naturalistic theatre so far that it became something else, something more like the older forms of theatre, like tragedy. Smith pushes modern sculpture so far that some of the power of traditional sculpture is restored. In both men, there is an eruption of the Romantic spirit, yet both are obsessed by a Classical strictness of form. Both men have a kind of primitive, tragic power in their art. To compare Tony Smith to the Primary Structurist sculptors in esthetic matters—volume, use of modules, the place of concept in the work—may make some things clear, but the most exact way I can think of to suggest the appeal that Smith exerts is to ask you to think of *The Marriage*, say, or *Die*, in the same way you think of *Long Day's Journey into Night*.

Smith has a number of things on common with the other geometric sculptors of our decade. But really, comparisons are unfair. What Fairfield Porter once wrote about de Kooning is the way one comes to feel about Tony Smith: his art "releases human significances that cannot be expressed verbally. It is as though his painting reached a different level of consciousness than painting that refers to any sort of program. [. . .] No one else whose paintings can be in any way considered to resemble his reaches his level."[12]

12. Fairfield Porter, "Willem de Kooning," [1959] reprinted in Fairfield Porter, *Art in Its Own Terms: Selected Criticism 1935–1975*, ed. Rackstraw Downes (Boston: Museum of Fine Arts Publications, 1979), 36–37.

Ronald Bladen (1967)

Review of Ronald Bladen at Fischbach Gallery, *57th Street Review* 1.3 (January 16, 1967): 2.

Ronald Bladen's *Black Triangle*, an "experimental piece for metal construction," is an inverted wedge nine and one-third feet tall. It stands alone in the gallery like a black ship riding at anchor. This opaque prism involves the viewer bodily with its balance or suspension, as did Bladen's falling three-part sculpture in the *Primary Structures* show (Jewish Museum) and his levitating white box in the current Whitney Annual. *Black Triangle* creates a daring, almost excruciating tension; people in the gallery do not come too close to it. You have no choice but to apprehend the piece as a whole (since it has no parts); nevertheless the attention tends to focus on its bottom, the edge on which it perilously rests. Its energy seems to be concentrated most sharply there, and to disperse in rising, so that, paradoxically, it is not at all top-heavy.

Still, it is a massive solid which "defies gravity," and thus has the thrill of fantasy, such as we feel when we dream that we can fly. It does provoke kinesthetic anxiety, but is also psychologically gratifying.

If the dynamics of physical inquietude were all that Bladen offered, his work would merely irritate. But it has not only a counterpoint between anxiety and imaginative release, it has as well great metaphorical power. Words to describe *Black Triangle* are "loom," "rise," "float"—expressive, evocative words. But Bladen's metaphor is not explicit; like the story in Balanchine's *Serenade*, it is in an unknown language. So the drama or poem becomes abstract.

Bladen has some affinities with Mannerist sculpture, the great dynamic pyramids of Giovanni da Bologna or Bernini reappearing inverted in *Black Triangle*. But perhaps the work which Bladen's latest piece most resembles, in its grand gesture, is the *Winged Nike* from Samothrace.

When Attitudes Become Form: Notes on the New (1969)

"Notes on the New," in Harald Szeemann, ed., *Live in Your Head: When Attitudes Become Form* (Bern: Kunsthalle Bern, 1969), n.p.

E.N.: When Attitudes Became Form *was a defining exhibition for conceptual, earthwork, and Postminimal practices. In this relatively short introductory essay to the catalogue, Burton adeptly juggled the divergent artists included in the exhibition. Due to the nature of the exhibition and the fact that Burton was writing from overseas, he focused primarily on New York artists. Of note are his emphases on temporality and on the viewer's situation as criteria for evaluating this work. Furthermore, one can see the incipient formulae for his durational performance works in his emphasis on time and for his functional furniture sculpture in his statement, "Art is still what is useless; for it to imitate the utilitarian is one way out of the plethora of decorativeness in abstract painting today."*

"Saying is inventing." —Samuel Beckett, *Molloy*

This exhibition gathers a number of artists whose works have very little in common yet also a great deal in common. The similarities are less stylistic than intellectual, at least among the participating Americans; a few major groupings may be made: multiformal or non-rigid art (Claes Oldenburg, Robert Morris, Eva Hesse, Frank Viner, Richard Tuttle), conceptual or ideational art (Edward Kienholz, Lawrence Weiner, Joseph Kosuth, Stephen Kaltenbach, Douglas Huebler), earthworks and organic-matter art (Dennis Oppenheim, Neil Jenney, Michael Heizer, Richard Long), geometric abstraction (Carl Andre, Sol LeWitt, Richard Artschwager, Fred Sandback), procedural or "process" art (Richard Serra, Keith Sonnier, Robert Ryman).

Grouping artists by intentions or their choice of materials will create communities otherwise unrelated. For example, it seems to be the aim of both Artschwager and Huebler to frustrate the viewer's method of information-gathering, but how different is a work of forty separate and widely distributed parts (Artschwager's "blps"), from one containing information (package wrappers, registered mail receipts) substantiating the work's dimensions in thousands of miles. In neither case is it possible to perceive the work in its spatial entirety or its extension in time (in Huebler's case, about 40 days; in Artschwager's, however long it takes to locate all the separate parts). But the two hardly resemble each other further.

The geometrically regular designs shared by Sol LeWitt and Carl Andre confer on the pair a stylistic relation which is then contradicted in their work. Andre's piece is completely variable since its separate parts are exactly alike. It is of no importance whether square x and square y change places. This formal arbitrariness links Andre thematically with the users of flexible, thus variable materials. LeWitt, on the other hand, is not only making geometrical designs, he is making them directly on the wall in order to *eliminate* variability. His wall drawings are like both a great Italian mural and a wall graffito: if they do not exist in a fixed relationship to their environments, they do not exist at all. LeWitt's work, unlike Andre's, cannot be altered in any way without being destroyed.

Richard Serra, an artist of a very different sensibility, also creates works to exist *only* in one specific place. An amount of molten lead poured directly on the floor cannot be transferred from place to place, obviously, but unlike LeWitt, Serra focuses our attention on the manipulation of the properties of matter. The location decided upon for the distribution of a *fluid* material unavoidably affects the manner or means of distribution; for example, the height from which Serra pours his lead will affect the very size of the result. Serra's splash pieces are as situationally specific as any architectural or relief sculpture was ever meant to be, but by a very novel and simple means.

One of the few general characteristics of the artists in the show is how they relate their work to location. Generally, the choice is between a totally fixed position or a totally free relation of work to site. Carl Andre has used the term, "post-studio artists," to describe himself and others who do not actually make their own art but have it fabricated. The phrase is equally applicable to artists like Serra or LeWitt, who make their own pieces though not always in their studios, as well as to Kosuth or Weiner, who may use typewriters and telephones, but eliminate the production of objects entirely. Weiner's "wall removal"—a work in which absence constitutes presence—has already been seen in New York and Europe; both showings, according to the artist, are the same work. Its identity lies in its idea, which can exist just as well as a "statement" on the printed page. Serra's splash piece has also been seen in New York and Europe; in this case, however, the artist insists that the two are completely different works of art. Identity lies in its actual presence, a position paralleled by the impossibility of moving the work from its site.

Both Weiner and Serra are "right." What matters is not so much the esthetic position in itself as the extremity to which it is taken, and this exhibition includes some of the most extreme art ever produced. The modern obsession with going as far as possible is demonstrated again and again; relationships between art and idea, art and site, art and material, art and methodology are pushed to their limits by these artists. Perhaps the only quality that unifies the artists in this show is their urgency.

The super-cool ironies of Bruce Nauman and the almost Expressionist pathos of Eva Hesse are two versions of that part of the modernist temperament which is Romantic. The early Romantic, whether Percy Bysshe Shelley or Caspar

David Friedrich, felt himself to be a tiny dot in the vast cosmos; Oldenburg's vastly enlarged objects create a similar haptic response—one's body suddenly shrinks. The fact that Oldenburg is parodying the relation between self and the universe makes him even more of a Romantic; his desire to create monuments is consistent.

To Robert Morris the uncontrollable forces of nature are embodied in the law of gravity, which dominates his drooping spasmically curling lengths of felt. More than method, process becomes product itself when, as in Morris's heroic and helpless cloth pieces, the work itself can be altered. Unlike an Andre floor piece, any change in a Morris work may be noticeable, though only to someone who has seen the piece in an earlier state. Memory is essential to comprehension in this case.

Again arises the crucially important subject of time in the new art. The unambiguous forms of Primary Structure sculpture tried to be like painting by inducing instantaneous perception; all information about a Donald Judd box is obtained as quickly as possible. But the new art generally does not try to defeat or deny its existence in time, but instead makes the viewer highly aware of it.

It is still "minimal" in its actual presence; note the avoidance of mass in Sandback's string pieces, the flimsiness of Sonnier's hanging fabrics, the reluctance to delineate volume clearly in Saret's crumpled balls of wire fencing. Much of the new work looks vulnerable, not only spatially insubstantial, but dominated also by the effects of time.

Though non-rigid art may at times refer to the weight and degrees of energy of the human body, it is not "humanist" because the viewer so often feels excluded, deprived of some states or parts of the work. In a similar spirit, Bruce Nauman's steel slab is said to have a mirrored bottom, but because it is hidden, we can only believe him. Yves Klein's day in Paris as a work of art is less an exuberant gesture than the presentation of an event that is impossible to perceive completely. Mere perception becomes a metaphor for cognition. The conceptual, categorical ambiguities of the new art stand in sharp contrast to its direct occupation of space or specific demonstration of physical laws.

The most fundamental law of nature is that everything that exists in space also exists in time; artists today work with that knowledge in unforeseen ways. A Bill Bollinger rope piece does not change from day to day; indeed, its fixedness, its tension as it stretches between two anchoring bolts, is its very point. But what happens to it when it is disassembled? Does it still exist? If so, does it exist as rope, as potential art, or as art? Its installation is made synonymous with its existence, whereas a painting or fixed-form sculpture, no matter how radical its esthetic, does not literally cease to be when it is in storage. The ontological instability of the Bollinger piece introduces, on the psychological plane, an experience of anxiety about being, which has been the chief subject of philosophy since Descartes. Consciousness as proof of existence is translated in esthetic terms: conception as method of creation.

Another Bollinger work (seen in New York in January) consisted of an amount of graphite strewn across the gallery floor. The spectacle of a work in several different parts is not unfamiliar, but here is a work in hundreds of thousands of different parts. Of equal relevance is the spectator's necessary participation in its form; when one walks across Bollinger's graphite-covered floor, it is inevitably changed in its distribution of volume. This is both willed and accidental, a combination stemming from Duchamp and Dada, but recently more familiar as a compositional device in the work of John Cage, Merce Cunningham, Robert Rauschenberg, and, before them, the Abstract Expressionists, particularly Pollock.

The artist who explores chance any further today has almost necessarily to use time in his work. Morris has announced his intention of working on his next show every morning before the gallery opens so that it will be necessary to visit it every day in order to keep up with the multiple changes. If Morris does this, his performance will be at least as relevant as the work's tangible elements.

What is happening to form is what happened to order when it was subjected to chance by Duchamp, Arp, and others; it proves capable of apparently infinite extension. (It is significant that several of the new artists use flexible or extendable materials like rubber. The interaction between time and material also determines the artists' continuing interest in "common," "non-art" materials — cloth, plastic, dirt and organic matter, industrial flocking. These things are mutable, perishable, sensitive to manipulation to a degree that more usual materials like stone and wood are not. Several years ago Rauschenberg said, "I try to act in the gap between art and life," for that gap continues to narrow. Art has been veritably *invaded* by life, if life means flux, change, chance, time, unpredictability. Sometimes the only difference between the two is sheer consciousness, the awareness that what seemed to be a stain on the wall is in fact a work of art. Or a trench in the snow, or a pile of scraps, or a hole in the wall, or a hole in the desert. After all, if a de Kooning painting is the record of a series of *acts*, why not act directly upon the world by cutting a three-mile-long swath in the snow, as Dennis Oppenheim has done? (Robert Smithson has developed the dialectic between site and work of art to a high degree of wit and complexity. Smithson's "non-sites," consisting of photographs, maps, and piles of rocks or dirt in his handsome bins, document his particular version of industrial archaeology for the gallery audience. Both his direct use of the landscape and his system of documentation implicate him centrally in the new directions of art.)

What we are witnessing is a new naturalism or realism born of extended collaborations between the artists and nature, chance, material, event, the viewer. The nineteenth-century manifestation of realism (especially in Europe, which was not under the Arcadian illusions of contemporaneous America) was not only a style but also a preference for a certain kind of subject matter—the raw, unpleasant, ordinary, ugly, proletarian. A similar preference is felt again and again in the torn, flopping "anxious objects" in this exhibition. But the humbleness of Richard Tuttle's wrinkled dyed, nailed-up pieces of cloth is rivaled only by their grandeur of conception—they have no back, no front, no up or down, they may be attached to the wall or spread out on the floor. Imagine making an object which will maintain its integrity in all circumstances yet which exerts absolutely no demands on its situation.

To see the superficiality and profundity of similarities and differences between the artists in this show, compare the Tuttles to the paint-on-paper works by Robert Ryman. The latter are glued to the wall in a certain arrangement and though they are as flat and insubstantial as the other's cloth works, they are about the conventions of a particular art—painting—rather than about the idea of art itself. It is not possible to say whether a Tuttle is a painting or a sculpture; it uses properties of both and is probably neither. But the Ryman must be seen in a strictly pictorial context, and especially one of recent American abstraction.

As American paintings have gotten larger and larger, they have also become thicker (primarily in Frank Stella) through the use of extra-heavy stretcher bars. Painting has asserted more and more its objectness through these means, and also in the departure from rectangular shape in many cases, and even in serialism, which emphasized physicality through sequence. Against all these Ryman reacts to make works as physically modest as they are conceptually demanding.

The deprecation of art, as in Serra's demonstration of something we all know—that one object will pin a sheet against a wall if the tensions are correctly (not pleasingly but correctly) deployed—is only apparently a deprecation. Art is still what is useless; for it to imitate the utilitarian is one way out of the plethora of decorativeness in abstract painting today.

But particularly interesting in relation to modernist abstraction is the new emphasis on time, the introduction of duration and performance. Categories are being eradicated, distinctions blurred to an enormous degree today. The difference between painting and sculpture has gone (following that between poetry and prose in verbal art). The tremendous critical intelligence demanded from the ambitious artist is bringing him closer and closer to the intellectual; art and ideas are becoming indistinguishable. The intention of some of the younger poets is nothing less than the blending of visual and verbal art; words are looked at, pictures are read, poems are "events," plastic or visual art is "performed." In dance, the difference between skilled and untrained body movement is dwindling. The only large esthetic distinction remaining is that between art and life; this exhibition reveals how that distinction is fading.

More precisely, is the occasion for the *mimesis* of that fading. No afunctional act can really be anything but symbolic, but it is compelling to see, at least, the continuing dilation of art's limits, to watch the quotation marks get further and further apart. In 1913, Marcel Duchamp wrote, "Can one make works which are not works of 'art'?"

Time on Their Hands (1969)

"Time on Their Hands," *ARTnews* 68.4 (1969): 40–43.

Two current museum exhibitions, the Guggenheim's *Nine Young Artists* and the Whitney's *Anti-Illusion: Procedures/ Materials* offer recent work in which the temporal dimension is crucial to both concept and appearance.

All art exists in time, of course, like everything else, but today time is often incorporated into the work of art by means so direct and so simple that it seems sometimes to be the paramount element of the work. To the composer, choreographer, and narrative artist, including the film-maker, playwright, and novelist, there is nothing new about the esthetic employment of time. (The main inaccuracy of the "formalist" criticism which calls much recent art "theatrical" is in the conservative assumption that the adjective is pejorative.) Perversely, artists, trained in the reorganization of physical matter to produce art objects, are today going against the grain of their mediums, so that what was once painting and sculpture has become as important for duration in time as for location in space. "Literalism" has been extended to modes of temporal existence; painting has been swallowed by sculpture—at least, insofar as the painter depends on the physicality of his work to elicit interest—and sculpture, always apparent in its temporality since merely to see the entire work takes time, is using time in new ways.

The interest in time was anticipated by the older generation of both painting and sculpture. In 1962, Tony Smith made a small sculpture, *The Black Box*, which is a box but which is not black but rather rust-colored. It is of untreated steel and is an outdoor piece; the rusting is intentional. Although occasional applications of linseed oil retard the process of oxidation, Smith's is a work which some day (in 200 or 300 years?) will no longer exist. Unlike patina, which "adds" to a sculpture, rusting takes away—literally. Jean Tinguely's self-destroying machines had a deliberately limited existence, too, but Smith chose instead to employ a natural (and very slow) process to determine his work's life span. Esthetic choice—in this case, as in Robert Morris's mirrored cubes, involving the appearance of the work's surface—is shunned. This is not just a new version of "truth to materials" but something more, an alignment or identification of the viewer's time with the work's. The two become continuous; the fictive time of art gives way to *our* time, to "real" time.

By a different method, the late "black" paintings of Ad Reinhardt accomplish a similar temporalization of plastic art. How long does it take the eye simply to see that there are colors in these pictures? How much longer to see how many there are? To see what colors they are? We may look as long or as little as we please at most painting, and see more or less in it regardless of style or period, but Reinhardt uses time neither in the depiction of moments in subject matter nor in the traces of fabrication which embody time in Abstract Expressionist painting, but rather in a very direct and simple way: his closely valued late paintings do not exist for us *at all* if they do not take up at least a few minutes of the viewer's actual time.

Any technological art, such as neon sculpture, makes us think of time because it has two primary states, on and off. When it is turned off, it is dormant. Intermittent or limited existence is a feature of some recent non-electronic art as well, where it is the result of a more complex rethinking of the relation between three and four dimensions. The ancient notion that life is short and art long has been challenged by artists as diverse as Richard Serra, Bill Bollinger, Richard Tuttle,

Bruce Nauman, and Robert Barry, all of whom create in some way "short art."

Serra (at both the Guggenheim and the Whitney), whose sensibility is as American as scrap iron, has produced in his *Prop* series a number of sculptures dealing with the physical problem of supporting objects. In these works, the parts are vitally interdependent (in *Close Pin*, a long, narrow metal cylinder holds a short, wider one up against the wall) yet the parts do not permanently adhere to each other; precariousness and a potentially violent rearrangement (given the weights and sizes he favors) underlie Serra's matter-of-factness in demonstrating the various ways, all perfectly obvious, of propping things up. Serra removes the functional and thus the rational justification for such activities as leaning one thing against another. He is content to reveal, and refrains from using as well. This intention depends on the avoidance of fixed physical relationships, within the work or between the work and environment. Material instability creates impermanence.

Serra's *Splash* pieces, made by pouring molten lead along a length of the intersection of a wall and a ground plane, whether in a room or out of doors, are interesting not only for their application to sculpture of principles of painting (derived specifically from Pollock's and the later stain and spray painters' fidelity to liquidity) but also for their—again—impermanence. As obviously rapid in execution as a de Kooning or Pollock line, a Serra splash of lead has nothing like canvas to mediate between it and the floor or wall, so it cannot be moved without being destroyed. As anchored to its site as any fresco or architectural relief, it is nevertheless anti-situational not only in its indifference to architecture—any planar perpendicularity will suffice—but also in its implied deprecation of permanent installation. (Compare Sol LeWitt's recent permutational squares of diagonal lines penciled directly upon the wall; their rigor of concept is accompanied by an equally intense fragility of both duration and appearance.) Like Michael Heizer, Dennis Oppenheim, Richard Long, and others who go out and work directly in the landscape itself, and also like Neil Jenney, Rafael Ferrer (both at the Whitney), and others who, with less grandeur than the earthworks artists, use organic matter (fruit, leaves) in their work, Richard Serra stamps the word "perishable" across his art, though his mediums are the orthodox ones of sculpture—metal, wood, glass, rubber. Serra is as concerned with the results of (human) activities on materials as he is with the properties of those materials; naturally, the two are mutually determinant but Serra's production (including series involving folding, sawing, hanging and balancing also) is as assertively in our time as a Donald Judd box is in our space, by virtue of its emphasis on both its past (its identity as a result) and its future (its potentialities).

Bill Bollinger (at the Whitney) gives his rope sculptures similar existence in time. They not only cut up space like all sculpture but are also explicitly temporary; their chief quality being not their linearity but their tautness—their pull between two points (these being the grommets screwed into the floor or ceiling). Such work might be called "post-Soft" sculpture because, though it uses flexible material, it subverts material's nature by drawing it so tight as to make it nearly inflexible, as well as subverting its purpose of holding things together.

Bollinger's floor pieces (the floor is the most likely place to find recent art) take a further step toward impermanence. When he strews graphite flakes or industrial sweeping compound, a gritty green substance, across a floor, not only does Bollinger produce landscape-like sensations of great beauty (the graphite work is like walking into a Seurat drawing), but he also makes something which cannot stay in any one state for any determinable length of time. These sculptures, with their hundreds of thousands of separate (and possibly modular) parts, are not isolated but walked right upon by the spectator, whose body thus becomes an active accomplice of the transient and limitless formal possibilities of the work.

As predecessors of variable-form art like Bollinger's "Pointillist" floor works, the earliest that come to mind are Calder's mobiles. These are not only changing in form (though in a fixed if enormous number of relations) but also take advantage of a natural process, the air current, to effect their shape-shifting. The wind that revolves the metal leaves and branches of a Calder mobile is the same wind which blows away the helium, neon, argon and other gases released out of doors by Robert Barry in his "inert gas series." The same medium is used by Michael Asher (at the Whitney), who makes "air columns," invisible but tactile works (produced by blowers) through which the "viewer" walks. Warhol's flying silver pillows are a cousin in this family and the grandfather is the author of *20 cc. of Paris Air.* The great-great-grandfather is J. M. Turner, a specialist in gale-force winds. Such a thematic cross-sectioning makes clear how a Romantic sensibility—the interest in ethereality, in vacancy and absence—is still with us, whether in the guise of "conceptual" art like Barry's or "process" art like Asher's. Such comparisons also reveal the extremism of younger artists, who discard even the confining flask of Duchamp's air work, to say nothing of the purely metaphorical or depictive method of the painter of air. Barry's gas works extend, in his words, "from a measured volume to indefinite expansion"; here is not only another instance of art where spatial totality is not measurable, but a product, as well, of three generations of environmentalist thinking: Barry's work becomes part of the global environment, the very atmosphere of the earth, and his sense of scale and proportion as expressed in the relation between something so vast and the tininess of the artist, his work and gesture, is reminiscent of the early Romantic theme (*vide* C. D. Friedrich) of the dwarfing or overwhelming of the individual self by the cosmos.

Bruce Nauman (at both the Guggenheim and Whitney), whose Dadaistic wit seems a far cry from the earnestness of a Novalis or Shelley, is nevertheless related to this Romantic tendency to temporalize plastic art because he constantly uses the most impermanent of all artistic mediums, the self. The author of *Portrait of the Artist as a Young Man* would have been amused by the conception of Nauman's photograph, *Self-Portrait as Fountain*, in which water spurts from the artist's mouth. *From Hand to Mouth*, a sculpture cast from Nauman's own body, is not only a comic device of misapplication (an idiomatic expression taken literally to determine the work's image) but also an indication, like his neon sculpture of his own signature distorted, that the self or consciousness of the artist is still a subject able to sustain a variety of inventions.

As anyone who follows any of the performing arts more than briefly understands, the artist's own body is not an enduring material. Artists like Nauman or Robert Morris, in his box with photograph of his nude self, begin to blur the traditional distinction between performing and producing arts; that is, between art as service and art as object. If a work of plastic art can exist as a gesture (arid not just as the result of a gesture) then critics of the most recent art are right to feel threatened by the "theatricality" of temporalized work. The chief characteristic of live performance is that, after it is completed, there is nothing left to quantify. The witness is forced to examine his own impressions and thus his own psyche instead of being able to pretend to a formal objectivity. In Nauman's self-cast, the form is as arbitrary as in Bollinger's floor works, or as in Richard Tuttle's wrinkled, dyed octagons of canvas (at the Whitney.) Neither the irregularity of the permeation of color nor the myriads of folds and creases were put there by Tuttle (which is not to say, of course, that he did not choose and so in effect create them); he even allows the factors of which way is up, of which is front, and of placement on wall or floor to remain open. And, like all non-rigid work, Tuttle's can be folded up, whereupon it resumes its condition of potential rather than actual art. Here, too, we find art's existence in time stressed, as we do in any three-dimensional work which can sustain morphological variability. This is the ultimate (at least, the current ultimate) in the idea of art as "imitation of life"; not to aspire to an impossible permanence is at once audacious and humble.

II.
ABSTRACTION AND ALLUSION

David Weinrib: See-Through Sculpture (1967)

"See-Through Sculpture," *ARTnews* 66.1 (March 1967): 36–37, 66–68

David Weinrib's recent sculpture [at the Royal Marks Gallery, New York; March 4–April 5] charts a new direction for him and perhaps for others. He still works in colored plastics, but now molds and tints the forms instead of fashioning them from ready-made sheets of the material. Formerly moved to "explore the implications of weightlessness in sculpture" by spilling large fragmented constructions from the ceiling or projecting them unsettlingly from the wall, he has turned to sculpture that supports itself on bases or the floor. The earlier anti-gravity works abruptly juxtaposed linear and planar shapes; the new Weinribs are all solid volume. "Solid" is accurate only literally, for Weinrib's new sculpture is also transparent. He has introduced transparency "in order to give a new aspect to volume; specifically, I have been working on forms that assert their materiality in space, while at the same time allowing space to flow through, as if to eliminate their existence as material." He accomplishes this dematerialization through a consuming interior radiance.

The pioneers of "new mediums" were Gabo and Pevsner, who first used plastics, but a programmatic enthusiasm for technological advance does not motivate Weinrib, even though a Constructivist or even Futurist predisposition makes itself felt in his art, now as before. But this is contested, in both his forms and his composition, by equally strong organic elements. A key work in Weinrib's development has been Duchamp-Villon's bronze *Horse* of 1914. Robert Rosenblum's characterization of it as "an organic fantasy of mechanized forms" is appropriate to Weinrib as well—though some of his pieces might better be called "mechanized fantasies of organic forms." In any case, the tension is rarely absent; Miró, Arp, Gorky, Giacometti in his early *Femme Egorgée,* even Calder, are also antecedents. Sometimes the biomorphic wins, as in *Pink Center* with its tumescent blue "flower," and sometimes the geometric, as with the three-dimensional parallelograms of *P-1.* In more complex pieces like *Statium*, the two coexist in a balance as precarious as that of the piece itself, poised on its two wedges.

An ambition to synthesize the two traditions is probably not, however, overriding to Weinrib. He has turned to something else—color-light. If you isolate the formal properties of *Statium*, for example, energetic lateral tensions impress you. The Boccioni-like arcs spring away emphatically from the wedges, and rhythmically oppose each other, too, while the wedges themselves thrust away from each other powerfully. Yet on their illuminated glass base, these unstable, bottom-heavy masses are stilled and seem to float on a field of light. But mainly, dissolution is effected by the clear color. Luminously rose and blue, like an amethyst, *Statium* lures the entranced gaze into itself. Consciousness of form, of everything but its scintillating interior, is suspended. The experience is exclusively sensuous (and highly pleasurable) but *Statium*'s combination of muscular counterforces and weightless balance, of chunky, awkward forms and delicate, iridescent color, give it a paradoxical character not unlike that of a Pollock—as "cold and passionate as the dawn."

Weinrib's method of composition has and has not changed. Structurally, his pieces have always looked arbitrary and eccentric, so loosely related, part to part, that the very idea of composition almost seems absent. He likes to "accent the separate nature of each form," to assemble them "so that the spatial effect is very open." In *Polychrome, 1* biomorphic, deep-hued parts fight against each other: the amber spoon lies poised under its red "male" correspondent arching threateningly over it; this sexual metaphor is wholly dissociated from the neighboring ovoids which swell apart; they are contradicted by the dark "vertebrae" rising over them toward the impassive Brancusi-like head, which, though the apex of the piece, is not its formal climax. Description makes these actions sound sequential, whereas in fact, they, and many more, are apprehended simultaneously, with equal force, and in no particular order. This "breakdown of the whole idea of domination-subordination as a compositional theme" (as Max Kozloff analyzed Weinrib's earlier work) refers not only backward to Abstract Expressionist painting, but also perhaps forward to the "gestalt" sculpture of Robert Morris and others, in that equal-relation is close to no-relation.

Polychrome, 1 is one of his first pieces in which a new molding process is used; since then Weinrib has produced several works more regular in form, in a single color (often the clear pink of *Statium*), and serial in organization. The small four-part *P-1* and a larger piece, of five almost identical anvil-like components aligned on the floor in a casual row, are attempts to compose systematically with geometric modules. In such work, rationality, or its parody, is necessarily part of the subject-matter, and Weinrib's strongest work is much more Surrealist, irrationally *automatiste*. The very recent 7-foot long floor piece (his largest molded work to date), which grew out of *Statium*, has five bizarre feet springing at irregular intervals out of a large up-ended wedge and resting in a shallow V-shaped trough. Thought it has regularized forms and is sequentially ordered, these elements are subsumed enough into the general conception of the sculpture to make it more successful than the four- and five-part ones.

When this apparently monochrome pentapede is lit, a surprising spectrum of ravishing colors comes to life—oranges, roses, violets, blues. In the polychrome pieces, subtleties of light and color are even richer, as they play against each other inside the work and spill onto their bases. The effect is so hypnotically seductive that it brings to mind the intentions, if not the vertiginous results, of so-called "psychedelic art."

Another quality of Weinrib's color is in its industrial, technological associations. One writer described his previous imagery as "Space-Age Coney Island," and the sense of "American place" still informs his color, which manages to be both vulgar and lyrical at the same time. If no longer in the very use of plastics, then certainly in the "man-made" colors, our urban environment, with its neon displays, instrument panels, rainbowed juke boxes and mixed-medium beer-ads, is consistently echoed by Weinrib. As it is by much of the abstract painting of the '60s. Because of this and the crucial role color plays in his sculpture, an analogy between Weinrib and the "color-field" painters suggests itself. However, the relation of form to color in painting is, obviously, a different problem than it is in sculpture, with its literal form. Polychrome sculpture is hard enough when color defines the surface of the work, and Weinrib has complicated rather than eliminated the difficulty for himself by introducing color *into* the transparent mass. This move is something like staining or spraying pigments directly onto unsized canvas: the painters who do that seek to create an inseparability of color and surface, but Weinrib's form and color, even though the latter is no longer treated as skin but infuses the volumes, do not, ironically seem related enough (although in juxtaposition they may give the work a paradoxical interest). The pleasure one takes in Weinrib's incandescent interior color could as easily been derived from a simple cube or sphere of the same material. In multicolored pieces the problem is less apparent, but still, color is not integral to either the individuation or the unification of shapes. And the shapes in turn can dissipate the chromatic power. Not even Weinrib's securely sculptural idea, the dematerialization of volume through transparency, depends on color. But if his use of color is fundamentally pictorial, its sheer beauty drugs the mind in the presence of the work. Only after the "trip" do questions of esthetic coherence arise.

David Weinrib is only two years or so into his current style. This is obviously a period of exploration and expansion; he seems to look on all his new sculptures as works-in-progress. If he can find a way to make his volumes and colors necessary to each other, his art will benefit. And so will American sculpture.

Ralph Humphrey: A Different Stripe (1968)

"Ralph Humphrey: A Different Stripe," *ARTnews* 66.10 (February 1968): 36–37, 53–56.

E.N.: *In this, one of his first feature essays on abstract painting, Burton put forth the idea of a tendency—that of the "Abstract Allusionists"—as a distinct alternative to the dominant presumption that geometric or minimal art should be neutral, unemotive, regular, and systematic. Offering an alternative to these formal pretensions to objectivity and the pragmatic, Burton advocated for artists who deal with "affect rather than idea"—a theme that also underwrote his writings on Tony Smith in the previous years.*

Ralph Humphrey's new series of paintings [at Bykert; Feb. 3–29] is hallucinatory, almost visionary in character. The number and kind of formal elements we meet in it may be the established pictorial conventions of the decade, but we are accustomed to seeing them treated in a highly self-conscious, quasi-objective manner. Humphrey, however, though he resembles the minimalists or reductionists in morphology, utterly diverges from them in sensibility. His painting is spare, geometric and systematic in design, but it is really only negatively similar to that of artists like Stella, Noland, or Kelly. It brims with a distilled lyricism, a measured exultancy as far from the scientistic mode as from the expressionist.

Humphrey's new pictures are shaped canvases. Squares or horizontal double-squares, they are rounded at the corners and not entirely flat but slightly beveled or sloped at the edges so that they are more than ordinarily thick. But instead of emphasizing the painting's object-ness or making it architectonic, Humphrey's departure from rectangular two-dimensionality makes the painting, paradoxically, less of a sculpture-like object. Rather than a crisp, clearly demarcated shape, the eye is presented with a softly bulging convexity much more difficult to calibrate or fix. Shape here helps to dematerialize the painting; it abets the illusion rather than denying it.

The illusion is multiple and animated. Far from being allowed to exist only on the surface, the picture space seems to be not just behind the canvas but also in front of it, expanding outward into the room. Such inverse illusion is familiar, but again Humphrey offers a personal modification: his space swells gently and slowly forward instead of jumping out aggressively, as is more usual. This buoyant frontal pulsation is achieved not only through the shape, which impels the painting toward one, but also through the employment of atmosphere. Here again, he is untypical; much prominent geometric art today is non-, even anti-atmospheric, but Humphrey's areas of color, though having legible perimeters, act less at a short distance as discrete planes than as translucent containers. (Up close, their surface and opacity are restored.) Form, like shape, is dematerialized. Color is not treated as an isolated, detached sensation—atmospheric color is inescapably referential, weather-like—but aerated and made luminous, turned into a bright, spreading *sfumato* through which we see the "actual" forms and shape.

The forms themselves are simply rows of stripes—horizontal in the smaller, square paintings and vertical in the larger ones—on cirrus-thin, apparently monochrome fields. These stripes, although at first they too appear to be of a single color, bear hues more quickly separable than those of the fields. The subtle nuancing of the expansive fields is almost more a matter of value than of color. The stripes tend to be brighter than the grounds as well as more clearly multi-colored.

Endicott, five by ten feet, is typical; it has a yellow field with a darker yellow cloud gathering at the center. It is almost imperceptibly tinged with green. Across this bodiless field run nine, hardly heavier pink stripes. Vertical and somewhat closer to the top edge than to the bottom, they hover, seem on the verge of shooting upward. The middle ones are a lighter pink than the others, and some are yellowish, as if reflecting the fields. At their edges, several of them have a penumbral lavender-blue. Humphrey's combination of acrylic and Day-glo paints (applied with sponges) makes the stripes' color changes look as much like a prismatic scattering of light as like accretions of pigment. In *Endicott*, as in several of his other new paintings, Humphrey's stripes seem, in both senses, pictorial.

In his design, Humphrey is not unlike a number of other Hard-Edge artists unconcerned with neo-plastic dynamics. He deploys his parallel and equidistant stripes symmetrically (or nearly so). When there is an uneven number of these ribs, the middle one coincides with the picture's central axis. The "layout" as such is static, non-relational or non-hierarchic, and is logically capable of extension beyond the edges, in fact, of infinite extension. The modules and intervals are as simply repeated and readily apparent as Judd's or Andre's. But Humphrey is not at all giving us a lesson in normative esthetics, isolating the characteristics "exclusive and proper" to the medium. His design is actually used as a foil against which the color plays, counteracting the uniformity of dimensions and placement of the stripes and refuting the negative, anti-art implications which often accompany such formal means. The pressures and gravities and temperatures of his colors make Humphrey's stripes begin to assume different sizes, to shift longitudinally or latitudinally and to advance and recede in relation to each other as well as to the field. And yet none of this is "really there." Humphrey's design is not what is arrived at, but what is started from, not a statement but a question—to which the response is chromatic.

(Treated this way, color gains, ironically, a greater vitality than it has in the more amorphous style of "color painting," where it often seems to grow exhausted by the structural burdens placed on it.)

The stripes are not exactly stripes. Almost line-thin, they taper to points at the ends, which gives them a kinesthetic energy, a suggestion of emerging from and disappearing back into the fields. But this makes them also slits as well as stripes. When they are seen that way, of course a figure ground reversal occurs, and we find ourselves looking into what we were formerly looking at. Yet Humphrey does not deal in conventional figure and field ambiguity; his fields are too weightless and fleeting for that. A painting like *Warner* has a double organization of luminosity—not only the effulgence of the blue field but also an intensely glowing orange which we glimpse through the interstices. What makes the effect uncanny, visionary, is that even when the stripes open up into apertures, the field does not really reverse itself and solidify into a "wall" but remains intangible—so that we are looking at a void *within* a void, one sky *through* another.

Humphrey's poetic quality is not of the attitudinizing kind. His palette is almost wholly pastel—baby blue, powder pink, soft lemon yellow, apricot, pale orange, warm rose-grey, violet, an apple green. The colors are vowels rather than consonants. They are feminine and perfumed, some of them edible. Humphrey transcends rather than avoids preciosity. The prospect is so delicious that you lose your appetite. It is a bit excessive. Because of the Day-Glo and the cosmetic sweetness, Humphrey comes close to Pop Art, which seems a strange thing to find in such a refined style. But Humphrey is not exercising irony, not putting his beauty in quotation marks. It is really the makers of lipstick and lingerie who imitate him, not vice-versa. His color imagery draws on the subtlest effects of nature, as a comparison with the next good sunset will reveal. If it resembles the girls in the ads, Humphrey is not responsible, but he would probably enjoy it; for a long time, modern artists have looked at cities and clothes and movies the same way they look at bodies and flowers and weather. Humphrey's is an urban pastorale, but a pastorale nonetheless.

Furthermore, the strain of vulgarity in his work gives it its poetic character, in a way the author of the *Painter of Modern Life* would have understood, conviction and freedom from affectation. Only a real lyricism can afford to ignore "taste."

This new series of paintings has grown directly out of Humphrey's last, shown a year ago at Bykert. It also used stripes on fields, but the pictures were rectangular and flat. Each had three horizontal stripes which quartered an immaterial field. The colors were even more "sickeningly sweet" than the present ones, but the floating and glowing stripes had a similarly apparitional effect. These pictures began to take off from the surface and project out into the room, and with the new ones, Humphrey has gone even further in that direction. His development has always been extremely consistent internally, however little some of the periods (he tends to work in series) resemble each other.

Humphrey's first show, at Tibor de Nagy in 1959, consisted of monochromatic paintings. Large and thickly painted in dark pigments, their color unity seems to be the result of a process rather than an *a priori* choice, and a slow process at that. A black picture, today in the collection of Mr. and Mrs. Tony Smith, is discovered on patient inspection to contain a number of other colors gestating under the surface. Far from suggesting Kelly's intergalactic purity of means or Yves Klein's brash fiats, such a painting is entirely consonant with Abstract Expressionism, particularly its unselfconscious duration in time. Imagine Pollock's *Scent* carried further, for example, to get an idea of where Humphrey's sources lie. From the beginning, minute color differences, whether of or within any one color, have characterized his style.

Another striking thing about the pictures of this earlier period is the concern about their relation to the space front of them, the viewer's space. To seize on the color inflection, one must be very close; even a few inches away, they subside and vanish—and one might just as well be 10 feet away as 10 inches. The illusion of recession and remoteness is as strong as in a Giacometti sculpture, and has equally little to do with the viewer's physical proximity. A decade later, Humphrey is still discovering new aspects of this kind of unfixable space.

From the monochromatic paintings, Humphrey derived a new concern: he began to introduce narrow, irregular edges around the main color. This dragged margin of a different color and value produced both a rudimentary figure-ground reversal and a distinction between color and form—both of these qualities becoming more and more pronounced as the margins became more and more discrete and regularized. Humphrey's well-known "frame" paintings, shown at the Green Gallery in 1965, were the result of this.

The frame pictures are as deceptively simple as the monochromatic ones. A border, often of coral or salmon, frames a square or rectangle, often grey. But the variations and complexities which Humphrey managed to find within such severe limits were many. Differences of border widths, either within one painting or from painting to painting; slight or pronounced tonal differences between the two colors; differences of paint thickness between the frame and the internal rectangle—all contribute to the powerful specificity of each picture. The number of readings is also larger than one might think. The picture may be understood as two concentric rectangles, the edges of the larger one coinciding with the physical edges. Or the frame may be seen as just that—a window through which we see a more distant, empty field. Or the opposite, a rectangle positioned in an unlimited space. Or finally, two symbiotic forms poised together on the same surface.

The frame pictures are "badly" painted and have "dingy" colors. These are almost their best qualities. The edges are not neat and not always quite parallel, the surfaces are not impeccable, the colors are not quite muddy but they are hardly clean. Without depending on clichés of personal facture, Humphrey nevertheless uses these factors to make the frame paintings extremely subjective. And troubling: the bareness, the manic pink against the bleak grey, the "imperfections" of execution create an image, at once vivid and covert, of desolation. These pictures are closer to Hopper than to Albers.

After this group, Humphrey moved on to a series of "band" paintings. Using only lateral divisions which extend all the way across the surface, he produced a strong sensation of verticality with only horizontal means. When narrow enough, the bands became stripes, which led to the pictures shown in 1967, where the stripe is halted before it reaches the edges. In the band paintings, too, Humphrey started using the sweet pastels, the pistachios and spumoni colors which he is still tasting today.

His career demonstrates not only a durable consistency of evolution and considerable powers of formal innovation, but also a steadily rising emotional range. From the deep, slow heaviness of the blue-black monochrome paintings, through the ambiguous personal impersonality of the frame paintings, to the soprano lyricism of the present work, Humphrey's "voice" has become higher and higher, verging at moments on the inaudible.

He reminds one very much at times of Turner, whose ship spars floating in a rose-yellow haze resemble the abstractionist's similarly misted-over stripes. Humphrey's coloration, if not intention, is reminiscent too of the Impressionists. And there is a real connection with the Symbolists, especially Redon and his hallucinatory apparitions on barely tangible pastel fields.

The whole Symbolist esthetic is revived in Humphrey—its preoccupation with the ineffable and transcendent, its search for "correspondences" between the visual and other senses, its fascination with the void, with absence, its "meta-sensuousness." Baudelaire's "hyacinth and gold" or Mallarmé's "infinite azure"—either can be found on Humphrey's palette. Closer to home, he shares of course the disposition of Newman, Rothko, and Reinhardt, toward the most rarefied, heightened sensations or states imageable.[13]

In this tendency, Humphrey is joined by a number of other artists who currently practice geometric abstraction but whose use of it is much more expressive than conceptual. As Lucy Lippard wrote: ". . . System, simplicity and clarity are not exclusively the property of impersonal, highly theoretical stances." Limiting it to artists who use a minimum of forms, and those strictly geometric, I would include in this group Al Held, Doug Ohlson, Larry Poons, Agnes Martin (there are others), and, among sculptors, especially Tony Smith and Ronald Bladen. As dissimilar as some of them may seem—e.g. Held and Martin—they share qualities of feeling, of emotional reference expressed in a vocabulary in no way illustrational. They are "abstract allusionists," sometimes dramatic and grand, like Smith or Held, sometimes quiet and contemplative, like Martin, but all dealing essentially in affect rather than idea. They are image-makers, not art-makers, allowing full expression to the subjective or passional impulse which has intermittently shown itself in the haunting strangeness of certain Stellas and Robert Morris's, but which is fundamentally counter to the methodical cerebrations of, for example, Judd or Noland. Though minus the Expressionist anxiety or anguish, these "romantic minimalists" (as they have been crudely but accurately called) should make us less quick to

13. [This is Burton's neologism, i.e. "able to be imaged."]

declare a "radical," overnight change in American art. There exists in these artists a real temperamental continuity with Pollock, de Kooning, Kline, Still, as well as Newman, Rothko and Reinhardt. Humphrey's shiny female-pinks, for example, have the same excitation and intimacy as de Kooning's. Though this kinship is a subject which demands a great deal more space (as well as a criticism which acknowledges the primacy of sensibility over formal techniques), it is impossible to resist mentioning it in an essay on a painter whose work so clearly demonstrates it. Ralph Humphrey's paintings couldn't be more minimal—nor more mysterious.

Al Held: Big H (1968)

"Big H," *ARTnews* 67.1 (March 1968): 50–53, 70–72.

A show of 20 paintings by Al Held, all from the 'sixties and including the giant *Greek Garden*, recently closed at the San Francisco Museum and is on view at the Corcoran Gallery in Washington, D. C. [March 16–April 21]. Sponsored by the San Francisco Museum, it was organized by Eleanor Green of the Corcoran, who wrote the catalogue.

In today's context of anti-heroic irony, Held aspires to the heroic mode. His painting grows steadily more ambitious, monumental and public. It is determined to be not only available but inarguable—a paradoxical intention; both aristocratic and democratic at the same time. Held's style is appropriately synthesizing; his aim has been to unite the major impulses of mid-century painting into a new whole which, if greater in its aims than the sum of its parts, reminds us that resolutions have a way of turning out to be beginnings.

To a codified vocabulary of geometric shapes, Held adds the Abstract Expressionist undertones of personal gesture; subjective choice and emotional weight. Particularly, his sliding, ambiguous, often explosive picture space and his tough, obviously *painted* surfaces carry this charge. Also, a spontaneous painterly style is operative in the "drawing" of the shapes. Done free-hand, their edges bulge slightly, as though responsive to the pressure of a search for a precision that would be the opposite of mechanical. A further Abstract Expressionist element lurking in Held's art is that of gesture. Individualities of arm-movement have been sublimated, if precariously (documentably, over the past decade, and still now in the execution of each picture, one supposes, glimpsing from close the torrents of brushstrokes under the surface), but the kinesthetic quality of gesture is rarely absent from his shapes. Though stabilized, they have a directional energy like a Kline or Pollock lash. For example, the white swath of *Siegfried* veers agilely up and across the canvas. (But *Siegfried* is also two red L's, one of them reversed and inverted, facing each other down across the DMZ of the white interstice.) Or similarly, *Mao's* orange 0, which looks so immediate, as if done in one fell swoop.

However Held does not actually draw with the brush, or if he does he doesn't leave it at that. Neither do his paintings emphasize any longer the traces of their own execution. He used to leave, underneath the color-skin, quantities of ridges, ghosts of abandoned forms, which he now mostly removes. As his surfaces have become hard, regular and sealed, his pictures have eliminated studio autobiography. They are brought to completion, removed from development in time. Such terminability is very different from the continuous presentness of a Pollock or a de Kooning, which is always happening before your eyes and looks suspended rather than finished. For all their spatial skirmishing, Held's paintings finally "click"; they fall into place and, though theirs is a stasis arrived at rather than started with, ultimately disengage themselves from us—rejecting, as insistently as they have demanded, our participation in their visual enactments.

Especially unlike most Abstract Expressionism is Held's "composure." The self-distancing or decorum necessary to the idea of heroic style is not in his case punctured by the obsessive, exacerbated self-exposure—the anti-decorum—at the core of the Expressionist temperament. Held does not make himself, his own "flayed nerves," the subject of his art.

Another modern tradition (also usually antithetical to a heroic enlargement of life) which Held has integrated into his style is that of picturing the common and contemporary. His loud, glossy, almost hubristically anti-natural colors, his billboard scale and blown-up typographical motifs, recall obviously the urban, industrial ad-scape pressing in on us. The eyes of Dr. T. J. Eckleburg, Fitzgerald's oculist—eyes "blue and gigantic, their retinas one yard high . . . looking out from a pair of enormous yellow spectacles"—must have looked very much like an Al Held. Yet the painter does not make such references in either a social-moralist or a let's deflate-art spirit. Rather, he picks out from this subject matter what has *élan*, what can be used for visual zing, and leaves the invective to others. And actually, the further away he, and we, get from the domination of Abstract Expressionism, the more the Pop connotations in his painting seem to drop away, like booster rockets which have served their purpose.

Compared to other Hard-Edge artists of today, Held is notable in his avoidance of over-all patterning, equalized formal relationships and "absolute" flatness. His geometric abstraction has been deeply informed, despite the qualifiers, by both the drama of Abstract Expressionism and the big bright look of here-and-now art. In his confident stylistic synthesis, in his exceptional refusal to create himself out of nothing, Held demonstrates very clearly the scope of his intention. He rivals history without setting out to annihilate it. For a serious contemporary artist to prefer evolution to revolution is rare and, ironically, hardly prudent. It would be difficult to call Held's omnivorous, hyperbolic style conservative.

The public aspect of his art is closely related to his interest in mural painting. He worked in expanded scale well before he was actually commissioned to do murals. Not only the need for large unbroken areas to paint on (sometimes the inevitable but difficult-to-ignore panel divisions of his larger canvases annoy the eye and interfere with the painting), but also the very content of his work, led him to the mural. He has spoken of using "scale as content." Relationships of internal parts to each other and to the size of the whole, and the relation of the latter to the viewer's size, are constants, but what happens between the picture and its architectural surroundings is variable—except of course in the case of murals. Held works deliberately with "vulnerable" forms; the fewer and simpler, the more crucial the nature of the space around them becomes. To check the attenuation of their impact demands a specified and permanent location. Deprived of communal subject by the very nature of abstract art, Held turns that art inside out and forces confrontation and communication between his painting and the world-surrogate of the room. It is anti-intimate; the individual viewer does not feel that his size is particularly necessary to activate the painting's scale. If Held's tree fell in the forest with no one around to hear it, it would still make a sound.

Even when one of his larger works, say *Greek Garden*, is not done for particular conditions, it is still more than an "inflated easel painting" because of its very sensitivity to environment. Daring to risk its strength—no picture can dominate every kind of situation—Held is nevertheless successful conceptually because he insists on the paramount importance of the interaction between painting and place. Even if he did a mural for a private home, it would be externalized, public. It might be said that the content of Held's murals is the idea of murals.

His smaller pictures, too, where the issue of mural-scale does not arise, are dedicated to the same spatial usurpation. Whatever their size, their volumes turn out to us rather than in on themselves. The motifs are starkly simple—circle, rectangles, triangles; letters: N, X, D, A—but they over-reach their stations, stretch beyond the framing edges. It is the antithesis of cropping, which is to pull the eye inward. Here, the eye is directed outward to try and complete the swelling forms, especially the letters and circles. The paintings seem even larger than they actually are. (Macaulay said of hyperbole that "it lies without deceiving.") The air around is charged with the implications of persisting volumes, as in *The Big D*, whose reversed white curve, if completed, would augment the painting's width by about half.

The eye makes this effort also when it is not a question of familiar shapes. In *The Red Gull*, one accepts the top of the canvas as defining the upper edge of the angled red line. Because we know its width from where it dips down, we assume that its painted edge coincides with the physical edge, the constancy of dimension giving the form integrity. But the yellow triangle, about which less is known, acts very differently. There, the physical edge is a little shocking. Something is missing; the yellow may be part of a larger form impinging from above which we are frustrated from seeing. Integrity is purposely withheld from the yellow. It presses down and pulls up at the same time. (On further examination, this contradiction is contradicted: because it is credible as a triangle and because it is locked up by the red V, the yellow can also be seen as an entity in itself, holding its own.) Almost all of Held's paintings reach beyond themselves.

The putsch is frontal as well as lateral. Forms charge out at the viewer. Sometimes it is done by overlapping, as in the inverted telescoping of *Mao*, whose yellow behind maroon behind blue behind orange behind white makes it hard to keep the painting on its surface. The vestigial yellow field, shoved into the corners, starts the ball rolling, in an aggressing series of big and little bounces, out *at* you, until your reaction is finally to duck.

When he is not illustrating the domino theory with overlapping planes which cascade forward, Held's intense, volumetric colors still trespass on our space. They snap off the thick surface and vibrate in front of it. Thus, the picture refutes its own heavy corporeality. Though the colors are sealed in their "flesh"—their obdurate envelopes of pigment—they are also weightless and intangible (but not atmospheric). They won't stay down.

In identity, if not in behavior, Held's colors are unambiguous. He makes them all look like primaries. They do not waver in the spectrum; a blue, though mixed, never threatens to become a green, nor an orange a red.

The light also is unwavering. It does not alter speed or intensity in different parts of the painting but emanates imperiously from everywhere all at once. Occasionally, a quasi-naturalistic tonality occurs. The broken white fragments of *Greek Garden* and especially of *Circle and the Triangle* link up with each other to provide a light background in front of which the huge forms in black and other colors turn into silhouetted masses, the way buildings stand out starkly against the sky in New York. But only a rigid theorist would object, because the drama of these rows of dark, looming, mutually indifferent things is quite strange and ominous.

Also, such figural distribution of value is strongly perceptible only in black and white photographs; looking at the actual paintings, one must squint to catch it because the surface is so self-insistent, so tough. It back-stops the whites and prevents them from turning into voids. The only instance I know in Held's large body of work where a color does not hold is the yellow upper part of the Whitney's *Dowager Empress.* Obstinately recessional despite the surface and the usual tendency of yellow to leap forward, this exceptional passage makes one realize how generally successful Held is at forestalling and reversing the conventionally illusionistic qualities of color and value.

These are paintings which tend to pull the viewer apart. The earliest one in the show, *Ivan the Terrible* (1961) and *I-Beam* have absolutely nothing to do with each other; and lower parts of *Ivan* and the left and right ones of *I-Beam* have absolutely nothing to do with each other; neither colors nor design make cross-references. Held's investigations of dissociation as a formal principle culminated in the great 1963 *Genesis* (not in the show), which has one painting—a head-on orange cross bordered in green—juxtaposed discordantly next to a whole other one—two enormous black ripples on a white ground. In his more recent multiple-image works, like the tripartite *Greek Garden*, organization is less "willful" but there is still a disturbing and fascinating discontinuity in the relation of the major parts to one another. Each exists imperturbably in and for itself. The effect is as anti-casual and irrational as in module-repeating art, but minus the non-hierarchical passivity. Held does not pretend to abdicate the role of choosing and making.

But again, his paintings offer a plurality of readings. For it is equally true of them that there is internal continuity. Energies spill over borders in a visual *enjambement*. *Greek Garden* revolves monumentally around a central axis, not unlike Gauguin's *Where Do We Come From? What Are We? Where Are We Going?* The black and white rectangles near its middle are frontal, while the red and ocher circles pull out and bend away to the left and the green and yellow triangles do the same thing to the right. The painting is as cogently unified as it is disjointed.

Held's single-image paintings, like *Siegfried*, are no less complex. The planar dialectics of figure-ground interchange have long intrigued him, and in his hands what has become one of the most banal spatial habits of abstract painting receives a new viability—because, I think, of the extremes to which he takes it. Nowhere is positive-negative ambiguity pushed further than in the daring *The Big N* (which, compared to the similar upper part of *Ivan*, clearly reveals Held's impulse to follow his ideas to their extreme limits.) Initially, we see a white plane with two small nicks in it, almost squeezed out. It even verges on three-dimensionality because the blue and yellow of the nicks are so placed as to make the N look like a solid letter with blue sides on a yellow wall. But suddenly, there is a switch: two triangles come to the fore and engage in a staccato interchange across a vast bare stage. What is so convincing about this reversal, which might seem an obvious device in the repertory of a less audacious painter, is the exaggerated disproportion in scale between the white and the other parts. Here, the tiny stalagmite and stalactite control the positioning of an area about 30 times their own size.

In fact, delicacy and fineness are as typical of Held as are aggression and tension. The way *Dowager Empress'* red ring just grazes the yellow plan above it, the way its green circle slightly spills over the bottom edge of the canvas, the way the black square's two lower corners barely protrude from behind the red—these are matters of one-fourth to one-sixteenth of an inch, in a picture eight feet high and six wide. Held eschews the intermediate in proportion; everything is either monumental or minute. Indeed, he makes the two define each other: would *The Red Gull's* blue, already large, become so boundless without that small yellow goad from above? The leaps of internal scale are made gracefully and at times insouciantly. Held's paintings escape looking labored and ponderous because their heavy volume, both emotional and spatial, is tempered with a feeling for "niceties," for subtle refinements which abstain, elegantly and lightly, from calling attention to themselves. The best Helds look effortless.

Just as the little parts make the big ones bigger, the intimacy implied in the artist's attention to hair's-breadth adjustments and overlappings authenticates the external, super-personal face of his art. To satisfy its sense of credibility, the modern disposition insists on ferreting out the man behind the mask, the "I" under the image. One of Held's most interesting achievements has been to plant hints—in corners, along edges, under surfaces—of the private consciousness without abandoning the heroic role or style to which he has willed himself. His paintings are in many ways open and vulnerable, in many closed and untouchable. They are both immediate and aloof. In the fact that so many tensions, ironies, ambiguities, surround it, Held's is a characteristically modern style, but in its potentialities for a more than rhetorical grandeur, a more than private intensity, it is a style which makes a large claim to a new, a "post-Modern" phase of art.

Adja Yunkers: The Eye's Edge (1968)

"Adja Yunkers: The Eye's Edge," *Studio International* 175.899 (April 1968): 203.

Adja Yunkers's "Aegean Series," shown recently in New York at the Rose Fried Gallery, is a Russian's response in an American idiom to a Mediterranean experience. Yet these large abstract collages (canvas and acrylics on canvas), almost all white with strips of ultramarine blue and an occasional, extremely pale grey, yellow, or pink, are much less dependent on reference to traditions of sensibility or on the associational value of subject matter than on the purely optical experience they induce. It is through what happens to his eye that the viewer is most persuaded by Yunkers's reticent but expansive, simple but secretly complicated new pictures.

Not that simile is excluded from them: their "Aegean-ness" is instantly apprehendable in the brilliant white light, the deep, "wine-dark" blues, and the spare, horizontal landscape—and seascape—like configurations. But they are more than abstract versions of a particular geography; Yunkers's subtle deployment of his highly limited formal means impels the viewer to search the pictures as slowly and carefully as he is able if he is not to miss a great deal of what is there. The act of looking, sheer looking, becomes so central that one has a sense, when the painting has finally yielded itself up, of being somehow capable of seeing better than before. The vision has been expanded, the eye widened. At their core, the works in the Aegean Series operate metaphorically—they establish a unity between the literal (physiological) and figurative (psychological) levels of the experience of sight.

Yunkers's main sight-enlarging device is the big, irregularly-curved form of cut-out white canvas which he affixes to his white field. The color or value equality between figure and ground makes the central pendant difficult to grasp. Its edges keep disappearing and the eye has to focus in on the canvas weave itself to apprehend just what is on top of what, and where. Limits are elusive, almost unreadable. Abrupt changes in physical substance, a usual feature of collage, are here avoided in favor of a receding, equivocal relation between the two layers of material. The ghostly contours, when we locate them, we experience almost more as drawing than as relief, so intent is the artist on suppressing the corporeality of collage.

The physical cognizance we lean forward to take of the self-absenting central form is further forestalled by the way Yunkers pushes our eyes out to the framing edges. Hardly nebulous are the frequent swathes and peninsulas of resonant blue, or sometimes yellow, in the Aegean pictures. But they are almost never to be found centrally; only at the very top of bottom, or veering in from the sides. Making strong claims on the attention, they disconcert the eye, almost playfully, in its attempt to "pin down" the collaged canvas. Even if he refuses to be distracted, the viewer has nevertheless a gathering awareness of this peripheral activity which is taking place, as it were, at the edge of consciousness. At times, the superior layer of canvas is tinted grey or pink, but so softly that Yunkers's inversion of traditional composition is not broken. That is, instead of a dominating central image and a lessening intensity toward the edges, Yunkers gives us weighted outer areas with his stronger colors and contours, and allows the heart to remain apparently empty. (Actually, there is no point at which we can safely call any particular area positive or negative.) Rather than resting secure or turning in on itself, the picture space seems to open itself, to spread outward. The eye becomes engrossed in trying to keep up with it.

Yet another optical activity we are drawn into is discriminating between painted and "real" or cut-out edges. Only up close is it possible to do so, and even then, there is a cache of variations. For example, a painted and cut edge may coincide and run along together for a while, then separate. Or if the collaged canvas has been painted before being cut, its perimeters are reinforced by the difference, however small, in color; here, painted and cut edges do not coincide but are identical. Again, Yunkers will make an area of paint slightly overlap a physical contour, so that the latter becomes an episode within the painted plan, whose edge then assumes the function of demarcating the cut-out form. It is the growing assertion of such "minute" adjustments and variations that makes one feel finally that his very ability to perceive has been increased. It is a feeling, needless to say, productive of exhilaration.

Their subtlety makes Yunkers's visual effects unphotographable, but also included in his recent show were some smaller collages, paper and acrylic on paper, which register more broadly. Though independent works, these often serve as sketches for the large canvas collages. *Collage: Blue, White, Yellow*, for example, contains the river and rivulet of white spilling down a medium blue field which reappear in the big *Blue and White* canvas collage. The latter, however, has lost the ragged horizontal yellow at the bottom of the paper collage, and so becomes an image of absolute verticality. Though its extreme value contrast makes it untypical of the Aegean Series, *Blue and White* is like it in its demonstration of Yunkers's tendency toward radical elimination. The very number of pictorial elements he retains counts as a visual factor in itself, multiplying as it does the import of what is left to look at. The two tiny, almost unnoticeable triangles at the lower right of *Aegean V* gives some idea of the series' fineness of inflection, as does the momentary coincidence of the edges of the dark horizontal strip and upward-bulging grey form.

Doug Ohlson: In the Wind (1968)

"Doug Ohlson: In the Wind," *ARTnews* 67.3 (Mary 1968): 38–39, 67–70.

The new paintings of Doug Ohlson [at Fischbach; May 11–June 8] have a strangeness and complexity not immediately apparent—in fact, almost hidden. At first glance, they seem, with their modular panels, uninflected surfaces and restricted palette, to be well-behaved specimens of the Minimal type, but one discovers that they really are something else. They are inward paintings, taciturn, unintimate, slow to reveal themselves. Yet, in their remoteness, they are not images of indifference. They can be witty, though drily so, sometimes brooding, but always open and expansive, secretly expressive and moving.

Ohlson practices the strictest economy. The only elements he works with are the panels—tall, narrow palisades of one color—and the squares painted on them, all in one other color. The former, often 18 by 90 inches or one to five in proportion, number from three to twelve per painting and are hung on the wall two and a half to three inches apart. Horizontal paintings are made out of vertical shapes. The squares range along the bottom or top of the rows; when they are raised or dropped, it is no more than their own height. So far, none have appeared toward the middle. The equal margins they make out of the field around them approximate but do not duplicate the intervals between the canvases. The colors (acrylics applied with sponges) are more opaque than transparent but stay thin, neither quite infused into the material nor lying pronouncedly on its surface; tactility is not an issue.

These paintings are not fantasies of renunciation or of rigidly controlled order. Their tight-lipped Purist aspect (of which the square is almost a badge in modern art) coexists with a high sensuousness breaking through in the eloquent color but strongly tempered with intimations of melancholy and solitude. *Mâtho* is a five-panel nocturne whose deep, clear midnight blue and darkly silvered grey lie together in unbroken silence. To *Mâtho* as day to night and twice as wide, *Cythera*, with its luxuriant almost orange-yellow field and intense pink squares, has a Southernness so brilliant and warm that only a Northerner could have imagined it. *The Gates* is both somber and burning, its dull ocher field and deep red squares making together a shadowed incandescence. An untitled painting, Ten panels of medium grey with pale blue squares only at its far right, is tranquil and light by contrast but is touched by a mood of desertion.

In short, Romantic. To find such feelings in such forms—it is as if Keats had written concrete poetry.

Of the several things about Ohlson's work that are paradoxical or apparently self-canceling, another is the way in which his monochrome grounds are and are not fields. They are, as with a number of other painters, both flat, inert planes and illimitable, intangible stretches of color and light. But they are also literally not fields because they are divided, in accurate and sensitive proportions, into non-contiguous parts. However, the shared color of the panels is as strongly unifying as their interstices are separating. One major way the viewer is drawn into Ohlson's paintings is in his alternation between seeing them as parts and as wholes, as units or as unities.

If one thinks of the fields as illusions of void, there is a nice reversal in the role of the interstices. When the field remains a simple plane, the spaces between the panels are what is missing; they are the not-there. But when the fields themselves are experienced as empty or open, then the interstices interrupt and recall the eye to physical actuality. They represent no longer the absent but the present. Ohlson's fissures are their own opposites, in something like figure-ground reversal but fresher.

The interstices are a unifying factor instead of a disruptive one when they are compared to the internal forms. They are regular and predictable, and the distribution of the squares is anything but. Here is not just the standard good-design rule of repetition with variation, but something more extreme—the repetition is patent, the variation seems haphazard and willful. Ohlson strews his squares intermittently over the panels as if he were throwing the dice but never abolishing chance. The large *Sterne*, for example, has light blue squares at the bottoms of its first four ocher panels (reading from left to right), then raised ones on the next three, and then, as if perversely, none at all on the last two. Even odder is *Cythera* (which will be seen this summer at the Museum of Modern Art in "The Art of the Real: USA 1958–68"): pink squares appear low on six panels in a row, but disappear for three, then return with a muffled exclamation both at the bottom and the top of the last panel. *The Gates* has, except for the first two, a straight row of squares at the top which does not make it all the way across; the last panels are blank. There is no logical progression or programmed order to be obtained from these groupings. They could not be predicted beyond the painting's limits, unlike the panels, which if blank could be repeated indefinitely. The apparent randomness of the squares, contrasting with the even beat of the panels and interstices, gives the paintings an intensified rhythm like that of a line of verse in which the stresses are played out *against* the meter. Ohlson's "prosody," surprising and supple, makes the lateral unfolding of his paintings into slightly quixotic skirmishes between chance and control.

But laterally or sequentially is not the only way to look at them. Another way is a frontal, simultaneous apprehension. The eye hesitates between a temporal viewing, passing from panel to panel, and a spatial one, encompassing them all at once. Usually when we look at a painting we see the whole first and afterwards lose ourselves in its parts, but with Ohlson we first see the parts and afterwards lose ourselves in—that is, discover—the whole. It is then that the squares group themselves into an order, not a logical one but an intuitable one. They look no longer arbitrary or capricious but reveal the painting's inner unity and justness.

Looked at all together, the squares align themselves, forming an invisible imagery of large, wholly unconstrained gesture. All of them, not just the ones in rows or steps, fall into place. Motion generates itself and soon we find that we are watching an implied skein extended, S-curving, suddenly flicking, hardly veering, through a no longer dormant area. That area has begun to stir. Triggered by the squares, it takes on an animation as if from inside itself. Ohlson calls this a "contraction and expansion of the field," but perhaps metaphors of wind are best for describing what happens, for there is no organic muscular exertion but rather a massing of immaterial energy. It fills the painting, transmitting itself across the breaks; it gathers force, slackens, swells, rises and drops. At times scattering the squares before it as well as being guided by them, it turns sinuously back on itself through a narrow funnel of margin to billow forth elsewhere, or is released in all directions at once. This evocation of energy without a direct imprintation of it is perhaps the final sensation of Ohlson's paintings. Since it reaches over the entire surface, it is the source of internal unity.

What at first appeared to be an architectural diction (the rows of panels as the standardized façades of modern buildings and the squares as their fenestration) is replaced in time by an impression of breadth and distance relatable only to the open scale of nature, of landscape as well as air. (The two seem fused in his paintings.) Ohlson says, "My subject matter isn't squares."

He is not the only painter around who possesses this wide-openness, but it seems particularly imbedded here, present in spite of the artist, because his discontinuous panels challenge the existence of the field in which the sense of spreading space is loosed. Yet it prevails.

The squares, their individual and combined areas and their placement, contribute to the extended scale. So do the taller than human heights and vision-filling widths, though these are not emphasized by any boundary-recalling device — the vertical panels are too unlike the over-all shape to reinforce it, and the interstices, because there are so many of them, do not bind the sides. The colors, especially, work as releasing agents for space-expansion, not in a push-and-pull interaction but in a way that language cannot imitate.

Ohlson was born in 1936 and raised on a farm near Cherokee, on the little Sioux River in north-west Iowa, where his Swedish grandfather settled in the nineteenth century. The empty, endless landscapes of the Mid-West and the Northern Protestantism of his upbringing must have influenced, but do not "explain," his art. He studied painting at the University of Minnesota. In 1961, he came to New York and graduate school at Hunter, where he now teaches. This show is his fourth at Fischbach since 1964.

Ohlson's style has been geometrical since his student days; it is a natural rather than an evolved mode for him. Within it, his investigations have been intensive. He very early decided that figure-ground ambiguity was exhausted for him, and it would be a mistake to look for that in his work. He has hardly ever used more than three or four colors in a picture but never went all the way down to one, either. Moving from static, frame-oriented symmetry to design in which the forms began to "float, freed from the edges," in his words, he found his colors getting at the same time darker and more and more tundral, until most of his paintings came to have black fields.

Too, each came to have only a single rectangle or square of another color, close in value to that of the field. Dissatisfied with the overwhelming illusion of recession in the dimness, he made the paintings more concrete by dividing them into two stretched canvases of equal height but unequal width. These were the same color and were joined, so what was created was an internal edge—an "undrawn line," he calls it, or a thin vertical dissociated from contour since optically it separated nothing. After these paintings (shown in 1967), which were charged with impendence, the gap widened and multiplied. That, and a renewed exuberance of color after a dark period, have gone into producing the current series.

Ohlson has recently received a Guggenheim and a grant from the City University of New York to investigate the possibilities of paintings that will take in more of their surroundings in more ways. He keeps spreading out. As Edwin Denby wrote in another context: "Americans occupy a much larger space than their actual bodies do; I mean, to follow the harmony of their movement or their lolling you have to include a much larger area in space than they are actually occupying."

Leon Berkowitz: Color it Berkowitz (1969)

"Color it Berkowitz," *ARTnews* 68.1 (March 1969): 32–33, 72–73.

E.N.: *One of Burton's most important art teachers was Leon Berkowitz, with whom he studied as a teenager. Berkowitz and his wife Ida Fox were important confidants and mentors to the young Burton. By the time of this review, Burton had grown distant from them and his attitudes toward painting had been expanded through his tutelage in realism over the course of his decade-long relationship with John Button in the 1960s. In this 1969 review of Berkowitz's exhibition at the Corcoran Gallery, Burton kept a cool remove in his writing even as he advocated for his former teacher and, indeed, the significance of the alternative to New York offered by Washington-based abstract painting.*

Berkowitz, born in Philadelphia in 1919, has lived most of his adult life in Washington, D.C., a city whose hard-won esthetic sophistication has roots in the locally famous Washington Workshop Center of the Arts, a school and gallery of the early 1950s of which Berkowitz was co-director until 1955, when he went to Spain to concentrate on his own painting. He developed out of Abstract Expressionism a poetic personal style—fast, soft, gestural, strongly suggestive of land, sea and sky in its shifting lights, stains of atmospheric color and lifting lateral sweep and recession. For a decade of forays from Washington to the Welsh coast, the eastern Mediterranean, the American desert, Berkowitz's response to nature sustained his romantic abstraction; but by the mid-60s he evolved his current idiom of high-intensity colors flashing like revelations in a format of vertical bands reminiscent of the light spectrum.

The earliest paintings at the Corcoran are from Berkowitz's *Chasuble* series (1965–67), so named because its partial diamonds hang in their four-cornered white fields like bright outspread robes. Most numerous and complex in design is the *Cathedral* series, large paintings all having the same essential arrangement: two major mirror-image groups of stripes leaning toward each other. These halves are halved; each is internally symmetrical with a core of maximum-intensity color-light around which the reverse duplication revolves. Berkowitz's *Cathedrals* are like vertically sliced cross-sections of concentric cylinders of color. The white ground remains only in long triangular slivers at the tops of the sides and in the center's upward-pointed white triangle, which is as tall as the painting—taller, in fact, for its apex is or would be still higher. A third series has two parts—the *Verticals*, narrow shapes so tall (126 inches) that the eye cannot keep the top and bottom in focus at the same time, and the *Obliques*, similar in proportion but parallelogrammatic in shape and vertically bisected at the center by bright stripes perpendicular to the horizontal edges. This series creates interesting perceptual distortions, but seems less full expressively than Berkowitz's other paintings. His most recent group, the only one which varies in size and design from painting to painting (and varies considerably), is the *Coronas*. Hardly a series, it has nevertheless certain persistent concerns, especially very intense, almost lurid colors deprived entirely of background. The *Coronas* eliminate the prismatic figure or image in white space which gives the *Chasubles* and *Cathedrals* an impression of vision-activated expansion. The *Coronas* are made up entirely of shafts of color-light coalescing into and fading out of the range of the visible. What Berkowitz seems to aim for in this group is an experience as close as actual painting can provide to the sensation of the disembodied.

Berkowitz seeks to replace form with light by manipulating their common property, color. He not only takes advantage of all chromatic possibilities (like the after-image) and the myriad values created by layers of color-transparencies, but by color's very temperatures. The main thing he talks about doing in his painting is making a warm "run" (film) over a cold one, "pulling a sheet of color" across one of a different degree of heat. Form in Berkowitz's paintings is not only depicted in dissolution (the soft shadowy edges) but also apparently gets out of optical control: the yellow, magenta, and emerald of *Cathedral, 14*, for example, destroy the stripes' boundaries; they disappear into the air. Though this is geometric art, its color and light are as close in feeling to the way nature operates—unpredictably, open-endedly—as to the binary alternatives, such as "off-on," "right-left," "yes-no," of the constructed world. The complicated doublings and quadruplings in the *Cathedrals* reverberate in a profuse harmony with the multiple actions of width and edge of stripe as well as temperature and intensity of color. These paintings ring like gongs, sending out echoing waves of color instead of sound. A dark vermilion will occur three more times as the eye scans across but there are too many similar and different colors and values for this repetition to make the order easily graspable.

The multiple implosions of, say, yellow-green meeting cadmium orange on one side and aquamarine on the other blind the viewer for a split second so that the painting disappears physically, leaving only colored light behind in the air. This effect is closest to Op Art in the *Coronas*, where the sight of a viridian-green stripe splitting an ultramarine-blue field is apt to stun the eye. Sometimes the dazzle is a little over-insistent but a lyrical delicacy usually persists in the midst of the streaks and flashes of light.

Berkowitz is "painterly" in that one is drawn to look at his actual painting; that is, the pigment in and on the surface. The vulgar idea that painterliness means messy brush strokes is best forgotten; indeed, many in the canon of the "post-painterly" have been among the best handlers of paint in American art. Characteristics of surface can never lose their potency, but the power of sheer paint to please or annoy is not critically acknowledged, often because it is impossible to account for. Berkowitz's thin washes or runs of oils, eight or nine per painting, over well-primed canvas give him an ingratiating façade, strong, slightly dry, but very pure. He does not like to talk about his method of paint application but it's obviously controlled without being over-mechanical.

One's first reaction may well be, "Not more stripes! Especially not from Washington!" But Berkowitz's temperament is in a somewhat different tradition from the sensuous corporeality of most "color art"; the only Washington painter he resembles at all is Morris Louis, whose dramatic, magical-looking imagery is as physically charged as Berkowitz's hieratic radiances. Berkowitz's stripes have their fellows in the variegated wings of early Italian angels or in the unworldly glow of Blake's visions rather than in the suave urban images of Stella or Noland.

Curiously, several characteristics of "psychedelic art"—its maximum light, convulsive color and assaulting spatial ambiguities—seep into Berkowitz's primarily contemplative paintings. The sensory overload we like so much today is the technochemical age's version of the Romantic quest for ever-increasing intensity of experience. An art whose experience-units are brief but vivid, often discontinuous, illuminations, like esoteric communication, is offered by Berkowitz's epiphanies for the eye.

Willem de Kooning's *Gotham News* (1969)

E.N.: *This text was printed on the back of the box for Springbok Editions' 1969 jigsaw puzzle featuring Willem de Kooning's* Gotham News. *It was one of a series of complex puzzles based on Abstract Expressionist paintings that the iconic company released in the 1960s. The puzzles were often accompanied by such texts commissioned from art critics to introduce a general audience to the artworks.*

The large, dramatic *Gotham News* is Willem de Kooning in the process of shifting his weight from one foot to the other, at the beginning of a major change in a career of restless changing. Painted in 1955–56, *Gotham News* still contains elements from the series of *Women* immediately preceding it. (The huge-breasted, huge-eyed dames of the first half of the fifties—only one of de Kooning's several series of figure paintings before and since—are the pictures which, along with Jackson Pollock's "paint slinging," first drew wide public attention to advanced American art.) But *Gotham News* also points ahead to the liquidly painted, loose and broad "landscape" abstractions of the late fifties and early sixties. Indeed, another work in de Kooning's 1955 production is called *Woman as Landscape*, and is just that—figure (seated woman) *as* ground (the space surrounding her), the two depicted in the act of merging. De Kooning's rapid, expert drawing with charcoal and a full, wet brush obliterates our certainty as to what is woman, what landscape.

The same doubt or ambiguity about solid and void remains in *Gotham News*, though not by means of conflation of images or "dissolve" of figure into ground. By means only of treatment of color and surface, especially the latter, de Kooning here intensifies the spatial ambiguity. In addition to the illusions of concave and convex spaces, *Gotham News*, as its title humorously reminds us, strongly asserts its flatness. Along with the impasto, the stains, the splashes, the draftsman-like lines describing contour, the purely gestural lines and strokes, the palette-knife scrapings and trowelings, the collage-like conjunctions of dissimilar passages, *Gotham News* contains yet another means of paint manipulation—its absorption, as a liquid state, by newspapers. Thomas B. Hess, the closest-range observer of de Kooning, has described the artist's working process in this period: "In order to slow the drying of the paint ... de Kooning placed sheets of newspaper over the surface, peeling them off the next day. They left offset images of columns of type and advertisements in the paint and, where de Kooning did not rework, he let the ghostly images remain ... he decided he liked this intrusion of the art of the streets into his work."[14] Though de Kooning may not have deliberately sought to augment the kinds of handling in this picture, one of its greatest pleasures is in its scope of painterly activity. Except for actual collage sections (de Kooning has frequently rearranged pictures by cutting them up), *Gotham News* bears, as do so many of his works of the mid-fifties, just about every method of marking that an artist makes on a surface. The "mechanical" method of transference of printer's ink to wet paint provided, furthermore, another type of image—mass-produced, unconnected with "fine art," utilitarian—whose flatness and connotations both contributed to the then imminent avalanche of Pop Art.

In color, *Gotham News* is (again like the *Women*) full of mixed but never muddy whites; a trail of reds running from high-key crimson through the cadmium oranges to shining,

---

14. Hess, Thomas B. *Willem de Kooning*. New York: The Museum of Modern Art, 1969.

soft pinks can be followed among the several lemon yellows; flecks of green and blue accompany the different blacks of charcoal and paint in their perpetual motions into and across the picture.

Though no longer organized around a figural imagery, the de Koonings of the middle of the decade do suggest in their structure a recognizable theme, that of landscape. It is not the simple horizontal spread of open or flat spaces which, in Duccio as in Rothko, is the essential out-of-doors pictorial organization. The image in *Gotham News* is much more peculiar; not only is the major thrust vertical, but the painting is also as heavy, as full of incident, at the top as at the bottom. The shapes are tilted, crowded together. The "clearings" or negative spaces are sudden and erratic. The flying planes, slicing lines and knots of volume alternate with or turn into weightless, translucent passages wholly without rationale—the luminous white patch shot through with the palest of sea blues and greens occurs *below* the more apparently "empty" space (at the upper right) in which the angular signature floats; yet that white, in relation to the scarlet and white defiantly flat scrapings still further below, becomes a secret disclosure of an infinite bright vista.

Pressing together with such lyrical, nature-inspired moments are less serene impressions of objects which are disturbing in character. The flesh-colored, partly rounded mass at the lower left is reminiscent of the Expressionist theme of menaced and anxious humanity as revealed in, for example, Soutine's large slabs of raw meat. The very spatial ambiguity of a de Kooning has a disorienting, hence disturbing effect, as does the obvious urgency of the act itself of making a painting—an urgency manifest in the speed of attack and the multiplicity of possible methods and readings. In tenor, *Gotham News* is very much of its period in de Kooning's *oeuvre*: it is high-pitched, intense throughout, both poetic and witty, informed with equal amounts of aesthetic skill and emotional pressure.

Generation of Light, 1945–70 (1969/1971)

"Generation of Light, 1945–70," in Thomas Hess and John Ashbery, eds., *Light in Art* (New York: Collier Books, 1971), 39–54.

E.N.: *This survey was initially written for the 1969* Art News Annual *special volume on "light in art" and then, when that issue was reprinted as a book, slightly updated to 1970. Burton exploited the topic to offer a wide-ranging and perceptive account of painting since 1945. He again demonstrated a strong, if opinionated, grasp of currents in contemporary painting, moving from Edward Hopper through to varieties of Abstract Expressionism to assessments of such artists as Philip Guston, Richard Tuttle, and Robert Ryman. His narrative is framed with brief discussions of representational painting treated comparatively. Such an approach was characteristic of Burton's desire to level stylistic differences and hierarchies.*

As does the painting of any period, post-World War II American art necessarily concerns itself with the depiction of luminosity; but really not to the degree that it can be said to be a unifying concern, and to a much lesser degree than many other movements and styles. The eternal element of light has, however, been as thoroughly reinvestigated and put to individual use by American painters as have been the elements inseparable from it: of color, in particular; form, shape, and scale; and method and concept. The profusion of innovations in the quarter-century of our art from the mid-1940s through the late 1960s may have resulted in no theoretical homogeneity, especially in regard to light as a pictorial concept but, and paradoxically, few phases of modernism have been marked by such sustained intensity in the exploration of luminosity. The achievements of our painters are diverse, but they are continuously brilliant.

For hundreds of years, "light" in Western art meant, of course, essentially one thing—the convention of tonality, the system of value gradations whose function is to represent volumes and spaces around them. When Turner and then the Impressionists freed light from its schematic identity as the opposite of "dark," they opened the way to our century's purely chromatic painting, for which luminosity is a result of the temperature and degree of saturation of hues, and therefore not quantifiable or subject to formulization but exclusively a matter of personal sensibility. Sensibilities have genealogies, and some case can be made, in the period here under discussion, for two major kinds of American light: one is urban, hard, often hyper-brilliant, artificial-looking; the other is pastoral, natural, much more atmospheric and "slow" or dim. Both are referential, both cut across stylistic and historical boundaries, both are generated by temperamental affinities of which the artists may even be unaware.

But before tracing these two main currents, we must remember that chromatic abstraction, whatever its "feel," is quite recent. Preceding it are both the late paintings of Edward Hopper, the last survivor of the first chapter of American modernism; and the well-documented, early phase of the second chapter—that is, the "black and white" period of Abstract Expressionism whose zenith was around 1950 and whose first and last, as well as greatest, masters were Willem de Kooning and Franz Kline. By different means, both Hopper and the black and white abstractionists provide a clear demarcation for later developments beyond tonality. The dialectical language of light-dark as used in a Hopper such as *Seven A.M.*, 1948, presents no critical problems, but it is a typically important and relevant painting for its metaphysical concern with light as time. The value system in it is entirely "retrograde," innocent of coloristic self-sufficiency, but Hopper is as precise and serious about his "anecdotal" light as Monet ever was about his purely observed light. The observer-less closed-off view is not only made more intense by the numerous darkening and brightening surfaces and recesses, but, with the quasi-eponymous clock, is raised to a transcendent illustrationalism as ambiguous and enigmatic as any Surrealist scene. Hopper's modernity is obvious in his smooth unification of Cubistic geometry and representationalism, but perhaps less apparent—and even more interesting today—is his emblematic or metaphoric bent, accounting for the unique notion of light, translated into time (a specific time of day), as the true subject of the painting. The straightforward American realist has Pirandellian depths.

Curiously, the painting least like Hopper's of the same period—wholly post-European art of the New York School, first generation—is fundamentally similar in its conception of light as value. De Kooning's *Night Square*, painted one year later than the Hopper, is also a tonal painting, yet it is a paradigm of the most advanced work of the time. Though its value scale is reduced to the simplest and most total contrast possible, pure black and pure white, *Night Square* exhibits an amazing multiplicity of luministic virtuosity within its bare, polarized means. De Kooning creates a light of sharp, dramatically shifting "shadows," obscure hollows and sudden, dazzling streaks of radiance which seem to come from behind the darkness as often as they split or float in it. The unpredictable interstices and dissociated lines of white act peculiarly in that they do not illuminate or lessen the darkness but rather seem to increase it; de Kooning's recurring tendency toward somber coloration (as in his *Men* and some of the earlier *Women*) is, though coexistent with an equally strong impulse toward coloristic exuberance, never more affecting than in his strange, murkily pristine black and whites. Along with Hopper and the whole Western tradition of light as value, de Kooning organizes here in a light-to-dark scheme, yet this is not grisaille painting but an art which conceives of black and white as two colors, or uses them so.

To jump ahead in de Kooning's career, we see the proof of this in such masterpieces of the 1960s as *Rosy-Fingered Dawn at Louse Point.* The allusions in the title to both Homeric prehistory and the local geography of the artist's Long Island habitat point up the matutinal freshness of his art after the dark-edged, charcoal-etched *Women* of the 1950s. The purity and openness of *Rosy-Fingered Dawn*, with its pink, yellow, and white skin, are prefigured in such de Koonings as the 1939 *Elegy* or the 1945 *Pink Angels*, but new for the artist—and for American art—after the late 1950s is the spiritual hedonism of organizing the painting wholly in terms of light. What unifies it, including its minor passages of greens, is the same thing which holds the black and white pictures together: sheer luminosity. Drawing, gesture, planar space—all art subsumed into an overriding brilliance, here as clear and untroubled as *Night Square* is tense and puzzling. In both moods, de Kooning's synthesizing principle is that of light; for all his spatial ambiguities and internal contradictions, he makes in both cases an optical world held together by form-obliterating radiance.

After de Kooning, the master of "no-color" was Kline, whose equally tonal light is bleaker and harsher than that of the several other painters who eliminated color from their palettes around the same time. Kline, with his great awkward structures which are at the same time black armatures in white voids, white forms in a far-reaching darkness, and planes of paint overlapping in a shallow space or in no space at all, is a Ryder of noon instead of midnight, and the heir of Eakins and Homer, native geniuses of unremitting, almost tragic clarity in their charged, oppressive pictures. Kline's broad, iris-confounding swaths of extreme brilliance and fathomless dark are not only the high noon of American black and white art, but also its twilight, for after Kline, no gestural abstraction is able to produce light as well as form from this binary resource.

The resource of color was of course never absent, even in the purgative period of black and white painting. Indeed, the American who comes at once to mind when the subject of light in American art is raised is Mark Rothko, who not only never eliminated color but elevated it to an unprecedented importance. Rothko's incandescent blocks of color-light, whether in the typically warm orange, yellow, and white of *No. 8, 1952* or in the cooler, shadowy blue and submarine green paintings (which together led to the experiments with a palette of heated obscurity of the later 1950s and the 1960s), are notable for their avoidance of exaggerated value contrasts as well as for their nearly explicit imagery of land- and seascape. The armatures—the soft frame around the perimeters of the individual color squares or around the entire work—and the sparely used horizontal stripes (like the blue in *No. 8, 1952*) are more differentiated on the scale of hues, departing just enough in value from their neighboring tones to perform a structural, "holding" function without, however, threatening by over-articulation the tentative existences of the colors weightlessly and as if momentarily settled upon the fragile surfaces. The steady, even light in a Rothko is its most tranquil element, whether in a super-radiant key or invisibly dark; the rest is reticent to an anxious-making degree. Rothko's tonalities are limited in their variety, necessarily reduced so that no wrenching will take place, no discreteness, but instead a recessive and underplayed adjustment of value, tending toward equalization and serving the needs of the colors themselves (without giving up atmosphere in favor of "pure" or flat color). In Rothko, light is made one with color and atmosphere; for this commanding synthesis, he is a pivotal figure between the Impressionist inheritance and the American painting of the 1960s, a seminal artist whose progeny include such diverse young painters as Ralph Humphrey, Agnes Martin, Ray Parker and other "romantic Minimalists," who uncannily combine defined edge or contour with abstract sfumato.

Among other major painters of the generation of de Kooning and Rothko, the non-gestural or "field-painting" wing of the New York School is further divided over the question of atmosphere. Rothko is the master of airiness; of his conceptual colleagues, Newman has shown less interest in atmosphere, Reinhardt was not to pursue it intensively until the latter part of his career, and Still's impulses took him in an anti-atmospheric direction.

Barnett Newman's work is hardly without light, however. The jarring verticals of color that split his monolithic façades represent, especially at their brightest as in *Vir Heroicus Sublimis*, an entirely new use of light in painting. Later to be explored by Larry Poons, most thoroughly, and also by many Pop and Op artists, Newman's color-light is presented in an epiphanic structure. The verticals exist as light only for an instant; the "illumination" is short-lived and soon the eye reduces the immaterial flash to corporeal pigment. However, scanning the vast surfaces, we then pick up once again in our peripheral vision the elusive, intermittent glow of the narrow stripes. Newman's light possesses an insight-like structure; it is momentary and recurrent, though not at the viewer's own will. While Newman's feeling for the value range is less strong than his unique sense of the optical volume of color, he is able, in his best works, to maintain a sourceless radiance throughout even the largest areas. This light coexists with the occasional blinding perpendiculars, rather than emerging from them. The middle-value stripes are generally related to the field tonally, and to the brighter stripes formally, and so they act as intermediaries between light and the material color-covered surface; this accounts perhaps for their ghostliness and even for Newman's invention of his strange "non-stripe," a form made by painting brushily across masking tape, then pulling off the tape so that there are two scrumbled columns around an empty center. These negative stripes are as light-conducting as are the positive verticals.

Clyfford Still seems a peculiarly lusterless artist, as it were; the disturbing body of his thick patches of paint, which exist as if in a state of peeling off or even sliding down the canvas wall, have, I think, contributed importantly to the recent invention in three-dimensional American art of soft, shape-shifting, disarrayed objects, but (doubtless intentionally) Still has eliminated any impression of overall luminosity, to say nothing of atmosphere, in his dry painting.

Ad Reinhardt also eliminates light, in the sense of brightness, but demonstrates that to do so is not to eliminate luminosity. From the time he reduced his forms to simple rectangles, he tended to make his colors, whether the reds of the early 1950s or the later black-threshold browns, blues, and greens, equal in value. Even before, in his overall paintings, the light had been dim and constant throughout, but more and more intensely until his death, Reinhardt sought an even and low light in his poised, anticipatory symmetries whose luminosity is as vivid (and as atmospheric) as the most burning, Turneresque Rothkos.

To compare the rectilinear art of Reinhardt to the brush-drawn style of Philip Guston is to see how light ignores formal boundaries; these extremely different artists are both painters for whom light is produced by atmospheric color relations. The "Abstract Impressionism" of Guston's trembling blues and efflorescent cadmiums and roses of the earlier 1950s has its source not only in French painting but also in the Mondrian of the waves and piers; Guston's constant swells of short verticals and horizontals, stroked and re-stroked with a restless hand, have an unfading shimmer which gathers in intensity (near the painting's center, usually) to provide another absolutely individual use of light as structure. It is impossible to tell whether the characteristic blues and reds mix more optically or more tactilely, but in any case we do not see such sheer luminosity successfully performing a structural function again until Jules Olitski's spray paintings and Sally Hazelet Drummond's mottled centrifugalities of flecks of color-light. Guston, after this "sunrise" period, turned to more separable figure-ground relations and more contrasted light-dark relations, and his light became generally much deeper and foggier; but in his thoroughgoing identification of color, light, form, and surface, he is a virtuoso of atmospheric light—even in his recent caricatureal pictures. He is insufficiently recognized for his early synthesis of gestural and colorist modes of abstract painting.

Perhaps the most ambitious American painter in this respect, the one most eager to synthesize modes, was Hans Hofmann, whose visual bombast in his most Teutonically rhapsodic manner has unfortunately obliterated for some his authentically sensitive, more thinly and freely handled paintings of the late years. Hofmann was crucial in American art not only for the living example he provided of post-Fauve coloration, of the "push and pull" of pure color, creating a non-tonal luminosity, but also for his pioneering incorporation of the whiteness of the canvas itself into the light of the picture. It has been made clear by various spokesmen for "stain painting" how the luminosity can come from behind the colors, but Hofmann, the champion of the "open" surface—one taken through the entire register, from heavy slabs of paint all the way to passages of untouched canvas—was as central (when he exercised a restraint in his attack) to this 1960s style as were Jackson Pollock, James Brooks, and, even earlier, Arshile Gorky in certain late paintings. When Hofmann washed an area so thinly that the canvas shone through with unhampered clarity, as he did as early as the mid-1940s in his Miroesque, automatist pictures, he pointed the way to a major new source of light in our art. The master of this kind of light was to be, of course, Morris Louis, whose lyrically clear voids of white brilliance contain the most translucent of colors in pools and tides which, even at their very deepest, rarely block all of the brilliant white ground.

A currently more emphasized precedent for Louis is Pollock, for his innovative brush-eliminating procedure of paint application. Pollock's methodic revolution created, too, an important change in the quality of his own luminosity; he was the first to discover the strong but soft, dappled light characteristic of so much later American art. The undulatory rhythm of advancing and withdrawing spots of radiance, liquidly fused together, in such Pollocks as *Autumn Rhythm* or *Lavender Mist*, allows the artist to recreate, at will and without reference to actual landscape images, an effulgence as weightless as Rothko's, yet, remarkably, with a use of paint as forceful as Rothko's is force-less. Pollock's indifference to calculated nuances of value is more than compensated by the omnipresence of his "visionary gleam," which is emitted from any and every point in the monumental suspended webs that mark his "classic" period.

Pollock's relentless search for the extreme boundaries of painting has provided American art of the 1960s with a further crucial precedent. So far, it has been light *in* painting that has been under discussion—i.e., depicted light—but with the advent of Minimal art, a practice of Pollock's which seems relatively minor to his total intention assumes new relevance. I refer to his use of richly reflective paints. A number of artists had already painted with Ripolin or Duco enamels but Pollock, (after abandoning his brief habit of forgetting cigarette stubs and paint tube tops in his surfaces) was the first American to use aluminum paint for its literalistic, surface-emphasizing property. The metallic threads in many Pollocks—from *Cathedral* and *Lucifer*, 1947, to *White Light*, 1954—reflect rather than represent light; Pollock's unprecedented deployment of light *on* the painting (instead of *in* it) takes us directly to the Frank Stellas of the aluminum, copper, and metallic monochrome series.

Along with his increasing assault on the rectangular format of orthodox thickness, the earlier Stella underscores the flatness or "realness" of his paintings to such a degree that they embrace one of the conditions of sculpture, its control of light with surface, almost leaving painting behind. Stella's near-300 sculptures are a link between Pollock's emphasis on presence (and the antecedent collage tradition) and the later work of young artists like David Novros, on whose iridescent fiberglass wall units the light of literalism shines brightly, or like Gordon Hart, who approaches even closer the brink of "objecthood." Hart's flat, white rectangles (of steel plating), which are flush to the wall like paintings but supported by the floor like sculpture, depend on light, on *actual* light, for their definition: without our discernment of the penumbral shadows of the three edges not touching the floor, we are likely to miss entirely these pure white planes.

But the painting of the late 1940s and the 1950s does not lead only in this direction—that is, toward literalism. Kenneth Noland and Ellsworth Kelly, though they both have relied heavily on physicality, still address themselves to "traditional" problems of painting. They seem increasingly (in today's context of "advanced" art's wholesale embrace of three-dimensionality) both more conservative and more successful. Noland, particularly, improves as he eliminates eccentric formats and large areas of unpainted canvas in favor of post-systematic, intuitively colored canvases. His enormous, eye-filling but not unconventionally proportioned support shapes, horizontally striped in the last few years (as in *Stria*), leave him free to concentrate on relationships of color to color; the resultant light is fabulously clean and somewhat more atmospheric than his Pop-tinged earlier palette. The exclusive horizontality of recent Noland suggests landscape, and perhaps not coincidentally, one feels a new cogency in Noland's art, replacing the earlier, uneasy mixture of hard, fast, urban sensibility and the more romantic staining derived from Louis. Stain painting was a procedure invented, after all, under the pressures of Louis's more hermetic and contemplative, not to say lyric, temperament; and Noland's is not Louis's character. His art will never possess the resonance of Louis, but his most recent period is his happiest—a new harmony of light, color, and surface offers itself in an amplitude of fertile variations. The thin translucent color in recent Noland has a painterly vibrancy no longer interrupted by conflicting demands of overly emphatic actuality or temperamental ambivalence.

More direct heirs of the Pollock-Hofmann-Louis staining are young innovators like Richard Tuttle, who goes beyond it to actual dyeing— a thorough, total saturation of the fabric. In Tuttle's wrinkled octagons of color, the accidents of slightly uneven dyeing produce variations in luminosity but, as with Gordon Hart, we are more aware of light on the work than in it. Another young artist—a painter, it is safe to say—who confronts issues of light in painting as directly as it is possible to do so is Robert Swain. His large pictures, each constituted of separate squares of stretched canvas, are "meta-color charts"; they present schematized scales of value, hue, and saturation in the manner, superficially, of ordinary color charts, but without even implied reference to those or any other object. Swain's is perhaps the purest painting possible; following the example of certain Kellys (both the early square-unit series and the later color-spectrum, contiguous-panel series), Swain concentrates exclusively on the properties of color to make some of the most luminous pictures of the decade. By antithetical means, Robert Ryman also achieves an outstanding light; Ryman uses only strokes of white paint, which, in their physical absorption by the paper or cloth support, cause a subtly shifting and atmospheric sensation harking back to Guston and to gestural abstraction's brushed inflections of tone. Ryman is not free of the literalism of our moment, however; eliminating stretchers in favor of stapling, gluing, or taping his pictures directly onto the wall, he creates an anti-illusionistic tension which contradicts the freely atmospheric play of his subdued white light. The now shiny, now matte surface further underscores Ryman's flirtation with literalism.

The only group of painters entirely unconcerned with objectness are the new realist and the figurative painters who have moved beyond French and Expressionist precedents to rediscover a clear and direct representationalism. The low-key, blurred light in a John Button cityscape, when compared to the glaring, even harsh light in a Richard Estes cityscape (full as it is of doublings, of depicted reflections) shows us how pastoral, atmospheric sensibility and the predilection for the man-made, artificially-lit urban scene are divisive even among a relatively homogeneous stylistic group. The opposing styles of Guston and Reinhardt have been seen to share a preoccupation with atmospheric light; conversely, the similar styles of Button and Estes are opposed in their kinds of light—the one romantically full of weather and gentle tonal play; the other as clear, fast, and urban as any Sheeler. Of the other important new realists, Philip Pearlstein, especially, has played a central role in re-identifying light with the value system while Alex Katz makes a brilliantly lit style which conjoins Matissean pure color and the "traditional" depiction of mass. They all have a common ancestor in Hopper; after one-fourth of a century of major accomplishment in abstract paintings, American art seems poised on the threshold of a return to figuration, from which we may expect a variety of lights to emerge.

Is there a New York light? The common subject matter of Button and Estes would indicate there is not, but the photographs of Rudolph Burckhardt and the blue-rose period in Guston's career both capture a phenomenon also present in "New York School" poetry like James Schuyler's whose "February" starts:

> A chimney, breathing a little smoke.
> The sun, I can't see
> making a bit of pink
> I can't quite see in the blue [. . .]

This trinity—photo, painting, poem—is too closely related for us to deny that yes, there is, at least *one* New York light, perversely a combination of the atmospheric, landscape-like tradition and urban inspiration. Beyond that, one cannot generalize: other lights gleam from individual eyes.

PLATES

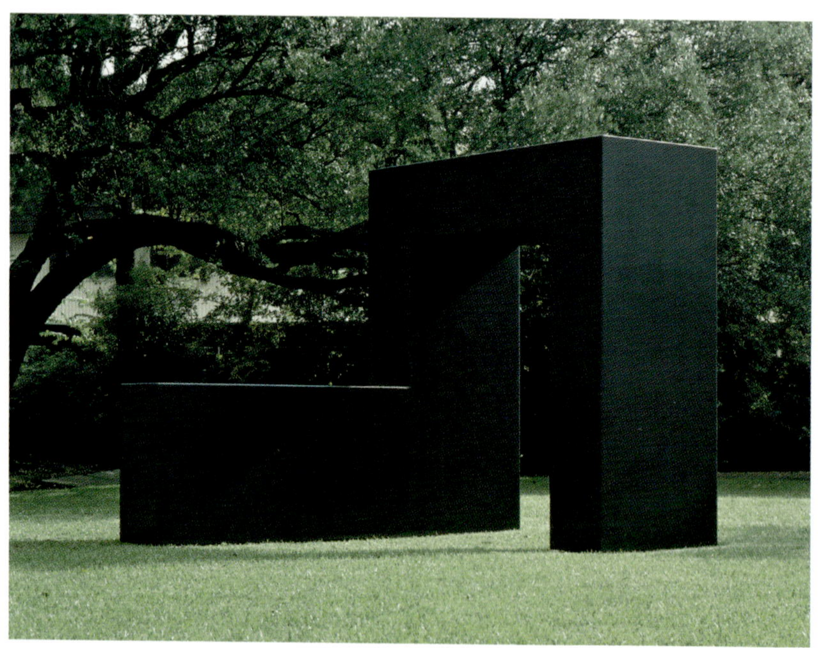

Tony Smith, *Marriage*, 1961. Steel, painted black, 120 x 120 x 144 in. (304.8 x 304.8 x 365.76 cm). © 2012 Estate of Tony Smith / Artists Rights Society. Courtesy Tony Smith Estate and Matthew Marks Gallery.

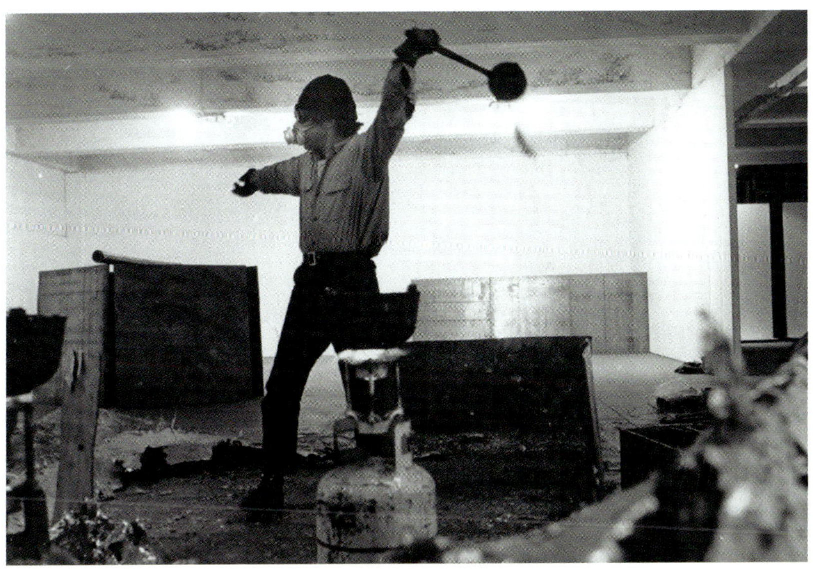

Richard Serra, *Splashing*, 1968. © 2012 Richard Serra / Artists Rights Society. Courtesy Leo Castelli Gallery.

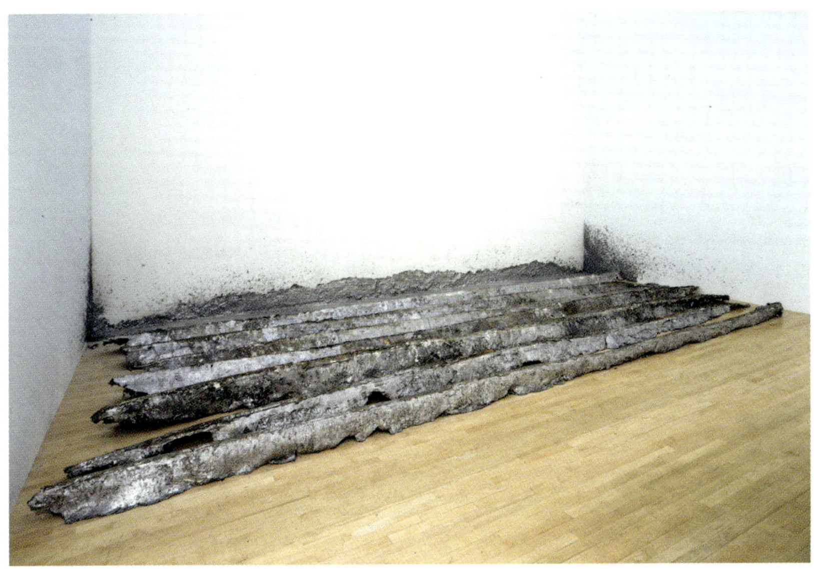

Richard Serra, *Gutter Corner Splash: Night Shift*, 1969/1995. Lead; 19 x 108 x 179 in. (48.26 x 274.32 x 454.66 cm). San Francisco Museum of Modern Art, Gift of Jasper Johns. © Richard Serra / Artists Rights Society. Courtesy San Francisco Museum of Modern Art.

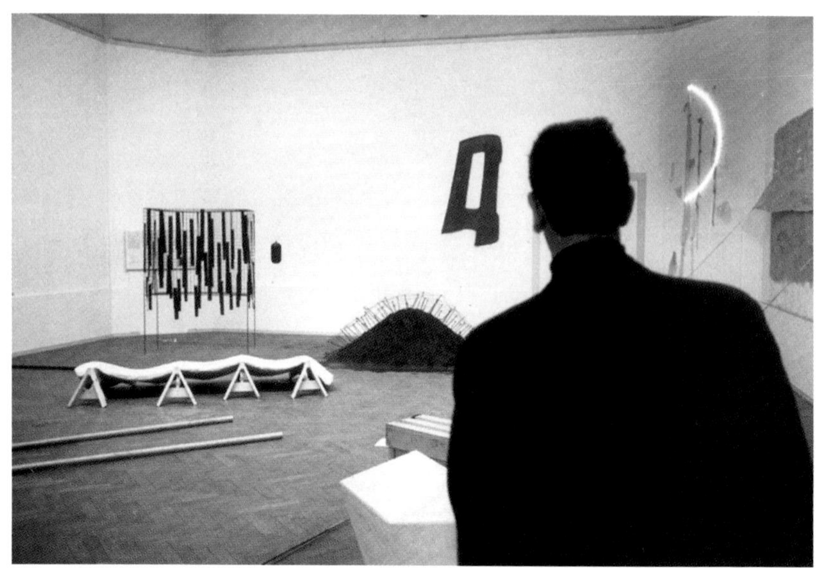

Installation view of *Live in Your Head: When Attitudes Become Form,* curated by Harald Szeeman, at the Haus Lange, Krefeld, Germany, May 1969. © Kunsthalle Bern. Courtesy Kunsthalle Bern.

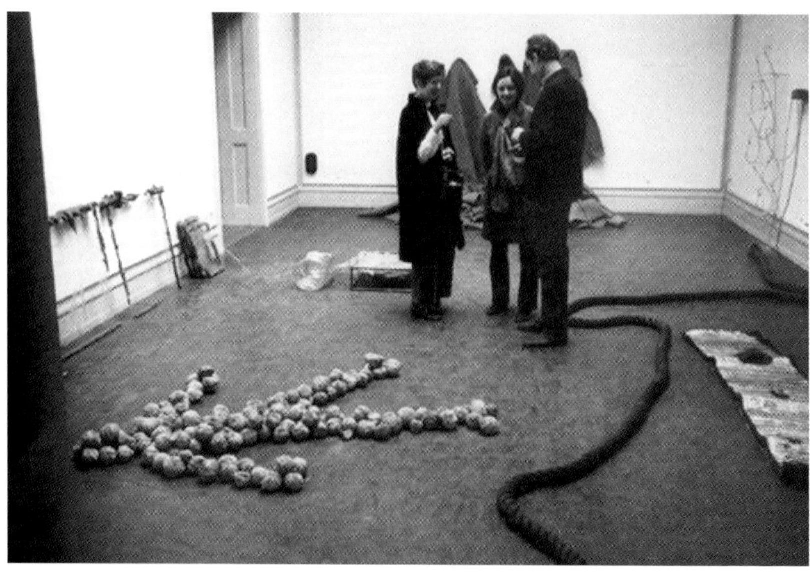

Opening of the exhibition *Live in Your Head: When Attitudes Become Form,* curated by Harald Szeemann at the Haus Lange, Krefeld, Germany, May 1969. © Kunsthalle Bern. Courtesy Kunsthalle Bern.

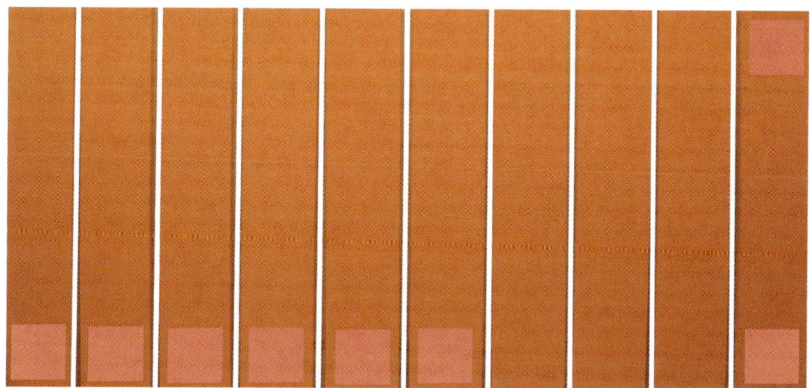

Doug Ohlson, *Cythera,* 1967. Acrylic on canvas, 90.875 x 207.875 in (230.83 x 528 cm). Courtesy Washburn Gallery, New York.

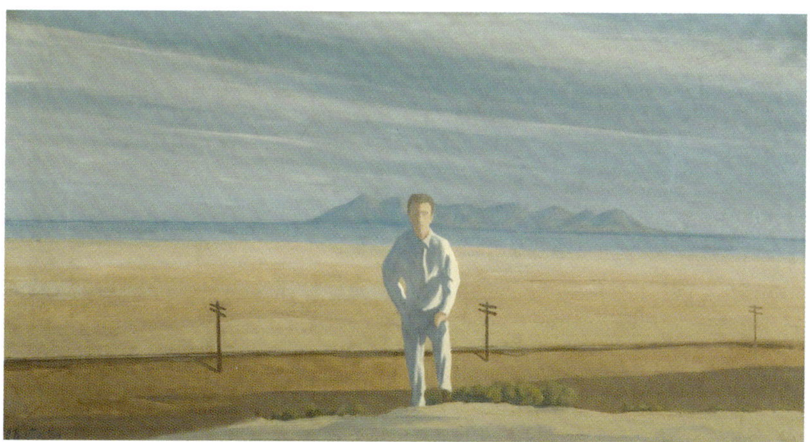

John Button, *Great Salt Lake (Self-Portrait),* 1964. Oil on canvas, 36.4375 x 68.125 in (92.55 x 173.04 cm). Utah Museum of Fine Arts, Gift of Sidney Talisman, 1989.032.001. © Allen Novak / Estate of John Button. Courtesy Utah Museum of Fine Arts.

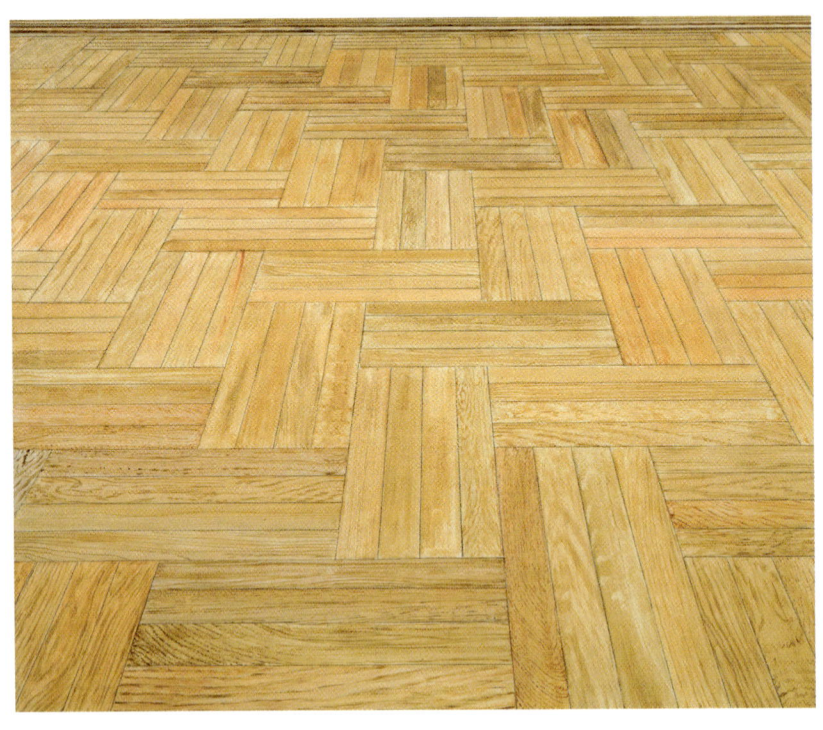

Sylvia Plimack Mangold, *Untitled,* 1969. Acrylic on canvas, 33 x 42 in (83.82 x 106.68 cm). Courtesy of Alexander and Bonin, New York. Photo: Bill Orcutt.

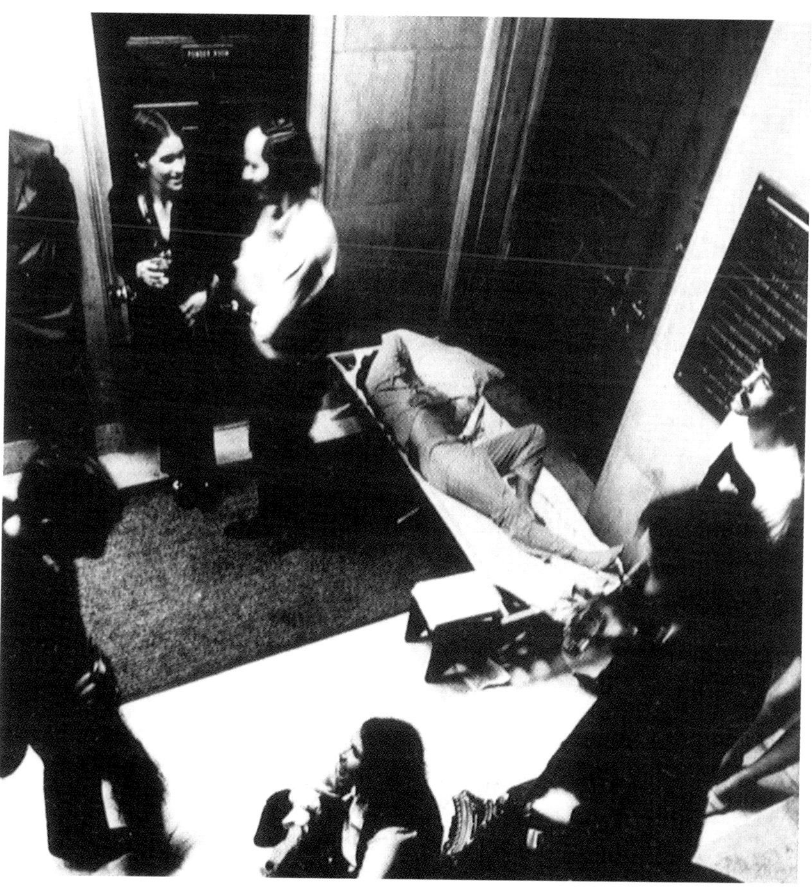

Scott Burton, Slide from *Lecture on Self* showing *Self-Work: Dream*, 1969. Performed at American Federation of the Arts, New York, October 1969. Scott Burton Papers V.12, Museum of Modern Art Archives, New York. Digital Image © The Museum of Modern Art, licensed by SCALA / Art Resource. © 2012 Estate of Scott Burton / Artist Rights Society.

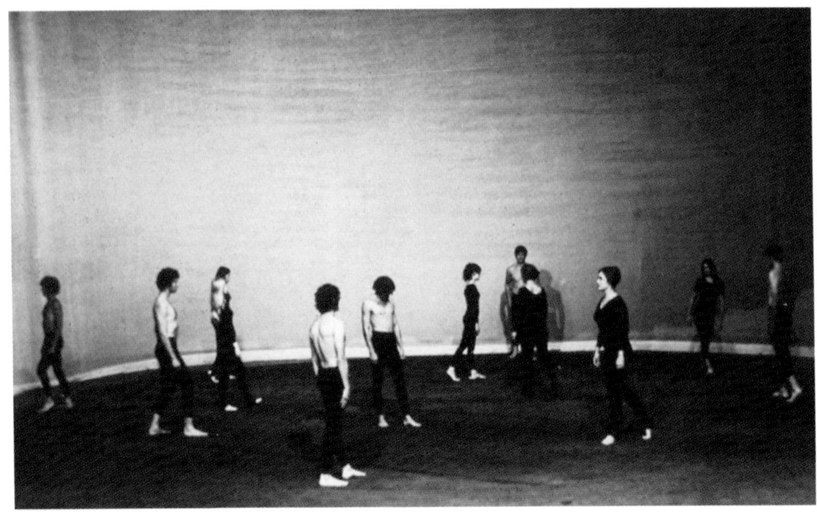

Scott Burton, Slide from *Lecture on Self* showing performance still from *Ten Tableaux: Theater as Sculpture,* 1970. Performed at the University of Iowa, Iowa City, 1970. Scott Burton Papers V.12, Museum of Modern Art Archives, New York. Digital Image © The Museum of Modern Art, licensed by SCALA / Art Resource. © 2012 Estate of Scott Burton / Artist Rights Society.

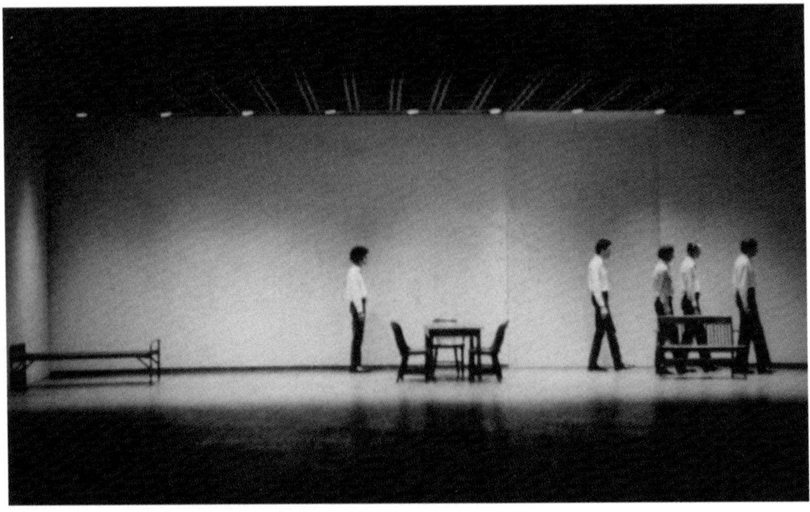

Scott Burton, Performance still from *Group Behavior Tableaux,* 1972. Performed at the Whitney Museum of American Art and American Theater Lab. Scott Burton Papers V.11, Museum of Modern Art Archives, New York. Digital Image © The Museum of Modern Art, licensed by SCALA / Art Resource. © 2012 Estate of Scott Burton / Artist Rights Society.

Themes and subjects ↓ / Materials and mediums →	OBJECTS	OTHERS	SELF
NARRATIVE, telling stories, depicting situations, representations, anthropocentric as conscious theme	MANNEQUINS AND THUNDER 3-MINUTE SCULPTURE FURNITURE PIECES RAPE OF SABINE WOMEN CHAIR DRAMA SLIDE NOVELLA	TEN TABLEAUX (WALKERS) 10 TABL. (MONTHS) 10 TABL. (NARRATIVE, RAPE) 10 TABL (DANCE) 10 TABL. (SLEEPERS) 10 TABL. FRIEZE SLIDE NOVELLA STATUES (FINCH) (succession) ALLEGORICAL TABL. VIVANT BEHAVIOR TABLEAUX ANIMAL PIECE	ST WK I (Schwitters) ST WK V (nude enactment)
ART, styles, forms architecture, sculpture, painting, theater, imitations, parodies, references as conscious theme	INGRES FILM - SCULPTURE THEATER CHAIR DRAMA	SIX CROSSES 30 COMPOSITIONS 10 TABL. (STATUES) 10 TABL. (DANCE) 10 TABL. (PEDIMENT) 10 TABL. (MONUMENT) 10 TABL. (FRIEZE) STATUES (FINCH) BATHERS POSES ALLEGORICAL T.V. (pty) BODIES	ST WK I (Schwitters) ST WK IV (dream part)
FURNITURE, ROOMS, HOUSES	FURNITURE LANDSCAPE. FURN. PIECES, CHAIR DRAMA	BEHAVIOR TABLEAUX	
CLOTHING		CHANGES BATHERS POSES DISGUISE PIECE	ST WK II (disguise) ST WK V (nude) FOUR CHANGES
SEXUALITY masculine, feminine roles - theme of Women - theme of the relation between lack of relation between figures, nudes, bodies, sexual-social behavior	INGRES FILM SCULPTURE THEATER MANS + THUNDER	30 COMP's 10 TABL (NARRATIVE, RAPE) STATUES (FINCH) BODIES CHANGES ALLEGORICAL T.V. BATHERS RAPE OF SABINES POSES DISGUISE PIECE BEHAVIOR TABLEAUX	ST WK II (disguise) ST WK V (nude)
SELF forms of self-portraiture portrayals of self personal symbolism	SLIDE NOVELLA	ALLEGORICAL T.V. BEHAVIOR TABLEAUX	ST WK I (Schwitters) ST WK II (disguise) ST WK III (deafened) ST WK IV (dream) ST WK V (nude)

Scott Burton, A page of notes (list of works completed through 1972) for *Lecture on Self,* 1972–73. Scott Burton Papers (II.52), Museum of Modern Art Archives, New York. Digital Image © The Museum of Modern Art, licensed by SCALA / Art Resource.

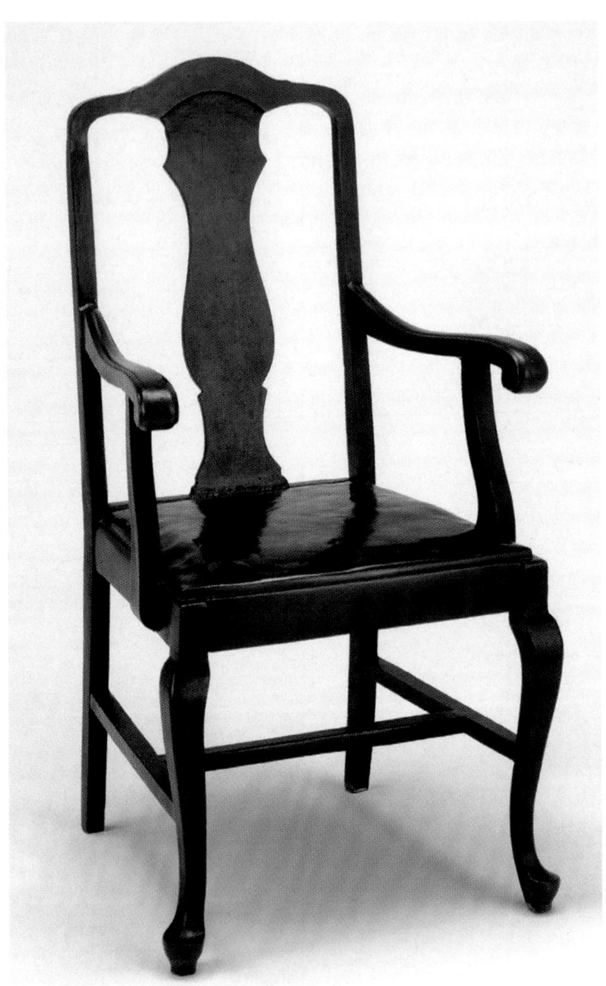

Scott Burton, *Bronze Chair,* 1972, Cast 1975. Bronze 48 x 18 x 20 in. (121.9 x 45.7 x 50.8 cm), The Art Institute of Chicago, Gift of Lannan Foundation, 1997.136. Photography © The Art Institute of Chicago. © 2012 Estate of Scott Burton / Artist Rights Society.

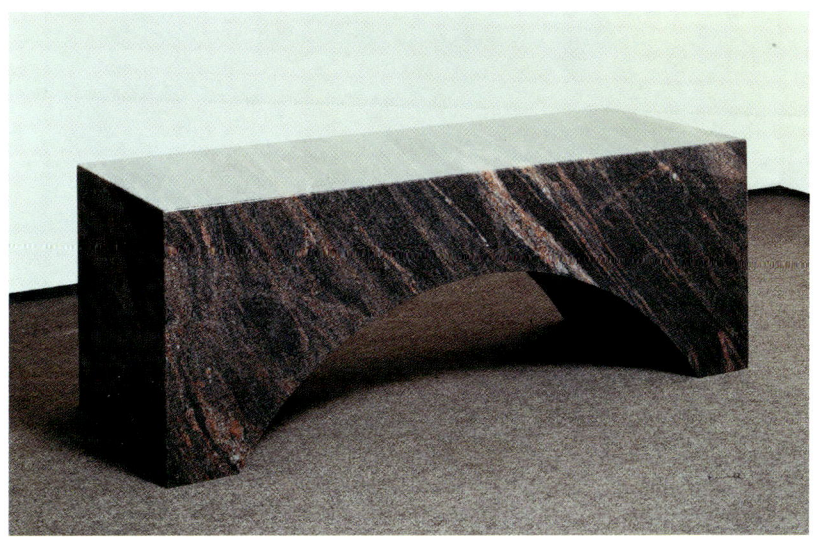

Scott Burton, *Low Piece (Bench),* 1985–86. Himalayan blue granite, 17 x 48 x 18 in. (43.2 x 121.9 x 45.7 cm). The Art Institute of Chicago, Gift of Lannan Foundation, 1997.137. Photography © The Art Institute of Chicago. © 2012 Estate of Scott Burton / Artist Rights Society.

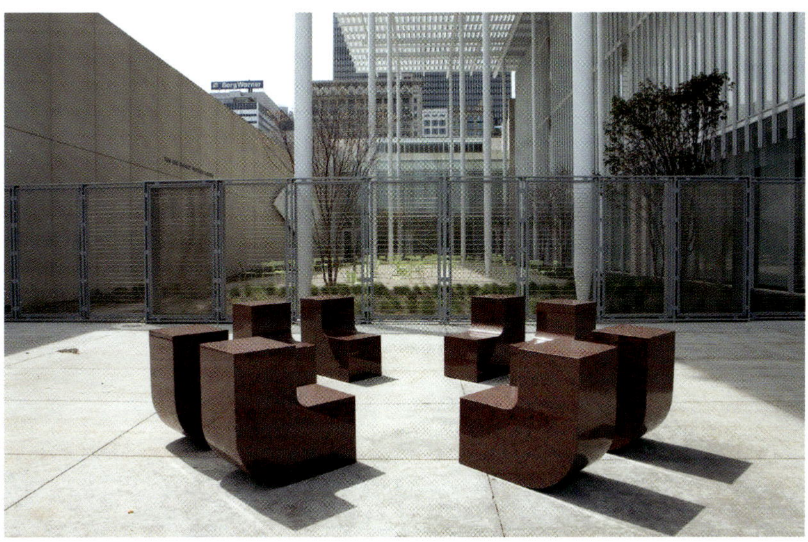

Scott Burton, *Seating for Eight,* 1985. African red granite, edition number two of two; each chair: 32 x 18 x 34 in. (81.3 x 45.7 x 86.3 cm). The Art Institute of Chicago, Gift of Fred Eychaner and Tommy Yang Guo, 2009.745. Photography © The Art Institute of Chicago. © 2012 Estate of Scott Burton / Artist Rights Society.

III. FIGURATIVE AND REALIST COMMITMENTS

Anne Arnold's Animals (1965)

"Anne Arnold's Animals," *Art and Literature* 7 (Winter 1965): 122–35.

The impulse to make art out of animals has come from various sources of energy throughout history. The cats and birds of early Egypt are deities, charged with religious energy. Religious, too, are the tapestried unicorns of medieval Europe, but at a remove; they are allegorical. As in the stories and drawings of the contemporary bestiary, no opportunity is lost to make analogies between animal and spiritual habits. But the bestiary is also inspired by another energy—the scientific. It is a proto-textbook of systematic zoological description as well as a religious guide. Much later, an apparently purely scientific impulse sent Audubon into America's birdlands to record their (then) infinite variety. He happened to return from the wilderness with beautiful works of art but it was left to others who shared his century to create animals from an exclusively artistic energy—to Courbet with his stags, to Delacroix with his lions. These beasts breathe an air far less domestic than the zephyrs to which certain other nineteenth-century animals were accustomed. The fauna of American folk art was shaped by an impulse not religious, scientific, or artistic, but simply functional. The horses were for children to ride on, the ducks for decoys, and roosters for weather vanes.

In our century animals have been trained to other roles. We do not worship them, our scientists inject them with strains of virus, our children prefer to ride on skate boards, and our artists visualize their own formal and psychological researches. Yet the animal population has exploded in the general culture: we have camels on our cigarettes, mice on our movie screens, tigers in our tanks, and at the polls we elect elephants and donkeys. The menagerie in modern sculpture is a scattered one—a goat (Picasso), some birds (Brancusi, Flannagan), a horse (Marini), a few bulls (Nakian, Nadelman), an occasional dog (Giacometti)—and all of them more relevant to the rest of their makers' work than to other members of their species.

I thought it might be useful to think about representations of animals because Anne Arnold, the American sculptor, uses them, almost always, as subject matter. Her animals are not gods, not subjects of scientific scrutiny, not functional. What energy is left? The exclusively artistic. Yet Anne Arnold is not the heiress of Courbet or Delacroix; her animals are not romantic plasm.

She cannot be placed in a tradition of depicting animals in modern art because there isn't one. Nor does she draw her images from popular culture; Larry Rivers's camel gallops right off a cigarette package, but Anne Arnold's doesn't smoke. Except for the marvelous American painter, Lois Dodd, Anne Arnold is the only artist today I can think of who consistently creates animals. (She *does* sculpt the human figure, all of it and in parts.)

You don't ask why she uses recognizable subject matter instead of being abstract. That is a donnée, like being a natural blonde. You can ask, though, why she chooses one kind of subject over another. For one thing, her strategy of using animals gives her a greater range of forms than using the human body would. For the realist sculptor, what other choice is there? There are few still lifes, no landscapes, in sculpture. And though the human body gives Giacometti or Henry Moore plenty of inspiration, their styles are more obsessive than Anne Arnold's. Animals give her a wide choice of available shapes.

They are also good material for a witty artist. Although not a fantasist—she makes no unicorns, no griffins, no heffalumps—Anne Arnold does characterize and exaggerate her bestiary with a humorous hand: her giraffe is mostly neck. With animals she can avoid a problem which haunts modern sculptors of the figure, whose variations on the human form, when not radically original, often look more like the mannerisms of caricature than genuine formal invention. Nadelman, Lachaise, Lehmbruck settle for or cannot overcome this look; Anne Arnold does not have to worry about it because human beings do not feel so intensely earnest about animals' figures as they do about their own. She has taken a subject which permits her a maximum of freedom—she has plenty of shapes to be interested in if she doesn't feel like making up her own, and if she does feel like making variations, she doesn't encounter any high seriousness about their formal justification.

From the beginning she has sculpted the human figure, in clay and stone as well as wood, and has never abandoned it. But quite early in her career she made two animal pieces which she considers germinal. They are a horse's head and a cat, both in wood, both done around 1957, but strikingly different from each other. The gilded horse's head is in the Brancusi–Arp family of organic forms reduced to their essence, but however elegantly and delicately simplified, it halts well this side of the abstract. Thrusting up equinely, it resists its base like the steeds of Helios from the Parthenon. The cat, painted a bright orange, is a member of a different family, the constructivist. With its geometric shapes, primary color, and architectural formulation, it is a distant three-dimensional cousin of Van Doesburg's cow. These two early sculptures resemble each other only in their relations to ultimate abstraction—on the way, but not there yet.

Anne Arnold has not remained with either of these styles, but both have informed her later animals, the style of the cat less apparently. In a recent cheetah, for example, the generalization of forms reminds you of the early horse's head, for while she arrives at the whole through detailed augmentation, her reduction of each detail remains dear. But in the same piece we can see vestiges of the orange cat; the cheetah is still constructivist in that its *construction* is not concealed. The forms are organic but the way they fit together and interlock is loosely reminiscent of post-Cubist art.

A third influence on Anne Arnold's animals, visible in the cheetah, is that of American folk art—those hobby-horses and duck decoys. She no longer hides the woodenness of her work: paint is sketchy; grain, knots, and chisel marks remain; urbanity is abandoned. Shapes refer, too, to Americana. The cheetah's torso calls to mind an ox-yoke or horse-collar, some functional piece of wood spontaneously incorporated into the sculpture. And as in naive art, the body's axis is stiff and straight.

This is about the cheetah and art; its relation to nature, to real cheetahs, if you compare them, reminds you that Anne Arnold's source and inspiration is more than art history. What she has produced is an observant, witty version of a jungle cat—absolutely still but bursting with potential mobility, streamlined and svelte but also undecoratively aggressive. All her animal sculpture is animated, like the cheetah, by her interest in its models' particularities as well as by her humorous eye, by her sculptural education as well as by her references to naive or folk art.

In her human figures, though, she does not seem to have found formal equivalents for her imagination. A recent full-length portrait of the artist as a swimmer has all the charm of the animal pieces—the pert immobility, the quickness of attack—but problems of psychology creep in. The figure is not conceived as if it were another member, merely a ranking member, of the animal kingdom, but rather as a conscious being, "the paragon of animals." This conception shows itself in the face, which although blankly staring and stylized, jars the viewer with its stubborn refusal to join in the whole. It is *too* interesting psychologically, is all too human. And there is insufficient variety in the body to distract from this distraction—no trunks or tails to lead the eye away. In fact, vivacity of shape is everywhere shunned: hair smoothed under bathing cap, limbs glued together, no dance of axes or gravities. The face on another of her cats, a recent one, also calls attention to itself but because it is caught in the same spirit as the askew plane of the breast, the quick-paced cluster of paws, and the independence of the ears, does not disembody itself. It can be focused in or out.

Anne Arnold does not, it is true, beg the question of human portraiture as Marisol often does by resorting to photographs, drawing, or life-masks, but in "facing" it, has not yet resolved it. This may be what has led her to breaking up the human figure, to making legs. Startlingly isolated from the torso and from each other, this high-heeled double-take does such lively things to space, to wood, and to legs, that it doesn't make us worry about man's place in the great chain of being.

What may be Anne Arnold's major pieces to date are her rhinoceros and elephant. Her largest, they look very light for their scale. Each is a chunk of torso supported by five columns—four legs and a snout—plus assorted tails, ears, and horns. In each there is enough interpenetration of void and solid to satisfy the most rigorous David Smith devotee, enough liberty with wood to please the grainiest Raoul Hague fan. Moreover, the two beasts are broadly characterized—the elephant as a kittenish monolith, the rhino as a front-heavy klutz. As great a pleasure as their personalities is the way they are put together, the simplicity of each form, the complexity of all the forms together. You want to count how many different pieces of wood there are in each animal. It would be enjoyable, like a puzzle or a game, to dis- and re-assemble them.

These two pieces, like all Anne Arnold's work, are highly unusual because their essential point has to do with pleasure. Our professionally anguished sculptors would not ignore the opportunity to make the rhino's horn or the elephant's tusks into menacing projectiles impaling man on his notorious condition. But Anne Arnold makes them entertaining as shapes—the elephant's tooth-pick tusks, for example, contrasting wildly with the world's-largest-living-thing attitude of its legs. It is spatial pleasure.

And its quality is never frivolous—even on purpose. It may not be the apocalyptic gratification afforded by Blake's Tyger, but it derives substance from its deliberate modesty. Anne Arnold's animals are as far from Bacon's mad dog as they are from Winnie the Pooh. It is amazing, the straightness of the course she steers. Compare hers with certain other modern animal sculptures: she never strays into Calder's marginal cuteness or Germaine Richier's Dracula expressionism, Baskin's suburban surrealism or Flannagan's homeletic mysticism. Her involvement with her subject matter is very direct.

This is another way of saying that there is no school or program between Anne Arnold and her work. Her only piece which might be connected to current art world currents is a large moose's head with proliferating antlers. If the how-to-do-it of pop art is the conversion of a banal image into subject matter or content, this moose might make you think of pop art. Mounted bodiless on the wall, it is closer to the taxidermist's product in the hunting lodge than to nature's product in the forest. But Anne Arnold's moose is not explicitly enough like a stuffed trophy to be accurately classified as pop; the process of hewing and hacking it out and piecing it together is too enjoyably in evidence.

(More on Anne Arnold and Pop art: after a century and a half of the tradition of the superiority of the liberated child to the repressed adult, a tradition which in painting has shaped our taste for such different artists as Klee and Dubuffet, it seems to me that Anne Arnold manages to use what is still viable in that tradition—its affirmation of pleasure—yet avoid its most recent, though ironically inverted, manifestation—namely, pop art, which is based, after all, on the premise that our collective mental age is six, and which, while it deplores rather than adores such infancy, is nevertheless programmatically stuck in the familiar tradition.)

Although Anne Arnold obviously knows what her result will be before she starts a piece, and so is not committed to the *coup de dés* of Action art, she never covers her tracks behind her. Because you can trace her experience in carving and assembling a piece, you can see her surely as a member of her generation of artists. She also uses accident, I think, if in a minor way. You have the feeling that, if she is making an animal's head and there happens to be a knot in the wood, then she allows that knot to become an eye. I doubt whether she ever "just starts carving" and lets herself be surprised by what comes out, but the result does retain the free look of improvisation. That look, rather than any pre-meditated whimsy, produces the impression of playfulness in her work.

When you walk into a whole room of Anne Arnold's animal pieces, you first think you have wandered into a children's zoo by mistake. Then you look learnedly around and realize you are definitely at the show of a modern American sculptor. But after that is established, then you are free to pretend that you are, after all, in some pleasing and amusing menagerie, where apologies to the intellect can be left at the gate.

John Button (1967)

"John Button," *Art and Literature* 11 (Winter 1967): 69–81.

E.N.: *John Button was Burton's partner throughout most of the 1960s and a formative influence on his attitudes toward painting. Written during the final years of their relationship, Burton's review in the influential but eclectic quarterly* Art and Literature *aimed to do justice to his partner's paintings, and he positioned Button in a wide range of contemporary practices both figurative and abstract. In these years, Burton was also developing a critical advocacy for abstraction (as with the Tony Smith writings in Section I), but here one can see the first mature formulation of a parallel strain in his commitments: his impassioned defense of figuration and realism. Significantly, Burton also foregrounds temporality—which he would argue to be the most important component of art of the late 1960s in his writings on Postminimalism—as a key element of Button's paintings.*

If it is permitted to talk about a figurative painter without going into the assumptions underlying the very idea of figurative painting today, then such would be appropriate in a discussion of John Button. He is much more a painter of perceptions than of conceptions, and is set apart from even his fellow figurative painters more noticeably by sensibility than by ideas. Fairfield Porter once wrote, in a sympathetic review of Button's work, "originality is not proclaimed." However, it is not shunned; Button does not borrow an historical style or use a deliberately banal one as does, say, Magritte. His non-ideational example is unlikely to be crucial in the stylistic evolution of modern art. Instead, he has found a personal way of painting which is inseparably both cause and result of *what* he paints—a style flexible but not virtuoso, reticent but not invisible.

Elements of it are almost casual. The composition of a recent cityscape, *Blue Windows*, includes only a vertical slice and a horizontal sliver of buildings, but this does not evince an ambition to become the figurative Barnett Newman or Ludwig Sander. Rather, it seems to be because Button knows just how much to put in for his purposes. He will cut his edges abruptly, not like Philip Pearlstein, who does it to make a conceptual point about picture space, but because he is concentrating on a certain kind of day—its light, its weather—and what buildings or roofs we see are sufficient to define the blue-gray-white atmosphere as it envelops and transforms solid surfaces as well as the sky. There is an instinctual economy, a restraint.

Critics and reviewers have tended to speak of Button's "modesty." They are partly accurate. But, cast back as we are on the artist's perceptions, we wonder at the description. Dramatic and ambitious, his paintings inescapably insist on themselves—on what they are about, on what they *are*. James Schuyler wrote that Button's "gift is to know what is emblematic of his most profoundly engaged feelings, and to paint it when he sees it." Button's subjects, though, do not function simply as occasions or excuses for the painting; they release the energy of his perceptions but they also contain it.

The character of these perceptions has to do with the sense of time, which always pervades Button's work. This sense does not depend on method; it is not the velocity of action painting (the sense of the time taken to paint the picture) nor is it the stillness often resident in paintings in which pre-calculated areas are dispassionately filled in. It does not emerge just from the depiction of things we assume to be poised in a sequence of change (clouds, someone moving), for it is equally present in paintings of things that don't move, like buildings. You feel that Button's sense of time is part of the perception itself. His adagio light spreads at its own pace across the canvas, even in a picture of a bright and clear day, preventing the eye from taking in its play quickly. His colors, though high in key and at times almost blatant, cannot be instantly comprehended, either, in their rich subtlety of variation. They do not deflect the gaze but absorb it—as they do, to the point of unification, the light. A Button reveals itself gradually, not through multiplicity of incident but through depth of concentration—which takes *time* to filter to the surface.

However, the mechanics of this operation or emergence are elusive, and not primary.

Button's isolation of particular moments out of their flow does add to the weight of time in his work. He paints assertively in the present tense, not in the past tense of memory or elegy. Whether a figure's suspended gesture, a façade's fleeting color at dusk, or a soon to shift formation of clouds, each moment is detached from the cadence of its neighbors. Such liberation from the chain of sequence is dramatic, but not melodramatic because the implicit sequence is itself smooth and measured. The past and future moments were not, will not be, violently different from the presented one. There is a "kinaesthetic continuity," as Schuyler wrote, "in which there are no transitional passages, or which is all transition."

So, by concentrating on an instant in time, Button expands it into timelessness. He does it with unique authority of sensibility.

John Button was born in San Francisco, California, in 1929, and grew up there. His move to New York in 1953 was simultaneous with a change from abstract to figurative painting. He first showed at the Tibor de Nagy Gallery, associated, now as then, with the group of figurative painters which includes—very loosely—Fairfield Porter, Jane Freilicher, Larry Rivers, Nell Blaine, Paul Georges, Jane Wilson, Alex Katz. This group has been infinitely more responsible than the now moribund "California School" for reviving or keeping alive figurative painting. Button, in fact, expressly dissociates himself from almost everything Californian—except its redwood trees. He is an ardent conservationist (today's term for "nature-lover"). An equally ardent traveller, his journeys throughout the United States, Mexico, England, Europe, Africa, and Greece are recorded in a series of gouaches as alive in their descriptive clarity as in their handling. Their directness of observation has something of the quality of that national genius for watercolor of the English in the nineteenth century.

In Button's painting, development has been not abrupt but steady. There have been no radical breaks but rather a constant personalization of theme, refinement of style, and expansion of both. In *Three Serious Ladies* of 1955, with which he feels he first started to hit his stride, his characteristic equivocality between the candid and the posed or arranged can already be seen (though the latter seems to dominate, in the confinement of the shallow, horizontal-vertical space as well as in the picture-album tone). But by 1961 and *Garage Space*, a greater freedom has developed, both of event and structure. Frontality still exists, but a deeper resonance of color, a more specific play of light, and a less intrusive geometry combine with the figure's unawareness of being seen to give the painting a self-sufficiency, an immediacy in which there is no longer any barrier of self-consciousness, any difficulty of translating the scene into the painting.

(Abstract Expressionism developed spectacularly its own methods to outmaneuver the "Shadow" which, according to Eliot's diagnosis of the modern situation, falls "Between the conception / And the creation"; finding such methods inapplicable to his work, Button has overcome this malaise in his own way.)

In *Garage Space*, too, Button is with the subject for which he may feel his strongest affinity, the subject perhaps most "emblematic" of his feelings—the city. For him, it is New York.

Representations of the city in art are complex, involving as they do not only stylistic history and iconographical traditions but also attitudes about society which, due to the nature of the subject matter, become almost overt. Long gone is the confident eighteenth-century assumption of the Guardis or Canaletto that their rational views of Venice or London, including major building, monuments, street life, are adequate and appropriate chronicles of the civic life of the times. After them, such schemata are abandoned. The Impressionists looked at Paris as if it were landscape—which means more than just that they painted city and country in the same manner. Their cityscapes are not comprehensive: views are partial; the angle of vision is fixed at pedestrian level, or if it is high, out a window or from a roof instead of omnisciently up in the air. Style begins its radical transformation of subject, to the point that Futurist examples of the genre must be called "urban environment" painting rather than cityscape. And if you consider Mondrian the greatest twentieth century city painter, the genre's history grows awesomely complex.

The precedents in American art are less daunting. The city paintings of Sheeler, Marin, Niles Spencer, and Stuart Davis, are addressed to what is nationally possible in a post-Cubist idiom, but often seem to use urban architecture almost opportunistically; the planes and angles are already in the subject matter, so it's easier to get them into the style. In this country, Edward Hopper alone created a style of city-painting which was neither provincial nor derivative, and it is with Hopper that Button has been most often compared.

Button may almost be said to be in direct competition with Hopper—the primal struggle of the son against the father. Though the younger painter might not have existed as he is without the older, he hardly lives off his paternity. While Hopper fought to emerge from American Scene painting, Button seems eager to immerse himself in it. Perhaps that is due as much to historical as to temperamental differences. It no longer occurs to the American artist to worry about being left out of the mainstream of modernism just because of where he is, and he can afford to paint America as well as Americanly if he wishes.

Like Hopper, Button has a way of painting that does not call attention to itself, and too, both love the instant of catching someone absently doing something ordinary, something which nevertheless seems to be significantly arranged. But Button sees the city itself in a way Hopper does not, more as Monet did, as if it were landscape. This means that the city is imagined chiefly as color and light and scale instead of narrative, and it limits the range of what can be painted—no gas pumps, night cafeterias, or movie house interiors. The light on a Button cornice could illuminate similarly a cliff or treetop.

And in Hopper, atmosphere, literal atmosphere, is missing. His windows never look as if there is glass in them; Button's smokily reflect the weather. In Hopper, the same bleak clarity pervades the whole space, and the picture's coherence is axial, while in a Button like *Downtown Street,* the modulation of atmosphere (through the shifting adjustments of hue and value) unifies the picture much more than does geometric organization; Button's design is as loose as his colors are precise.

In recent cityscapes like *Grand Central*, he has increasingly turned from smaller, older, more congenial buildings to large, new, "impersonal" or "hard-edge" architecture. This is not, I think, to take part in the up-to-date reaction against the "emotionality" of Abstract Expressionism, but instead to help maintain art's ability to incorporate the changes in our environment. Lichtenstein or Oldenburg probably have this intention, at least in part, but Button is without their irony or parody. In none of his cityscapes does lyric conviction ever cease to dominate.

When he adds a figure, half-turning or in the middle of a stride, to his city paintings, or to his nature paintings like *Coney Island, Summer*, the plot thickens—but does not congeal. Is this genre painting? It is either not quite or more than. In the beach painting, because the two men are not aware of each other, narrative content is avoided, almost explicitly. Yet you cannot feel that their mutual unawareness illustrates the clichés of alienation. There is the promise of incident but not its fulfillment. And the picture's space both invites us in and excludes us; it recedes, but it flattens. These are highly meditative or contemplative paintings—a state which genre painting, with its claim to typicality and its anecdotal impulses, does not accommodate.

Also, modern genre painting is often pressed into the service of social realism, and Button, though he paints working-class neighborhoods, does not do it ideologically. He makes them look too beautiful to be polemically useful. If the most powerful archetypes of community are the City of God and Babylon, the social realist must surely be portraying the latter, while Button's New York, like El Greco's Toledo, is the City of God—though now the god be color.

In landscape too, Button is closer to the Garden of Eden than to the Wasteland. He clings to the pastoral, unfamiliar and western as it may appear. In painting the Wyoming mountains, the New Mexico sky, or the Salt Lake of Utah, he states his version of sublimity, derived in part from Maxfield Parrish, and through him, our nineteenth-century painters of the Hudson River valley or the Yosemite or the Grand Canyon. It is paradoxical that a knowledgeable painter can use such sources today without deprecating them. Parrish's outrageous light on infinitely distant castle tops reappears without apology on the skyscraper in *Grand Central.* Even in his most postcard-like paintings, Button always paints the scene itself, never its reproduction. The sincerity is persuasive. Pictures like *Grand Tetons*, with their "impossible" subjects, render obsolete, I think, the hoary distinction between high art and kitsch. Lichtenstein's landscapes do the same thing, but where the Pop artist forcibly destroys the distinction by emphasizing it to the point of absurdity, Button does so simply by ignoring it. One reviewer disliked *Great Salt Lake (Self-Portrait)* because it reminded her, she said, of a Marlboro cigarette advertisement. She got it backwards; the ad imitates, in effect, the painting. In Button, feelings and attitudes long considered atrophied, fit only for mockery or exploitation, are discovered to be still viable.

There is something else pertinent in *Great Salt Lake (Self-Portrait)*. When painting themselves, most artists either eliminate setting to concentrate on interior autobiography or, placing themselves in their studios, represent themselves as professional, working painters. Button, as if allegorically, does neither; both the existence and the nature of the location are telling. He projects himself, The Traveller, into one of his "emblematic" settings, which here seems to play a double role. It is *in* the painting, and it *is* the painting, that is, both cause and result of the artist's "most profoundly engaged feelings." The gap between subject matter and content closes, making this, like many of Button's other works, seem practically self-generated—for all its involvement, also distanced, self-contained. And too, the ambivalent placement of the figure, both inside the scene and in front of it, cogently repeats this duality or unity.

Button's art is fundamentally one of balance, as the persistent "neither . . . nor" and "both. . . and" constructions of this essay indicate. His color is neither subservient to photographic tonalities nor the "pure" product of imagination or theory. His surface hovers between the transparent and the tactile. His space does not stress mass or volume; it flattens in the modern way, but not so far as to eliminate perspective. His perspective is often intense but is also mitigated, interrupted by the edge of the painting or an object within it, or softened atmospherically. The anxiety in these recessive vistas and isolated figures shades into the exhilaration of *presenting* (making present materially and in time). Impulses are equalized, even in Button's very adjustment of subject and style.

This balance may be construed ethically—as a metaphor or mimesis of civility. Button's poise between extremes seems to me to represent the idea of civility in its best, its moral sense. He builds a pictorial and emotional structure which resolves resiliently the conflicts of experience variously characterized as reality and fantasy, the social and the personal, others and self. In the implications of this reconciliation, Button reminds us how the painter "thinks with his brush," how art is a *visual* comprehension of experience.

Robert Beauchamp: Paint the Devil (1966)

"Paint the Devil," *ARTnews* 65.2 (April 1966): 26–27, 67–69.

The visionary or fantasist appears at every point in art history; his impulse may be autonomous, unprovoked by his culture's pressure, but its embodiment is of course historically specified. Redon's temperament, for example, may remind us of Bosch's, but stylistically the two are as different as Breugel and Monet. It is like the similarity and difference between a friar riding a donkey and a friar on a Vespa.

Robert Beauchamp's paintings, too, are both timely and timeless, both in and out of their particular historical environment. In situating this apparently eclectic artist, in relating him to other artists, we should therefore distinguish between parallels and influences: parallels are unintentional but caused, influences willed but accidental. And generally, parallels refer to correspondences of content, influences to correspondences of style. Thus, Beauchamp's relation to Redon is a parallel, generated by the continuity of the primal or archetypal imagination and not by Beauchamp's volition, while his relation to Hofmann is in the category of influence—historically given (you can't help when you were born), but deliberately accepted, and incorporated.

This is not to suggest that B(eauchamp) = ½ R(edon) + ½ H(ofmann), i.e. old wine in new bottles. The mysterious life in his painting could never be born from such programmatic wedlock. Without cognizance of this life, without an initial or ultimate suspension of the analytic, there would be little attraction to his paintings. In looking at them, several other parallels (Bosch, Ensor, Munch, Moreau) and influences (Dubuffet, Gauguin, German Expressionism) come to mind, but to ignore the force and individuality of the artistic personality which has synthesized them and moved beyond the eclectic is to ignore the essential, the mystery of what art is.

Robert Beauchamp was born in Denver in 1923. He studied at the Colorado Springs Fine Arts Center both before and after wartime Navy duty (1943–46), which took him to Australia, Arabia, Iran. From the Center, where he especially remembers studying drawing with Boardman Robinson, Beauchamp went for a year to Cranbrook, and then, in 1950 moved to New York for two years of study with Hans Hofmann. At that point, he painted abstract pictures which he says were like what you would expect from any Hofmann student, but his first one-man show, at the Tanager Gallery in 1954, initiated the series of on-the-scene reports from a nether-nether-land—its animals, natives, birds and landscapes—which he has continued to compile for more than a decade in a developing Expressionist style. In his latest show [Graham; to April 23] these flora and fauna make a full-cast appearance in ambitiously scaled *tableaux* of the psychic life. In his simultaneous creation, discovery and description of this New World, Beauchamp is our Audubon or Catlin of the Unconscious.

The new paintings greatly expand Beauchamp's iconographic and stylistic ranges (not that the two aren't functions of each other.) The "witches" and simians are familiar, but now all manner of fish, flesh or fowl (always exotic, never quite imaginary) invade the picture. The delineation of the images plays, too, in a wider scale: from a butterfly whose identity is nearly dissolved in a patch of yellow pigment all the way to a wholly explicit, almost *trompe-l'oeil* fly resting on a teacup; this range matches that of the paint surface itself, which runs the gamut from stain to slab. Beauchamp's articulation of the surface seems to derive, not just from Abstract Expressionism generally, but specifically from Hofmann (who prescribed it to his students), as do elements of his color and form. The purity and saturation, and sometimes choice, of color are reminiscent of Hofmann, though Beauchamp plunges dramatically into tonalities absent in the master. Hofmann is a great model too, for Beauchamp's (or anyone's) way of working wet on wet yet keeping the color brilliant. And certain shapes: the cock's comb of the "leaping fish" painting or the form caught between the curves of the snake and apple in *Eve* seem inherited from some 1946 and '47 Hofmanns. But Hofmann's version of Cubism is absent in Beauchamp, even though small geometric shapes have recently begun to appear in his work.

The Hofmann influence, in its specifics, seems relatively recent. Perhaps it was a way out of the primitivistic, *art brut* influence visible before, or out of German Expressionism. Stringy-haunched nudes, like those of Otto Mueller, still preside, but they no longer squat or swoon—they stride, stalk, crane their necks more freely in the picture space. Beauchamp's relation to German Expressionism has come to look much more like a parallel than an influence; if we are reminded of, say, Nolde, it is through certain clusters of feelings, rather than references of method. Devoted as it was to transforming the subject without relinquishing "rational" structure, German Expressionism must have outlived its usefulness for Beauchamp, who has turned to the more open or improved structure, image-less or not, provided by Abstract Expressionism. Thus, in one exemplary (untitled) painting, not only the inhabitants of the space, but the space itself have been transformed—into an over-all field, subject everywhere to equal diminution or expansion of episode and energy. We do not read the decrease in size of the figures from bottom to top as determined by perspective but rather discrete "complexes," each in its own scale, yet swept into the whole by color and paint manipulation. In the same way, some of the figures are flattened out while others are projected in illusory, if shallow, depth. The space keeps changing. And what circumstantial business has that infinite or flat space there at the bottom behind the skeins of paint and/or tail-feathers? In his incorporation of some of the pictorial conventions of Abstract Expressionism, Beauchamp shows us, as fully as do Al Held, Fairfield Porter, Lester Johnson, how fertile remains the ground broken by that style.

Sidney Tillim and Dore Ashton both have spotted "parody" [or] "spoof" in Beauchamp's work. Perhaps this is a way to skirt the issue of his diabolism. Certainly, horror has become rhetorical to us, even in its anti-art and shock-esthetic forms. But to me Beauchamp's art is neither ironic (parodying the demonic) nor melodramatic (dealing in gratuitous horror—remember the Chicago monsters?). Its humor is much more visceral, yawpy; and its derangement or violence is due not at all to stale literary associations, but to the jarring discontinuity of scale and the instability of an environment in which forms and figures crowd claustrophobically around, yet loom out of an undefined, potentially limitless mass. In other words, the vehicle of Beauchamp's psychology is, legitimately as we think, the painting itself, and not a set of props or cast of characters.

His images have, however, an ineluctable interest in themselves. Why do they seem so emotionally loaded? While Beauchamp, in conversation, disclaimed any interest in automaton, that method comes to mind because of the compulsive recurrence in his work of certain figures, separately or in any combination: the leering monkey, the harpy with matted hair, the Egyptian-Polynesian-Oriental nude. The charged sexuality of these creatures is spawned at some level of receptivity surely pre-conscious. You think, by the way, how daring it is of an artist to work in such an area today, after the depletion of Surrealism and the advent of the "Every-man-his-own-Norman O' Brown"–era. Beauchamp reverses art history; he comes to Surrealism (its "voluntary hallucinations") through Abstract Expressionism, and in doing so, replenishes his source.

Finally what is most interesting about Beauchamp as a Problem in Esthetics is his creation of a style which includes such different conceptions of painting a nude running past, a drip, a bird's wing turning into a splatter of paint, a geometric stripe next to a free passage of brushstrokes next to a tightly rendered teacup. A Beauchamp camel or witch has not the same relation to the abstractness of the painting as has Pollock's she-wolf or de Kooning's woman; in Beauchamp, the controlling action is not the emergence of a single totemic image. His images are fixed individually, and only in concert do they gain and lose denotative control of the painting. It is in this play or range, in its extent, and in the extent of the range of surface modulation, and the shifting play between color and tonality, as well as in the nature of the subject matter, that we are confronted with the inimitable presence of vitality of life. Beauchamp's images focus and subside, crystalize and fade, slip in and out of the visible (as well as temporal) spectrum.

His inclusiveness is not for the conceptual purist. His ability to join subject and style inseparably together is at least as mysterious as that dusky animal who pursues or is pursued by her creator.

American Realism: Letter to the Editors of *Artforum* (1967)

"Letter to the the Editors," *Artforum* 5.5 (January 1967): 4.

E.N.: *Burton wrote this letter in response to Barbara Rose's contribution to a special two-article feature on the opening of the Whitney Museum of American Art's new building at Madison Avenue and 75th Street. See Barbara Rose's "The New Whitney: The Show,"* Artforum *5.3 (November 1966): 51–55.*

Sirs:

Barbara Rose (in *Artforum*, November 1966) learned from the Whitney Museum's opening show "how American realism deteriorated from its apogee in Eakins to its nadir in the thirties and forties," and left the matter at that. Unfortunately, so did the Whitney; there is not one single work in the show representing the renewed vitality of representational painting in New York in the fifties and sixties. The advanced (non-academic, post-abstract, Pop-less) work of artists like Lennart Anderson, Leland Bell, Nell Blaine, John Button, Lois Dodd, Joseph Fiore, Jane Freilicher, Paul Georges, Alex Katz, Robert de Niro, Philip Pearlstein, Fairfield Porter, Herman Rose, Jane Wilson, is wholly ignored in a "survey" which pretends to be comprehensive. Because the Whitney gives the false impression that the books are closed on this kind of painting, as well as for the reasons she herself gives, Miss Rose is quite right to judge the "hip new uptown" Whitney worse than the "schmaltzy old downtown" one.

But as for Miss Rose, by not correcting this impression in her review is she not a passive accomplice of the change she describes and apparently laments in saying that it is "no longer the case" that taste is "formed by artists and critics?" Is she not allowing the Whitney to form, or at least represent, her taste when she ignores its omission of good recent figurative painting? Whether or not Miss Rose is personally interested in the above painters, she is surely aware of them, and should be a more conscientious historian than to permit their absence from the Whitney show to pass in silence.

Herman Rose: Telling and Showing (1967)

"Herman Rose: Telling and Showing," *ARTnews* 66.4 (Sumer 1967): 36–37, 68–71.

Herman Rose paints very small, quiet but vibrant cityscapes, landscapes and still lifes, and sometimes portraits. His latest show [Zabriskie; to June 10] covers five years of work and includes watercolors and etchings. Most of his urban pictures are of New York and environs—Yonkers, Brooklyn, New Jersey—but there are others of Rome and Barcelona, which he visited in 1962. Many of the landscapes are of Central Park but some were done in Charlottesville, Virginia, where Rose was artist-in-residence last year at the University of Virginia, and a few are of Cape Cod. His still lifes are of small objects: plums, shells, gourds, matchbooks, statuettes, vases, candlesticks. They crown the shelves and tabletops of his studio, and an impression of his ambiance is built up from the flotilla of small things much as the myriad of little touches coalesces to create the image in one of his paintings.

Though one senses in Rose a miniaturist impulse, there is nothing quaint or precious about his light-shredded distillation of the visible world, partly, I think, because they never look arranged or "stylized." Rose will go to some trouble to get to the place he wants to paint from, like renting a hotel room in Brooklyn or getting the City's permission to go out on a non-public dock, and once there, he never seems to leave out anything he sees. Instead, he summarizes certain elements of the scene. For instance, in a view of a Greenwich Village street, there is a diagonal row of parked automobiles in the foreground. They look jammed together, the way a telephoto lens would see them, and hump-backed. But rather than omitting them or coming back another time, Rose kept them in and dealt with them by generalizing them. In the finished painting, the cars are a little vague and in a looser focus than the rest of the things in the picture. But they are still there, revealing a basic loyalty to the actuality of the scene. (Rose always works directly before his model, returning to it again and again, which can stretch the actual painting time into months or even years.) The intrinsic demands of the picture appear to take second place to the outside dictates. Of course, this is not true, or rather, is an over-simplified antithesis, first of all because in the very choice of what to paint the picture is already begun before brush is ever touched to canvas. Further, because it is not just in "difficult" passages but throughout the whole picture that Rose generalizes or summarizes. In fact, such mediation is one of his strongest impulses, affecting his composition, color, light, handling, his very "tone of voice." Though a counter-impulse toward more dramatic arrangement and overt feeling sometimes breaks through, the drive to distance and compress what is pictured deeply informs Rose's style. The size itself of his format demonstrates this reticence, and since he leans to complex, panoramic subjects, the smallness is even more telling. It forces him to "synopsize."

The subject matter is not in itself arresting—views we all know or things anyone might have around the house, nothing novel. And the point of view, where the observing eye is located, contributes importantly to the distancing. It is not so much that you are looking from far away—the still lifes are in close-up—but rather that the angle of vision is indeterminate, not precisely placed. No table-edge or street in perspective is firmly fixed in relation to the sides of the canvas. Just how far away *is* that warehouse or that shell? All we can say is that it is "at a remove," discontinuous with the viewer's world.

Rose's way of handling paint, his touch, is also a powerful equalizer of what is seen. His mottled surface controls to a large degree one's perceptions of the images "behind" it. Spatial illusion is, of course, checked by the tactility of the pigment, in a manner long orthodox, but Rose's almost subliminally low relief has the further effect of leveling hierarchies in the relations between the various things pictured. Thus a sky is not a blank or smooth expanse acting as a foil for a complex of more heavily encrusted or more detailed buildings, but, as surface, is continuous with the buildings, equally tangible, equally activated—more so at times.

Rose's touch distributes itself without major discriminations over the entire surface; though his strokes are looser and more varied than they used to be (the influence of doing watercolors), they still provide a kind of filter through which the subjects are passed, to come out equally able to arouse our scrutiny. Rose summarily eliminates sharp contrasts between more and less intricate forms. In his cityscapes, for example, as many or as few windows are visible in the nearest buildings as in the farthest. Articulation of parts tends to be constant throughout; the back-cloth of a still life snags the eye as readily as does the conch shell in front of it.

Just as important to this tendency to generalize are Rose's color and light. There is no single-source illumination of either the striking "proscenium" or the scrupulously imitative kind. The light seems to come from nowhere—or everywhere, from the whole picture out to the viewer rather than from a set internal direction. (These days, we are more accustomed to seeing such halations in abstract than in figurative painting.) Cast shadows in Rose's paintings do not fling themselves, but spread osmotically across a street or wall, comporting themselves more as hue-changes than as tonal distinctions. These close-valued works have a diffused and dappled radiance which is, though here more and there less intense, still essentially even in its emanation from the rear of the painting, as if from the white ground itself.

In keeping with this gentle, intermittent effulgence, Rose's color is also pied or atomized. Not only are unbroken areas of single colors avoided, but in each picture, every color has something of every other color in it. The kettle in one of the still lifes is broken down not just into the stippled browns and oranges which the color of copper might be expected to yield, but also into violets and mauves—more of these than could be explained by the reflection of proximate hues. Not restricted to denoting the objects that originally suggested their introduction, colors are "let out of their cages," to fly and alight anywhere—a never-stilled chromatic aviary, but one without a "pecking order," for though an azure invades a yellow, it is in turn subordinate to a green. The method is one of homogeneity through variegation.

Too, the same colors reappear frequently from painting to painting. Rose's palette is fairly stable; "delicious," characteristically pastel, its rose, peach, turquoise, pistachio, mint and plum tones wander freely, though rarely straying into acidity, between polarities of crimson and blue-green. The hues are vivid, if delicately so, usually getting "paled out" with large admixtures of white. The high proportion of medium to pigment asks the eye to close in on the often transparent, glazed-looking paint to seize its many inflections of color as well as of surface.

Rose will often raise or lower the "volume" of local colors, as his picture of Central Park with the back of the Metropolitan Museum and midtown skyscrapers shows. The brick-red of the nearby Met is considerably diluted and the distant skyscrapers correspondingly sharpened in clarity and color for the sake of a muted atmospheric constancy instead of dramatized oppositions of color or space. Further, Rose only broadly establishes the time of day or kind of weather—an odd and telling fact about such a devoted open-air painter.

A particular compositional habit of Rose's is also synoptically undramatic—his "parade." He often marshals things in a horizontal sequence across the canvas, creating a kind of palindrome. This structural theme is obviously suited to views like that of New Jersey's factories strung out along the Hudson's shore (though which came first?) and is perhaps natural, too, in still-life, but the horizontal concatenation recurs as well in compositions that do not automatically suggest it. In *The Actor, Leslie Barrett*, the parade appears, somewhat altered, in the arc of objects that encircles the figure (from the containers on the floor at left, the still-life elements strewn across the table and shelf, down to the paper and phone at lower right). And in Rose's cityscapes, the pull of receding planes is often mitigated by the arrangement of buildings at the horizon in a lateral continuum, without the "beginning, middle, and end"—that is, the formal rise, climax, and fall—of dramatically valued structure.

However if Rose usually suppresses visual and psychological excitement in his work in favor of a reticent evenness, there are enough exceptions to suggest that the impulse toward more charged expression is strong. Several of the recent paintings present very directly intense states of feeling, accompanied by pictorial heightening. They are hardly Expressionist explosions (better, Impressionist implosions), and at first contact, you get but a whiff of the new energy that has broken through. Yet within Rose's fine range, the difference is marked. Sometimes the dramatic image seems unconsciously symbolic, sometimes expressly evocative, and sometimes it gains its import purely as a response to an arresting configuration in the outside world. For the latter, an indelible example is the picture of rocks and young trees in Central Park. The point of view is unusual for Rose: looking up from the bottom of a massive rock-hill, you see delicate tree-tops, but not their trunks, silhouetted against the sky; there is nothing else in the painting. The explicitness of the opposition of rocks and vegetation, as well as the exaggerated upward tilt of the vantage-point, gives the picture a directness and suggestiveness not at all "generalized." When there is apparent unconscious meaning, we can, without treating it condescendingly as "psychological projection," nevertheless recognize vivid subjective states which increase or are increased by the esthetic means. Such a picture is one of Cape Cod with a small boat on the water protectively framed by two rounded clumps of shrubs on the shore, and, in the foreground and to one side, a dead tree whose broken branch twists and yearns toward the distant craft. For Rose, this is a very precisely designed work. Its axial tensions, the tug between the tree and boat, the symmetrical placement of the shrubs, the isolation of all of them, convey a secret pathos unrelated to the actual subject matter. It would be merely sentimental if deliberate, but is, in its latency, a dramatic discharge of feeling.

Often the little nick of street at the bottom of an aerial cityscape will have the same effect, not only giving scale to the overview, but making the realm of human activity seem unattainably remote.

An expressly evocative painting is *The Actor, Leslie Barrett.* The theme of a man alone in a room is a recurrent one for Rose, and in this, the latest of the series, isolation and melancholy are palpable. The emotional significance is not disguised or muffled. Yet the conscious intellectual control of pictorial means is, paradoxically, at its strongest. The way that complicated areas are balanced against simpler ones, the way the left-hand part of the room is tilted up and in to keep it unified with the rest, the organization of a few major verticals and diagonals, these and other carefully worked out elements are there as if in compensation for the unusually "loaded" content. Picasso said that during the War he thought that poets would probably be writing sonnets. In Rose's case, certainly, the more intense or disruptive the emotion, the greater is the formal clarity and control.

In the Jamesian esthetic of the novel, much is made of the distinction between "telling" and "showing," or in Percy Lubbock's terms, "panorama" and "scene." In the former, the author intervenes between his characters and the reader, summarizing events and compressing time; he *tells* what happens. In the "scene," however, he *shows* events directly, letting the characters speak for themselves in something more like real time. Herman Rose seems to me to alternate between these two poles. He usually tells, and the pictures of this kind are beautiful, if remote; but sometimes he shows, and when he does, the point-blank confrontation with his revelations lingers in the consciousness.

George McNeil and the Figure (1967)

"George McNeil and the Figure," *ARTnews* 66.6 (October 1967): 38–39, 64–65.

George McNeil's new work makes it necessary to distinguish between figurative and figure painting. In the latter, an image of the body is clearly discernible, but identification does not extend to place. The figure inhabits paint. Such pictures, at once representational and non-illusionist, usually seek visual wholeness through attack. Painters like McNeil, with their Expressionist heritage, knit together figure and ground in strokes and streaks. The figure is affirmed as surface; the surround only hints at environment—room? Landscape? Night? If, as in the recent McNeil, the rectangular format is ignored, that other "modernist" article of faith, flatness, is crucial. When the right arm, say, of one of these figures is larger than the left, we are quick to see it conventionally, as being somehow closer to us, yet we are at the same time denied that interpretation by the artist's insistence on a tactile two-dimensionality. The ambiguity is apparent. Further, though you can't count the toes or fingers on a McNeil nude, you do see the right number of limbs, breasts, etc.; an ambiguity more than spatial is involved. The contest between expressive distortion and the representational impulse is more evenly matched in the McNeil than, say, a late Pollock head. However, in both there coexist two different types of painting.

The ambiguities of action-figure-painting, which McNeil faces with vigor, have challenged most of the Abstract Expressionists. The fraternity to which McNeil's recent work admits him has included de Kooning, of course, and Pollock, as well as Tworkov, Elaine de Kooning, Rivers, Marsicano, Lester Johnson, Beauchamp, Hartigan, George Segal, Cajori, and others. Though McNeil's images may remind one at times more of European styles—Appel, for example—than of American, he has been involved in the development of our native tradition for many years. Educated at Pratt, where he has taught since 1948, he then studied with Hofmann (1933–36). An early member of the American Abstract Artists, he become one of the "first generation" Abstract Expressionists. He was shown annually in New York by Charles Egan in 1950–54. Since about 1960, he has been painting increasingly recognizable figures; most recently, double ones.

Actually, what is more recent in McNeil's work than its representationalism is its deliberate violations of taste. His paintings always looked attractive: muted tonal transitions, large balanced forms, deep colors carefully worked, clear tempo changes. Now, however, not only do the figures look grotesque, but the surface is nervous, the composition willful, the lights and darks abrupt. The palette is discordant, a de-theorized Fauve range of acidulous yellows and greens, shrill reds and electric blues. It is as if the artist had purposely reversed himself.

McNeil's new aggressiveness avoids the monotonous pathos of much European Expressionist figure painting. His nudes are hardly passive, flayed victims. In fact, though working in a style to which gesture is central, McNeil has made the figures more gestural than the painting itself. In de Kooning, the figure is invaded by the tangled arabesques of the painter's act, and is opened up so far that it keeps disappearing. It bobs up and down on the waves of de Kooning's gestures, whereas McNeil's figure rests stolidly on top, dominating the picture and dictating its gesture. McNeil seems to paint out process in favor of the clear image, making it possible for his picture to arrive at a "finished" state, something foreign to a restless, ever-becoming de Kooning.

All Abstract Expressionist figure painting, whether McNeil's new *Dancer* series or de Kooning's *Women*, involves ambiguity of intention as well as of space. For over a hundred years, pictorial ambiguity has excited artists, be they representational or abstract. ("Abstract" and "illusionist" are not antonyms—witness the recent Stella.) But the esthetic of Action Painting joined with the representational impulse seems particularly two-sided. How does one accommodate the implicit spontaneity of a style like McNeil's with the conscious demands of portraying something? In other words, what is the figure doing there?

There are two possibilities: the artist *started* with a figure or the figure *appeared* during the painting. These have very different implications. In the former case subject matter is a catalyst, and is firmly established in the repertory of strategies to lull the awareness so that a deeper part of the psyche may awaken. A concise expression of it is James Brooks's 1955 statement (for the Whitney's *New Decade* catalogue): "Any conscious involvement (even thinking of a battle or standing before a still-life) is good if it permits the unknown to enter the painting almost unnoticed." The maneuver survives, *mutatis mutandis*, in Larry Poons, for example, who obviously begins with a system, however it is determined, but who so complicates (or simplifies) it that to figure it out becomes impossible. It is the aberrations, the departures—from the system or the still-life—which gives the picture life.

The second possibility, the slow or sudden emergence of an image under its own volition, might be called the Uninvited Guest phenomenon. Its appeal can be traced to the psychomythicism of the early phase of the New York School. Thus, de Kooning's women were for a long time classified as "goddesses" (and, indeed, they do have the obsessive presence and autonomous authority to convince one that the Furies behind the drawing-room drapes are *real*). Automatism is here considered a gateway to the archetypal; the creator "does not know what he is doing" until after he has done it.

To McNeil, the figure is there in the second way. He expresses surprise at the emergence of his images. He makes many drawings, from Hofmannesque still lifes; in these, it is clear that the subject matter is catalytic, provoking the hand and the imagination. But in painting, he seems rather to allow the figure to happen.

Then he seizes on it, traps it with heavy brush contours, isolates it by flattening and simplifying the surrounding color masses, until the figure asserts itself as the focal point. *Dancer, 6*, for example, swoops and flails her way across the picture, poised on one foot between a generalized face- and digit-less existence and a very specific human gesture. (The occasional inclusion of an illustrative detail like the white boot in *Caucasian Dance* reinforces in another way the specificity of McNeil's imagery.) Even *Angela* or *Marquise*, though they sit more inertly than many of their sisters, seem reluctant to exist only schematically. They are parallel to the picture plane, but not quite on it, and like most of McNeil's figures, begin to assert themselves as volumes. They participate in a vigorous contest of wills with their author about the nature of representational and abstract, of flat and illusionist painting.

Alex Katz (1968)

Exhibition catalogue essay for *Alex Katz at Cheat Lake* (West Virginia University and the West Virginia Art and Humanities Council, 1968).

Alex Katz's art is brashly "simple" and jarringly direct but also subtly distilled and secretly elegant, full of both obvious elisions and more slowly revealed complexities of choice and intention; his paintings and cut-outs have a swift ease of presence which couches their astute conception and rigorous construction. They seem to give themselves immediately and without reservation but prolonged attention to their formal devices uncovers hidden intellectual and expressive resonance.

Historically, Katz joins together several of the most persistent concerns of American art—the Abstract Expressionist insistence on high passion and scale, the Pop strain of vernacular urban irony, the "formalist" reductiveness and conceptualization of the nature of pictorial space. However, Katz is also one of the primary figures of what may be called "post-abstract" painting; like a growing number of other younger artists, he dares not only to paint representationally, but to do so unequivocally—i.e., to create illusionistic space, often very deep, in pictures, which, with their smooth, transparent surfaces, rely on neither the Expressionist nor the French (Impressionist, Intimist) sensibilities which informed the more "painterly" figurative art of America in the 1950s. The clear illusions of Katz and the other post-abstractionists make a direct challenge to the principles (by now, the orthodoxies and pieties) of modern painting. Especially in the current context of geometric and color-field abstraction, such unambiguously "objective" representationalism is as radical as it is energetic.

Katz is set slightly apart from most other new illusionists by his more apparent preoccupation with the very twentieth-century traditions he defies. In his work there is a temperamental continuation of, as well as an ambitious challenge to, abstract painting: the occasional explosions of skillful, "hot" brushwork; the reverberations of popular and commercial art's "appealing" imagery; the enlarged size, heightened color, and fascination with the conventions of depiction—these elements (all present in *Vincent and Sunny*, a double portrait of the artist's son and his dog) testify to a strong consciousness in Katz of his lineage. His verisimilitudinous yet larger-than-life people and places bear the pressures of a desire to be both modern and anti-modern (the latter in itself, of course, being a characteristically modern desire). One senses in Katz the impulse to encompass the opposites of the present and the past/future.

Within his illusionistic but near-optical (impenetrable) space, Katz's conjunction of suave humor and elevated presentation make his heraldic images at once ravishing and disconcerting. His special gift of temperament is the coincidence of a sincere, lyric response and a detached, almost parodic, attitude toward his subjects. His sitters may thus look both ennobled and quite eccentric. His lilies and daisies are both overwhelmingly attractive and slyly subversive of the whole tradition of floral painting. Of modern American artists, Katz is one of the most extreme in his combination of "irreconcilable" feeling-tones.

His subjects and formal themes are inextricable from each other. He works in loosely overlapping series, the most enduring one being of the human figure (from which he paints directly.) All of his figures are real, particular people; the one who recurs most frequently is the artist's wife, the sitter in *Red Smile* and *Smile Again* and a woman whose profile is as crisp and whose smile as delicate as these pictures indicate. Some of Katz's portraits are of only the face, often not even the entirety of that; some are busts; others are full-figure, whether single or crowded into tableaux vivants like *The Lawn Party*. In his earlier figure paintings, Katz put the sitter into or on what de Kooning called the "no-environment"—a flat, monochromatic ground which contradicts the volumetricity of the recognizable image. He has been moving away from this, as even the slight difference between the atmospheric and recessive ochre field of *Smile Again* and the relatively inert and heavier red of the earlier *Red Smile* will show. (However, perversely, in *Red Smile*, the axes of the bust are more suggestive of depth than is the schematic flatness of the other picture's large profile.) *Swamp Maple, 4:30* is an important painting in Katz's *oeuvre* for its summation of his obsession with combining frontality and flatness with sculptural forms in depth twisting away from—both in front of and well behind—the picture plane; the figure-ground problem, which has stimulated almost all modern artists, is stated in the most emphatic of terms. The figure of the tree is as if "nose-to-nose," while the landscape forming the ground is so distant that the eye is shocked, wrenched from its usual habit (and artists' usual habit) of making middle-ground transitions. Katz's elimination of any but very near and very far objects in this picture is entirely typical, and as "minimal" in its treatment of space as is the two-dimensional design, a slightly decentered cruciform. (The vertical axis is shifted to the right, the horizontal below center.) A further complication is the reversal of weight or incidental distribution—*Swamp Maple, 4:30* is much more active at the top than the bottom, which is accurate in relation to the subject of a tree, but is never the less exhilaratingly unusual in relation to the history of art. If the bottom third of the painting flattens out perhaps too much, the rest of it strikes a precise balance between depth (read in the atmospheric perspective of the simplified planes of the lake's shores) and surface grip. The white passage, reminiscent in its gentle light of Bingham, is just tactile enough to restore the surface without violating the soft blue distance. The picture's strange yellow sky reinforces the balance between observational accuracy and imaginative intent. The sharp-eyed particularity of the yellows, blues, and extensive range of grays (nearly from black to white) counterbalance the Newman-esque generalization of design to make this painting strongly emblematic, in tone almost elegiac. The botanical and temporal precision of the titles are both borne out and mocked in the summarizing fiction of this large and dramatic work.

There is little empty space, by contrast, in Katz's flower paintings. Though the mood of *White Petunia*, with its grand, surging arabesques and dramatic side-lighting, is not that of the "garish," hyperactive *Violet Daisies #2*, both (like most of the series of flowers) exhibit the tendency toward overallness, toward equality of emphasis throughout, which we find as well in American art from Pollock and de Kooning down to Kelly or Agnes Martin. For representational art to achieve such a freedom from compositional hierarchies, it must, as Monet was to discover, choose an appropriate subject, such as an expanse of water or some other field. Katz, by his typical devices of enlargement and cropping, makes us feel that the painting is both more (because larger) and less (because partial) than the appearance of its depicted objects. The negative spaces of the flowers may be come as noticeable as the petals, leaves, and organs. Suddenly we have no visual resting place. Everything jumps perpetually among the lilies but the backgrounds are controlled enough in their monochromes to suggest outside walls or shadowy distances. In figure paintings, this overallness is not possible to achieve but in the flower series, Katz has found a subject which can stand up to the pressures of modernist composition (specifically, omnipresent tension and pull) yet retain the integrity of directly representational art.

In his cut-outs, Katz deals with problems of form (in terms of figure-ground relations) by virtually ignoring them. These works are neither quite paintings nor wholly sculptures, but a combination as novel as Stella's shaped canvas or Andre's one-plane floor pieces; *One Flight Up*, with its dozens of portraits on a modern "altar," makes the most discreet of references to painting not only in the purely depicted volumes of the heads and shoulders but also in the few straight vertical edges which, like the straight horizontal edges emphasized by the elevation on pins, bring to mind the framing edges of a painting. Some of Katz's cut-outs are in effect cropped sculptures. Like the implied horizontal which holds down both the near partial figures and the distant whole figures in *The Lawn Party*, the strict alignment in rows of the busts of *One Flight Up* exerts a necessary control over an optically dense and ever-changing juxtaposition of faces. The complexities of *One Flight Up* (whose title derives from the fact that the studio where this work was made is on the second floor—countless sitters have been instructed to walk "one flight up") are conceptual as well as visual: the busts were painted and cut out individually but were then placed in unpreconceived relation to each other, so that the "psychological" element is as gratuitous as it is powerful. The quasi-narrative element (e.g. the odd sidewise look that the handsome blue-eyed young man in the back row is giving his older, white-haired and imperious neighbor) is as arbitrary as it is indelible. *One Flight Up* is one of those absolutely uncategorizable triumphs of American eccentricity, like the boxes of Joseph Cornell. Katz's free-standing cut-outs, like the self-portrait as sharpie, testify to the power of illusion; they combine, like the paintings, uncombinable elements—in this case, vividly illusionistic presences and obviously planar dimensionality. Too, the creamy luminosity which often bathes these countenances is a peculiar quality to experience simultaneously with the knife-sharp contours of the unyielding steel plating.

Whether in his groundless (literally) cut-out figures or his complexly organized representations of people and places in the paintings, Katz is a pivotal figure in the course of American art as it moves through European modernism, native varieties of abstraction, and forward to an open situation in which the formal and the expressive elements of art will once again be understood to be synonymous in figurative as well as in abstract styles.

Direct Representation (1969)

Scott Burton, *Direct Representation: Robert Bechtle, Bruno Civito, Yvonne Jacquette, Sylvia Mangold, John Moore: Five Young Realists* (New York: Fischbach Gallery, September 1969).

"Direct representation" is meant simply to indicate the broad stylistic quality that the five younger painters in this exhibition share with each other, and with a growing number of other figurative artists, only a few of whom are yet well known. Though all art is of course conventional, directly representational painting aspires to a conventionlessness, to a styleless transparency of depiction. The images in new figurative painting are not dominated obviously by formal, chromatic or procedural concerns or by distortive expressive impulses. Pictorial devices are covert, couched in a credibility of appearance; such focused clarity is able, it is being rediscovered, to accommodate a wide range of sensibilities and intentions.

Straight figuration is, I think, the only major mode now available to painting adequate for the expression of the fullest individuality. Besides a reinvigorated fidelity to the surface of the perceived world, the new representationalists share an historical situation in which, briefly, three-dimensional work has absorbed the premises of most earlier modernist styles and taken them to extremes where painting cannot follow. Abstract painting seems, for the most part, to be in a crisis of attenuation: its physicality and environmentalism, its logics of self-sufficiency, its conversion of facture to content, its dependence on innovation have led irresistibly to sculptural (whether Minimal or process) and verbalist or conceptualizing modes.

Painting has been turning (returning) increasingly to the resource of illusion. In recent painting of both geometric and chromatic persuasions illusionism has become more and more pronounced, and may now be generally admitted to be an inherent property in the nature of a picture, and not, after all, expendable. It is at this point that directly representational painting derives its art-historical coherence and its force as an alternative—not just in its commitment to figuration but, further, to unmitigated illusion. Most earlier non-abstract styles of modern painting have been ambivalent, to say the least, about this property; the recently American group of realists (an inadequate, inaccurate term) is the first modern one to go all the way forward or backward—to a total verism, to an unequivocal alliance of existential appearance and esthetic conventions. The phenomenon known as post-Pop, comprising pseudo-figurative painters who make images exclusively of other images, seems by comparison a weary and merely eccentric footnoting to, naming only the primary source, the earlier Jasper Johns. In current painting which incorporates images, the real vigor, the truly new energy is emerging from the risky embrace of illusionist precision, of direct representation.

That a retrograde academicist phase is *not* upon us is proven by the resilient ability of the new verism to sustain such a variety of achievements as this show (limited to younger artists not before seen in New York) offers.

Robert Bechtle, the oldest (mid-thirties) and the only one from the West Coast, is also the most easily identifiable as a new realist; his work is reminiscent in composition as well as theme of the amateur photograph—the family posing together, grouped candidly and centrally; the middle-class neighborhood, with its new cars and deserted streets; the baleful television set momentarily enlivened by a prismatic reflection—but this Pop-influenced element in Bechtle is, for all its updated American Scene-ism, no stronger than his reliance on the tradition of genre painting. (His sense of scale is reminiscent especially of seventeenth-century Dutch art.) The scrupulously neutral transmission of mundane information is tempered by Bechtle's softening, carefully atmospheric color, never vulgarly heightened, and by the immobile, oddly hieratic symmetries he favors.

Equally ordinary in subject is Yvonne Jacquette's series of interiors but here the artist's attitude is intense and heightening, monumental rather than neutral. Her repeated theme—ceiling, wall, door, a darkness beyond—is raised to a transcendent state sheerly by the artist's fervent vision; the limited subjects, the upward-looking point of view, especially the inexplicably glowing pale greens, yellows and whites—none of these violates the possible but nevertheless they produce an almost Surrealist tone, an enigmatic and ecstatic feeling which pervades these humanless habitations.

Sylvia Mangold is even more reductively exclusive in subject and angle of vision than Yvonne Jacquette, but here motivation seems more one of conceptual reappraisal of the relation between a picture and an image. These views of nothing but floor and ground planes also convey an alienation (in their lack of human activity) but are more clearly related to recent ideas in abstract art. The subject of floorboards is as normally non-relational as any gridded configuration in Minimal art—or would be were it not for the simple experience of perspective, which creates a steady diminution of unit sizes toward the horizons of Mrs. Mangold's edgeless or endless floors. The exclusion of objects which would give the painting a more hierarchic internal scale and the strange light coming from behind the paint instead of from a depicted, internal source are additional devices which relate this artist especially to recent abstraction; but it must be remembered that they are devices subsumed within a legitimately figurative intention. As proof of the latter, the attention to tactile surface, to the grain of wood, is the main vehicle. An equal attention to the surface of the canvas is obvious; the tension between the two planes (of floor and canvas) is extremely strong, representing a fascination with the idea itself of representational art.

John Moore, at first glance perhaps the least modern looking of this group because of his traditional subjects (nudes and still lifes in interiors) and his neo-Classicist, European taste, is nevertheless as involved as is Sylvia Mangold in the adjustment of concept and representation. In his case, however, the appropriate terms are "synthesist" and "perceptual." Moore, to a greater degree than the others in this show, is pursuing a unification of the verisimilitudinous and the stylized or summarized. To this end, he often chooses subjects whose forms (cones, cylinders) are already generalized or easily made so. Too, he approaches the suppression of tactile volume by his close-valued washes of form-effacing light, dimly brightening his elegant white rooms. Most indicative of Moore's synthesist intent, however, is the point in almost all of his pictures where two-and three-dimensional readings coincide exactly; the directly frontal presentation of one form, usually a nude's limb or a table leg provides a foreshortening of mass which is equally a flat plane. Necessarily unique to each picture, these points of planar and volumetric coincidence come to seem emblematic of Moore's larger ambition to synthesize the perceptual and the generalized.

The youngest artist of the group, Bruno Civitico, looks too to Europe for precedents, but much further back than the Ingres-to-Balthus predilection of Moore. Civitico's inspiration, despite the self-effacing modesty of his painting style, lies in an ambitious alliance with the traditions of the Italian Renaissance. Most apparently in his large roseate nudes posed in silvery Tuscan landscapes, but also in his small, figureless landscapes, he makes subtle alterations of form which never sacrifice detail but which make the images remote and idealized. Civitico's equally subtle sweetening of color transforms his views, even of New Jersey suburbs, into purified, troubled Arcadias reminiscent of the Venetians' pastorales. Its clarity and delicacy of form, its limpidity of color and light remove

Civitico's art from any connotation of realism, and yet in style his poetic work is perfectly compatible, to compare the two least alike in mood, with Bechtle's contemporary ironies.

All five of these painters are in fact highly individual, which may be construed as an indication of great vitality for representational art of the present and near future. Though (to summarize their dominant qualities) Bechtle is especially a vernacularist, Jacquette a visionary, Mangold a conceptualist, Moore a synthesist, and Civitico a lyrist, they have something of a common style in the directness of presentation which many other new young painters as well as older, exhibiting ones also share. This revitalized style, almost too inclusive to be called a style except insofar as it contains so many negative similarities, does not at all eliminate or make obsolete other varieties of painting, but does offer the audience a welcome expansion of esthetic opportunities.

The Realist Revival (1972)

Scott Burton, *The Realist Revival* (New York: American Federation of Arts, 1972).

E.N.: *The second of two shows of representational painting Burton curated,* The Realist Revival *was an important statement for Burton. After the catalogue was published, he began to revise and expand this essay independently. (Scott Burton Papers, (II.42) Museum of Modern Art Archives, NY.) In the early 1970s, he was advocating realism as he was developing his own Postminimal performance and sculptural practice. The characterization of realism as accessible and demotic underwrote both Burton's first sculpture,* Bronze Chair *(conceived 1972, executed 1975) as well as his first* Behavior Tableaux *performance (Whitney Museum of American Art, 1972). Burton considered both of these practices to be figurative and realist.*

Behind the title, "The Realist Revival," lie definitions and assumptions that should be acknowledged. The word "realist" is used here not with historical reference or to characterize all representational sensibilities, but to mean, very simply, two-dimensional but otherwise fully illusionist depiction. This definition is intended conceptually rather than stylistically and is based on only the most elemental features of morphology and intention common to a number of current styles. These features are: transparency of picture plane; internal illusion of space—of volume and distance; representation, with consistency of convention, of the color and light of the actual world. The realist's observance of these, and his related preference for pictures of easel instead of mural (or miniaturist) size, reveals his attitude of neutrality toward the painting as an object and his primary commitment to its iconic dimension.

Such neutrality toward the object implies opposition to the modernist tradition of self-reference of the work of art; but that is not to say that realism is not a product of the internal logic of advanced art. Indeed, only from a modernist point of view could the assumption, underlying this exhibition, be made that recent realist painting constitutes a "revival." The realist painter conceives his program as a post-abstract one; he makes a deeper innovation in his return not just to emblematic representation but to full scale illusionist realism than does, say, the recent "painterly abstractionist" in his return to pre-Minimal, spontaneous styles. During the entire century, no major American or European artist, with the unique exception of Edward Hopper, has demonstrated a more than ambivalent or intermittent return to realism—until now. Today, the inherent and proper content of painting is considered again to include the objects as well as the sensations of optical perception. The most coherent critical partisan of the realist movement so far, Linda Nochlin, has argued that "... the distinguishing feature of the new realism is ... the assertion of the visual perception of things in the world as the necessary basis of the structure of the pictorial field itself."[15]

Thus content adheres again to representation. Regardless of what is represented, or how, the members of the realist movement share the conviction that the role of subject is central. In its de-emphasizing of the material properties of the picture, the realist revival may be seen as a response not simply to abstraction, but more comprehensively, to three-dimensional art (in which, recently, "sculpture" takes its place with the "wall piece," the earth work, the performance, and the documentation of "conceptual" and "process" pieces). After the mid 1960s, no vital advanced styles of two-dimensional art emerged to equal the energetic innovations of three-dimensional work

15. Linda Nochlin, "Realism Now," lecture, Vassar College, Poughkeepsie, New York, 1968.

until the crystalization of the realist movement. A representational undercurrent in post–World War II American art has clearly become a “mainstream” movement, reviving the pre-abstract practice of unequivocally illusionist depiction. Perhaps in the early 1970s, we see no more than the opening phase of the revival completed, with the establishment of several major talents of the “first generation” (of artists around 40) and the arrival of several genuine younger realists to form a “second generation” (around 30). This decade will undoubtedly see a wide flowering of realism, and probably its hegemony (in painting, not in three-dimensional modes).

Its radicality of esthetic shift reveals realism as an evolution of modernism rather than a retreat from it, though *not* an evolution toward the ideal of communal style generated in a holistic society. The psychological characteristic is still individualist and subjective; it is the idea of esthetic means—image before object—that has changed. Choice and treatment of image separate the movement into three main clusters of sensibility: the perceptual, the synthetist, and the photographic. These groups form a triangle rather than a line, are not rigidly discrete but continuous and overlapping, and are more and more being integrated into one homogeneous and comprehensive style by the younger painters of the movement.

Perceptual style: The images in the paintings of this group give the appearance of being observed, by particular eyes, and painted in front of the subject, by a particular hand.

The perceptual style is descended from the “painterly” and traces of kinetic brushwork may remain, giving the execution an immediate character. This impression of spontaneity is not, however, taken so far as to interrupt the contours of objects; there is a strong concern for solidity, volumetricity. The weight of things is manifested in picture spaces very infrequently aligned in parallel or perpendicular relation to their surface planes. An insistence on the representation of tactility accompanies the invariable depiction of real light, usually sunlight and always, even if artificial, specific in source. And the perceptual picture is always atmospheric, this slightly softening its contours—it is not at all linear.

The preferred subjects of the perceptual realist are organic. Paintings of the human figure predominate, in a spirit of psychological naturalism. The naked men and women of Pearlstein, Perlis, Sleigh, and Wynn rest impassively, in informal poses, in specific moments of time — ever, in the name of verisimilitude, frankly modeling. Such implication of the presence of the artist and representation of actual time form, in fact, the overt theme of Sleigh's *Philip Golub Reclining*, with the quasi-actual (reflected) presence of the painter herself, and at an especially significant moment—the picture's inception. The kitchen chairs, hairbrushes and potted plants that also fill these pictures further communicate the real—that is, ordinary—life of the artist. Janet Fish's jars and bottles, though pictorially isolated from the domestic context, reflect it both literally in their surfaces and metaphorically in their homeliness. In his choice of artifact, the perceptual painter yet avoids the technological product: his cityscapes, for example, exclude the automobile. Neither Laderman, Murphy, nor Wilson turns the city into an emblem of urban industrial society. They all, instead, see cityscape as an extension of landscape, another "version of pastorale"; tending to incorporate actual landscape, they concentrate on the natural elements—atmospheric light and color—in their exact views of familiar looking cities. Similarly, in her views of floors Sylvia Mangold emphasizes the natural with her scrupulous depiction of the organic material of wood, as she does the commonplace with her choice of the "lowest" of subjects. Her concentration on concrete individuality (in the variation of woodgrain) is relevant to the fact that realist portraiture appears today only in the perceptual style. Pearlstein's are the most rigorous of the genre.

The attitude of the perceptual artist toward his subject, which seems to have been before him as he worked, is correspondingly "populist"—prosaic, non-Romantic. His subject is invested with more than merely descriptive interest, but the statement of meaning, instead of being metaphoric, is declared, direct, clear to all eyes. The tenor is demotic; the perceptual realist sees art as part of his daily waking life, and that life as a quietly disaffiliated part of a concrete and widely shared social milieu. That the disaffiliation is expressed by implication (through strict exclusion of any but private subjects) is corollary to the realist movement's partial return to shared pictorial conventions. Actual distortive impulse is contained; individualized habits of brush activity are almost completely suppressed. However, critical content certainly remains in the background of this sensibility. A residual Expressionism lies not only in the manual painting style but also in the occasionally cramped or awkward passage which testifies to "difficulty," to "authenticity," to the moral preoccupation of Abstract Expressionist painting. (The latent presence of this style is especially strong in Pearlstein's figure paintings with their disturbingly awry, Kline-like composition. In his further relation to Dada and Pop attitudes, reflected in his references to popular painting styles, this artist is perhaps the most complex painter of the first, the "heroic" generation of realists.) The Abstract Expressionist content of the presence of the artist in his work is retained by the perceptual realist, though transformed. An important step in this transformation has been the art of the Abstract Expressionist contemporary, Fairfield Porter, who revived interrupted practices of post-Impressionist painting and synthesized them with the spontaneous method of Abstract Expressionist style. After the 1950s, the way beyond the conserving nostalgia of Porter's subjects (small town backyards and New England landscape) was pointed by the still Romantic realist painter, John Button, whose nature-less, unpeopled, purely urban cityscapes parallel remarkably some of the subjects of the highly anti-Romantic Pop artist, Edward Ruscha. Ruscha's West Coast imagery leads him beyond painting to the mass art form of books of actual photographs—of parking lots, Hollywood highways, auto service stations—but this coincidence of new subjects for painting, like the anonymous modern high-rise in both Button's lyrically precise and Ruscha's ironically casual representations, marks an extension of the usage of depiction for us.

Synthetist style: In the paintings of this group, the image seems invented. Though conceived all of recognizable elements, the vision itself is frankly subjective and transforms what it represents.

The synthetist style prefers the sharpness of edge and lack of atmosphere characterized as "hyperreal." Though its forms curve pronouncedly in space, it is not a highly volumetric style, bearing an almost linear emphasis on (two-dimensional) shape. The resultant "unnatural" clarity is reinforced by a generalized luminosity; light more metaphysical than natural illuminates an heraldically arranged world: frontal composition, frequent shallowness, planes architectonically related to the picture plane and frame in general, symmetry and balance shape the synthetist image. The impression of simplification of visual incident is achieved with the relative suppression of the details of objects. "Incidental" complexities of form, tactile differences, and variations of color are minimized. Surfaces of objects, especially, acquire gleaming purity. And although very individual idiosyncrasies of drawing often remain, the synthetist's picture surface is perfectly smooth—so intensely as almost to become "painterly" in the degree of self-consciousness of application, of attention paid.

In this group, subject matter has the character not of being witnessed but of being imagined—conceived and then synthesized into appearance. The image seems not only to have been arranged, but to have been significantly, even symbolically, so. This characteristic is most fully realized in the remarkable phenomenon of recent narrative painting. Bruder, Butkovich, Civitico, Day, and Tillim give their figures deliberate, expressive poses and roles which dramatically restore *reference* to painting. Though not always strictly narrative, not anecdotal, the synthetist's figure compositions nevertheless refer unmistakably beyond themselves to extra-visual meanings. The uses of reference are various; they may be available, like Civitico's mythologizing and Butkovich's distillation of the theme of the nuclear family, or they may be private, like the modern-dress allegorizing of Sidney Tilim and the enigmatic dramatizations of Bruder and Day. But always, the realist commitment to the conceptual aspect of the work of art is explicit in the synthetist impulse toward symbolization. The figures turn "stylized," become in pose and feature generalized, living-statue-Iike. Action is outside of particularities of sequence, is frozen into statement. This quality is not absent even from the unpeopled rooms of Beal, Jacquette, and John Moore. Again, the deployment of "characters" in these object dramas is the vehicle of meaning (or, in the case of Jacquette, whose objects are encountered instead of manipulated, not deployment but an equivalent in her use of framing viewpoint). The things in these worlds, and as well in the still Iifes of William Bailey, are, for all their ordinariness and superficial informality of arrangement, still charged with associations of significance beyond their immediate identity. The perceptual realist associates significance with the known and the well-known: Fish's still lifes connect, through the representation of ordinary food, with the very physiology of life whereas Bailey's egg might well be (and resembles) marble; its reference is mental, to the historical tradition of mystical/mathematical esthetics. Without constructing actual symbologies, these painters of mutedly expressive interiors manage to suggest, in their precision of choice and arrangement of objects, heightened states, *extra*ordinary experience. Their rooms became metaphors of the interior of the mind, their objects embodiments of the states of feeling that furnish it. The taste for essence over appearance excludes subject matter too much associated with daily life: there is no factual cityscape, landscape is generalized and confined to minor passages, and the common mechanical object is virtually absent (again noting Jacquette's exceptionality with a fluorescent lighting fixture whose banality is utterly overcome by dramatic pictorial means—sharp perspective, compositional centrality, unusual and monumentalizing angle of vision).

The subjective representations of synthetist painting, with its lyrical, contemplative or oneiric affinities, form the major realist survival of Romantic art; an ineffable state of hieratic being fills the limpid spaces of synthetist images. This least naturalistic of realist styles derives, partially and at a remove, from "conservative" Surrealism—particularly Magritte (who created one of the largest styles, in terms of sheer representational ability, of the century) and de Chirico. And obviously Italian metaphysical still life is recalled. But, in the realist program, synthetist painting uses heightening devices only covertly—its world is always *possible*, conceivable, reconstructable. Its irrational quality is not exaggerated beyond the limits of credible experience, but is compressed into suggestion. Transformation is indirect; the method is to symbolize, not to illustrate, the extraordinary state. In synthetist painting, reality itself is estheticized. English Victorian painting is thus also recalled, along with (through the linking figure of Balthus) French Symbolist, Synthetist, and Nabi art. The cool, generalizing sense of shape reveals, too, the influence of Synthetic Cubism (and the classical Picasso of the early 1920s, as well); in fact, several qualities of geometric abstraction linger in synthetist realism: planarity, frontality, horizontal-vertical orientation of structure. These are, however, assimilated beyond ambiguity into wholly illusionist fields.

Photographic style: In this group, the image seems found. Though from the familiar world and not invented, it seems less observed than simply selected, chosen.

The photographic style is, expectably, the least tolerant of variations of drawing style or paint surface. The aspiration toward impersonality of facture results from the absorption of various mechanical processes of image reproduction. Whether human optical or manual functions are replaced, this style requires an "absolute" precision of formal detail. Its objects often appear to lack the property of weight; still the photographic painting contains unambiguous and often extremely deep spatial illusion. Conventions of arbitrary framing and schematic rather than analytic coloration (producing a transparency of atmosphere, some loss of "weather") reinforce the estranged quality of the image. Appropriately, the dominating formal interest of the photographic realist is in light, especially as it is reflected in the industrial materials of chrome and sheet glass; in this style, pure luster is salient.

The content of photographic painting is referential, though not to verbal but to other visual systems—to systems of image duplication which vary in type from the simple, non-professional snapshot incorporated into Robert Bechtle's way of seeing to the rhetoric of advertising-art styles assimilated by Parrish and Salt. The photographic painter is deeply drawn to technological subjects as well as methods. As have Goings and Eddy, Bechtle has exhaustively chronicled the automobile along with his California landscapes; and Parrish's motorcycle is a close surrogate. With the exception of Salt, whose wide-angled automobile interior image offers a version of human habitation (or entombment), the photographic painter places the mechanical chariot in its proper context—the urban-industrial "complex" whose growth has forced the residual pastorale from cityscape in the paintings of this group. They share such concentration on the automotive environment (painting highways instead of streets), that even a cityscape like Noel Mahaffey's, relatively traditional in its choice of subject (perhaps due to the survival in picture-postcard art of nineteenth-century iconographic traditions) is dominated by the barrier of the elevated highway. (This Jersey City would appear, too, to quote Hopper's *House by the Railroad.*) Richard Estes uses the photograph, he has said, as a "surrogate sketch"; his New York City cityscapes seem to catalogue the details of a number of photographs. Estes's style is most "photographic" in the sense of "photographic memory"—rather than duplicating specific visual effects of reproduced imagery, this artist strains for omniscience in his severely limited views (which exclude most noticeably the human figures that would normally occupy his day-time streets). Estes's unfoliated, purely man-made cityscape and Ian Hornak's tropical volcanic landscape provide through their diametric opposition a similar experience of complete dissociation of the artificial and natural worlds. Hornak's "picturesque" styling, after calendar iconography perhaps, records the loss of reality of landscape for us. A related theme in the "installation-shot" views of other artists' work painted by Richard Bernstein reiterates the photographic realist's preoccupation with the productions of man. The theme is ironically manifested in John Kacere's figure paintings; in "slick" magazine style, he portrays dehumanization of the woman instead of the environment. Generally the human figure is missing from work in this group (with some exceptional family pictures by Bechtle), and there is no still life (and little conformity to any familiar genre). Asymmetry is a major compositional value, reflecting the tensions of this style.

Though this group of painters has assimilated mechanical imagery into its style, it does not seek to replicate this imagery. This sensibility has been particularly impressed by the literalist aspect of modernism but still represents the realist shift away from the concretizing, reductivist principles dominant in the 1960s not only in abstract but also in Pop art. It is on the issue of the status of the work of art as an object that true realist painting differs from its closest representational antecedent, Pop. In their practice of imitating objects, of replicating them as opposed to depicting them, the Pop artists continued the literalist esthetic whose ultimate source is the Cubist collage. The "pre-Pop" sculptures of Jasper Johns and assemblages of Rauschenberg form part of the literalist canon, as do the "post-Pop" works of a number of artists sometimes not clearly enough understood as distinct from the (post-literalist) neutrality of object observed in realist painting. Thus, artists really closer to Duchamp than to Hopper include: Malcolm Morley, whose monochromatic and monotonal margins always cogently establish a bracketing, dominating flatness for his pseudo-illusionist images; Chuck Close, who rigorously imitates the mechanical lens with the in-and out-of-focus effects of his huge portraits; John Clem Clarke, who turns manual painting style into a subject rather than a method with his substitution of photographic silkscreening; and Richard McLean and Audrey Flack, who offer the heightened chromatics and tonalities of explicitly filmic processes. However close they may seem to realist painting of the photographic sensibility, these artists deal primarily with issues of esthetic mode, and only secondarily with representational *content.* The shared aspect of the imagery of mass culture does, of course, link recent realist art to Pop art, especially to the near photographic style of James Rosenquist. Another painter making an early contribution to the realist revival, Alex Katz, formulated in the transitional period of the late 1950s a unique representational style conjoining painterly treatment and Pop imagery. Of the current practitioners of realist painting, the perceptual style of Alfred Leslie shows the influence of Pop (and Abstract Expressionism as well) in its great enlargement of picture size. The industrial imagery in both the photographs and paintings of Charles Sheeler stands behind this sensibility.

(The issue of opposing attitudes toward the work's three-dimensional identity brings up the question of the renewal of realistic sculpture. Symptomatic of the critic's, though not the artist's, confusion is the frequent coupling of two sculptors, Duane Hanson and John de Andrea, who are in fact separated by Hanson's use, in the tradition of Segal and Keinholz, and Duchamp and Dalí before them, of real objects in his tableaux. This dialectic of reality and [in his replicated figures] illusion is a major theme of Hanson, but is absent from the work of de Andrea, who carefully limits his subjects to nude figures, entirely organic, without either replicated or "readymade" environment. De Andrea is perhaps closer in his purism to the non-Pop realist sculptor, Richard Miller. Miller, though he rejects the "found" forms of polyester casting from life, still demonstrates, in the ambiguous relation of his *Diane: Sitting* to its pedestal, the problematic relation in the present phase of modernism of three-dimensionality and representationalism. Painting has responded to this difficulty by relinquishing emphasis on its own objectness.)

The "triangular" relation of these three broad styles means that each shares certain characteristics with each of its neighbors. The photographic and synthetist styles share a hyperrealist look and thus, paradoxically, are clearly conceptual, "unrealistic," whereas perceptual realism is ostensibly unconceptualized. It pretends to be direct and objective in its vision but shares with synthetist style a deliberate personality of creation; whereas photographic painting seeks to conceal individuality of means. But like perceptual style, photographic painting avoids the Romantic, near-Surreal aura of synthetist painting, in preference for a secularized, materially oriented world.

All three styles have in common certain modernist features not found before the late nineteenth century and the breaking up of the historical style of Realism: the “close-up” and “blow-up” of only part of an object (reminiscent not only of photography but also of modern conceptions of sculpture as fragment); the filling up of the closest foreground zone of space, as far forward as possible without violation of the picture plane (unlike *trompe-l’oeil*); frequent use of a single, very restricted motif, painted over and over again in a way comparable to serialist productions; and finally, a restriction of range—no painter in the movement can so far offer a style flexible and authoritative enough to represent adequately more than one or two of the major subjects.

It is likely that the next phase of the movement will confront the issue of expanding representational range, and the concomitant integration of perceptual and conceptual sensibilities, of Romantic and naturalist philosophies.

IV.
SCULPTURE AS THEATER: PERFORMANCE ART STATEMENTS

Three Street Works (1969)

"Three Street Works," *0 to 9*6/supplement (1969): n.p.

E.N.: *In one of Burton's first acts of ironic mimetic representation, he offered the following contribution to Vito Acconci and Bernadette Mayer's* 0 to 9 *magazine. Burton's authored article consists solely of quotations from his then-colleague John Perreault's* Village Voice *reviews of the Street Works events in which they, and many other artists, did public interventions in a designated area in Manhattan.*

(for J. P.)

I. "On the corner of Fifth Avenue and 49th Street I met Joe Kosuth and two friends who had come to look for Street Works. He had just met writer Scott Burton who had asked him to select a piece of paper from the street. Burton then placed the paper in a plastic Baggie along with a slip of paper marked "Schwitters." This was his Schwitters piece."[16]

II. "Perhaps the most invisible and moat sensational work was 'performed' by Scott Burton. The ghost of Rose [sic] Selavy made her appearance. Burton walked the area in disguise and went completely unnoticed. He wore pink octagonal glasses with blue frames, a green floral print jersey slip-over with a large cowl (worn down), uncuffed navy blue elephant bells, a beige coat, low-heeled shoes with matching gloves. He also wore a short brown wig, pink-orange lipstick, Guerlain perfume, and carried a plastic, flower-printed shopping bag

16. John Perreault, "Art," Village Voice (New York), March 27, 1969, pp. 17-18.

and an umbrella decorated with white daisies. He was completely invisible."[17]

III. "Scott Burton walked around with his ears plugged up so that he could not hear."[18]

17. John Perreault, "Art," Village Voice (New York), May 11, 1969, pp. 14–15.
18. John Perreault, "Art," Village Voice (New York), June 5, 1969, pp. 16–18.

Literalist Theater (1970)

Unpublished transcription of a lecture given at the University of Iowa on June 25, 1970. Scott Burton Papers [II.27]. Museum of Modern Art Archives, NY.

E.N.: *Burton co-taught a class with Marjorie Strider at the University of Iowa in the summer of 1970 titled "Art in the Urban Environment: Theory and Practice of Post-Studio Art." The ambitious studio seminar culminated in an intervention by the students in an abandoned lot in downtown Iowa City where installations and performances were staged. In relation to the course, Burton gave a public lecture on his work. In addition to explaining the works done in relation to the* Street Works *events in 1969 (see the previous text), Burton further discussed his ideas for practices of dissemblance and the critical mimesis of behavior that would be carried through, in different forms, to his* Behavior Tableaux *performances, to his* Lecture on Self *piece, and to the furniture sculpture in the coming years. The present text was a transcript of the unscripted talk Burton gave (to which he made some subsequent additions). As such, it does not have the formality of his other writings or, indeed, of his other more carefully prepared lectures. There are many places where the transcription does not have full or correct punctuation. Accordingly, some minor editorial changes have been made to the transcription and its punctuation in order to improve its readability, but I have largely kept the impromptu tone of Burton's talk. Ellipses do not indicate excised text but rather passages where Burton seemed to trail off.*

It's only been within the last year and a half that I've been involved in doing works which are in public situations that are "literalist theatre." You might think, well . . . a painting or sculpture on display in a gallery involves literalist theatre in that sense but what interests me is the execution—that is to say, the performance—of the work in a public situation, not just the after-the-fact exhibition of the work. None of them have titles. I can only describe them. And I'd like just then to note some of my intentions—because I think those are paramount—and some concerns that interested me while doing this.

For one of the *Street Works* series that Marjorie [Strider] and John [Perreault] and Hannah Weiner organized, I wanted to do something invisible. I wanted to be there and not be there. I did this—and it sounds funny but it's not meant to be funny—by dressing as a woman. It wasn't drag. It was very ordinary. I carried a shopping bag and tried to be as inconspicuous as possible, and I think I succeeded because a lot of my friends looked at me but none of them saw me—saw *me*—you know? My interest was in controlling the way you present yourself and [in] your clothing as a language. And like language, you can [choose] not [to] use it. I tried to say something silent.

I did another piece as a *Street Work* involving silence: a removal piece, my negative sound piece. What I did sounds fancy, [but] all I did was walk around with wax in my ears to remove the condition of sound from the environment. Now, obviously, this involved only myself, but I want you all to do it. And if it's published, you know, the text . . . and the text of all of these constituted directions in some way for performing them. To read these things is not to experience them. You have to do a lot of them. I don't say you have to go around in women's clothing, but I do intend that the reader then put wax in his ears. That's the only way that he can experience the work as far as I'm concerned. Instructions, I think, [are] literature—as instructions. Anyway, I induced silence by putting wax in my ears and walked around, and it was very strange. It was. It made me feel very peculiar, and I don't know what to say about it.

I did some pieces called "street theatre pieces" or "theatre of the street." I have some examples of them. All of them really have to be performed not only to be fully experienced, [but] to be experienced. The performer has to approximate reality as closely as possible. They have to be . . . the degree of credibility has to be perfect because they're just doing. They're just pretending—doing ordinary actions by just pretending to . . . in a sense, doing them gratuitously.

For example, ten examples:

> Standing on a corner, waiting for someone, who does not come.
>
> Hurrying or perhaps running to a destination.
>
> Dropping some coins as if accidentally and then picking them up.
>
> Stumbling and tripping or falling and then getting up.
>
> Greeting a stranger, for example by waving or calling a name—in which case this becomes a piece involving mistaken identity.
>
> Laughing to yourself as if at your own thoughts, but in public.
>
> Asking directions as if you're lost and then going to that place.
>
> Walking down the street, stopping, and then turning and going back home or wherever you came from as if you had forgotten something or had changed your mind in mid-course.
>
> Looking behind you several times as you walk, as if you're looking at something of interest—moderate interest—[but] not enough interest to make you turn around.

> And the last example . . . (Incidentally, these are only examples. Anything you do without *having* to do it or doing it in the course of your life—just because you *want* to imitate ordinary life—constitutes another example, and an equally valid one, of this idea [of] streets and theatre.) Anyway, the last one is appearing to be deeply preoccupied while you're walking and not noticing anything at all around you.

The duration of these pieces is in some cases variable. I mean the one about picking up . . . you know, dropping the coins and picking them up obviously only lasts a certain time, but you can wait for somebody as long as you want.

I did another piece in the street as part of *Street Works*. The Architectural League of New York officially sponsored *Street Works IV*, and for that I did a public nudity piece—which you might think of as a visual removal. That is to say, I walked down the street nude. I didn't have the courage to do it on Fifth Avenue at high noon. I did it only a couple of feet late at night in an obscure neighborhood. Well, I'll tell you why: because the themes of this work, as far as I'm concerned, are madness and criminality, as well as the dream. I was told later that it was a classic anxiety dream. I, in fact, dreamed it. Walking down the street without your clothes on and everybody has theirs on and you feel totally terrified. . . . Well, you have the reason to feel terrified, I can tell you. But I wanted not only to enact a dream which I'd had . . . but, I don't know . . . I was preoccupied with . . . . Well, in the modern period, like in Dickens, the theme of prison is frequent and very haunting. And in Genet, the theme of the criminal . . . I think the idea—some future idea I have for art works—is that they must be illegal. This of course is illegal, but I think if art can help to undermine the legal system in this country, I think that would be good.

The public nudity piece was a companion piece to a work I did called *Dream*. Well, it isn't called *Dream* . . . it was having this dream. Many of my works are initiated to fit situations. [They are] not conceived and then executed whenever the chance comes up but fitted to the situation. This work, *Dream*, well . . . The Architectural League had a public art opening—not public . . . the [guests] were invited but it was a huge party with a rock and roll band and everything else. And I just took a cot and put it in the hallway and put on pajamas and dropped some—took some pills and went to sleep in public for two hours. The opening was two hours so that constituted the duration of the piece.

I think of my works as theater because they exist in time. I've done pieces for actual stages—which are not really relevant to urban environments in a way, except insofar as they require an audience. Anything else to say about the dream? They asked me for an explanation for their press release, and I said it was a combination of literalism and Surrealism-literalism in that I was using my own actual processes—my biological metabolic processes—instead of processes of my imagination. I really was asleep, and I really was dreaming. I really did dream this dream too. But body art—that's a term you're going to be hearing a lot of next fall—interested me at the time. That's the literalism part. Surrealism is the obvious thing: using the unconscious as a source of creating your art work. I wanted to dream up a work, and I dreamed a classic anxiety dream. You know, there are fictional elements in all of this critical analysis, obviously. But not fictional in the sense of made up—just fictional in that this is like a performance for me because I'm dissociating myself from myself. I'm talking in a critical way about works I've done, and it's very. . . . This is a schizophrenic work. I think that's all, thank you.

From Literature to Performances (1970)

Pamphlet for *Four Theater Pieces: Vito Acconci, Scott Burton, Eduardo Costa, John Perreault* (Wadsworth Atheneum, April 14, 1970).

E.N.: *Burton curated a small number of performance/theater events such as* Four Theater Pieces *for the Wadsworth Atheneum. What follows is the introductory text written by Burton and the four artists' statements about their contributions.*

These four pieces have their genesis in literature but seek to extend that medium. Although the writers' individual intentions vary (see their separate statements), all move beyond not only the printed page but further, beyond the word itself as the unit of expression. An important, often necessary, verbal element remains—whether in the formulation of the intention or the concept, or as an adjunct or a parallel to the performed part of the work—but in no case is there the verbal self-sufficiency of traditional writing, even those in non-traditional styles. These works are not in new style, but in new mode. Their visual and/or aural aspects are at least as important as the activity of reading, and usually more important.

Of equal importance here, and more innovatory, is the use of time. Other forms of literature, such as concrete poetry, have dealt with words as one more kind of visually apprehended information, but the new "performed literature" incorporates as well the element of duration. Their existence in time is essential to the very conception of these pieces. They are thus categorizable as "theatre," for they can only be experienced in extension, as processes or sequences in time, and they control the audience's length and rate of exposure (the opposite is true of reading a book or looking at a painting.) But these works for the theatre are unlike traditional dramatic art because they exist explicitly in the same, actual time as that of the viewer instead of offering fictive times and places. These are not illusionist but literalist theatre pieces.

For this reason they have a relation to the chief form of "abstract" theatre, the dance and especially, recent dance styles which mix genres or substitute one for another. Also related are the two dominant tendencies now in the plastic arts: "process" art, which changes or is changed throughout a span of time; and "conceptual" art, which replaces purely visual with verbal modes. However, the works on this program, whatever their genesis or esthetic parallels, exist first and last in the medium of live performance and explore systematically its characteristics.

Vito Acconci, *Learning Piece*

The piece is unrehearsed; the audience is a witness to a private learning session. In one performance, the performer acts on his own time; in the other performance, I am trying to keep in time.

Performing the present piece depends on performing (adhering to the terms of) another piece, which results in extending each term, time period, of my performance (behavior, manner of reacting to stimuli.)

Scott Burton, *Compositions*

My *tableaux vivants* imitate painting and dance, two arts I studied before starting to write. They are the nonverbal half of this work of autobiographical literature. (The 30 poses for 3 figures are the combinations of 5 body positions—standing, bending, kneeling, sitting, lying—and 3 spatial relations—very close, moderately close, far apart—in symmetrical and asymmetrical versions.)

Eduardo Costa, *You see a dress.*

My piece does not imply a strong belief in the importance

of physical objects or in the importance of visual over other kinds of perception. Also, it brings theatre closer to Hypnotism and Fashion.

John Perreault, *Anthology*

My piece is an anthology of images and sounds from previous pieces. The visual images are from "Bicycle" (8/68), "Solo" (5/69), "Roll" (9/6), "T-Shirt Alphabet" (10/69) and "Basketball" (2/70.) The sound sequences are for the most part from my continuing series, begun 6/69, called "Theatre of the Invisible." I as author-performer am not interested in exhibitionism. I act and my actions are my "writings."

The *Group Behavior Tableaux*, early texts (1971–72)

Unpublished texts from the Scott Burton Papers [II.43]. Museum of Modern Art Archives, NY. © 2012 Estate of Scott Burton / Artist Rights Society (ARS), NY.

E.N.: *Burton's* Behavior Tableaux *pieces were among his most well-known works in the 1970s. In these two unpublished texts, Burton provided preliminary plans for the work that would become* Group Behavior Tableaux *first performed at the Whitney Museum of American Art on April 19, 1972 (repeated in October of that same year at the American Theatre Lab).*

Notes on "body language" piece (1971)

Description: A performance or theatre piece of about one hour. A room with a door, containing table, chairs, cot. Five male performers who do not speak. A series of unrelated episodes in which various possible relationships between members of a group are enacted. Situations expressed only in "body language" and arrangements of "personal space." Postures agree or vary, groupings change—revealing rank, degree of acceptance, tenor of occasions.

A seated; B enters; A rises; B sits, A sits. C enters; A remains seated; B remains seated; C remains standing.

Theme is psychology but not of "characters"—specific fictional individuals. Not drama. A sequence of moving tableaux vivants; performed sculpture. Not verbal but plastic and visual. But not abstract; behavior of performers imitates actuality. But not illusionistic (pantomime). Pseudo-real gestures and poses, *without* the specialized or symbolic movements of dance. "Narrative." Attitudes rather than emotions.

Requirements: Six male performers (one back-up), close in age and physical type. Actors not necessary; no acting is required. Stage manager for timing and simple off/on light cues. Performing area with back and side walls, frontal to audience but not necessarily proscenium.

35 to 40 rehearsal hours.

Theatre Project for Whitney Museum / Application to Jerome Robbins Fund (1972)

This piece has six performers, all of the same body type—tall, thin men, who seem to inhabit a large, very bare room with only a table, chairs, and cot. We watch the men interact silently, revealing their relationships to each other and to the group. There is no dialogue. B enters the room and A rises; C enters and A does not rise. D is in the room alone but stands in its very corner, facing the wall.

This is a theatre piece closely related to dance because the performers' psychological relationships are stated only through their movements, gestures, and spatial behavior. Their feelings are conveyed, as they would be in sculpture as well as in dance, by the forms, movements, and positions of their bodies in the shared space. The kind of movement is not abstract, specialized, or spectacular, as is dance movement, but is instead realistic, universal, and ordinary—walking, sitting, standing. However, the actions are performed stiffly and formally, with no naturalistic emotional expressiveness at all. The pace is slow and exactly timed. Only one confrontation takes place at a time and they follow each other without building up an overall story, as a play would. But there *is* content—the emotions of these men, toward themselves and toward each other.

The length is about one hour.

Lecture on Self (1973)

Unpublished text of a performance lecture entitled Lecture on Self, given at Oberlin College on May 5,1973. Scott Burton Papers [II.52]. Museum of Modern Art Archives, NY © 2012 Estate of Scott Burton/ Artist Rights Society (ARS), NY.

E.N.: *In the catalogue to the Oberlin exhibition for which Burton performed this piece, he offered this description: "In a solo performance of about one hour, Scott Burton will give an illustrated critical lecture on the performances of Scott Burton, who will then appear for questions."*[19] *Burton had first devised an early version of this performance in 1971 as part of his works at Finch College. A fragmentary note from 1972 indicates that he returned to it as the basis for the expanded text below. The notes reveal some of the other directions he was considering: "Autobiographical piece. / deliver lecture on own life / photos of self. / question period (combine with nudity?) / poetry reading / use lecture on self (art)?"*[20] *Burton first presented the* Lecture on Self *at the Museum of Fine Arts, Boston, on April 10, 1973. On April 25, 1973, in New York, Burton premiered an artistic alter-ego which, as his most recent work, was included as the culmination of the ultimate version of the Oberlin performance two weeks later. At the end of this lecture, he appeared as his alter ego, the "Tragic Priapic Modern American Artist," to answer questions. Given the length of the slide list, the performance likely lasted more than an hour (in keeping with the endurance tactics that he incorporated in to his earlier performances).*

The text itself offers a complex statement of Burton's attitudes toward performance and an account of the field, referencing the work of Vito Acconci, Allan Kaprow, Joseph Beuys, and Gilbert & George. I have separated the text into two sections. The first deals with his general theories on performance

---

19. Scott Burton, "Lecture on Self," Allen Memorial Art Museum Bulletin 30.3 (1973): 134.
20. Scott Burton Papers, (II.38). Museum of Modern Art Archives, NY

and his discussion of his precedents. The second section, which would have been presented continuous after the first, only exists as slide notes on Burton's own work. He narrated his earlier work in the third person, referring to himself as "this young American artist," until he names himself at the very end. In the second section, I have indicated (or added) in italics the titles or categories of the works he discusses. There were often multiple slides within each category.

The manuscript text was prepared with varying levels of completion, from some highly structured opening commentary on the nature of performance art to more abbreviated remarks on his own works. I have reconstructed the present text from the existing versions of the lecture and accompanying notes. The meticulous slide list that Burton prepared was very helpful in confirming the order of the final sections. I have integrated the structured and unstructured notes into a single document that approximates the talk given at Oberlin. Some minor editorial changes have been made in the second section to aid readability, including the correction of punctuation and the replacement of those articles, prepositions, and other connecting words Burton omitted in his note-taking style. More significant editorial additions are signaled by brackets.

Overall, the text is riddled with ironic comments about his own self-importance, all of which were mobilized to make this lecture a work of mimetic parody of the self-authoring artist and of the genre of the artist's talk. Despite this aim, the text nevertheless offers his most considered statement on performance art and the best account of his own works from this period.

I. Sculpture as Theater

Performance is, most essentially defined, sculpture as theater. By sculpture is meant no longer the stable object but simply three-dimensional visual art—whatever is offered in an artistic context that is not painting. Recent examples of this category of transformed sculpture have included not only aggregates of mutable or impermanent materials but also works of plastic art that are not constructions at all but made instead of language (conceptual and information art) or of photographs, films or diagrams (documentational art) or of theater (performance art). By theater is meant simply art in time—whatever is offered sequentially that is not music or dance or drama. Recent examples of this medium of appropriated theater—of visual art whose primary dimension is temporal— have included mobile and kinetic art, light art and technological art, materials process art, and now include performance art. Performance is in medium a form of theater but in category a form of sculpture.

This esthetic innovation is not merely formal but indicates a new cultural value, at least metaphorically. The performance artist initiates a transactional or situational relation with the viewer. The viewer becomes a member of an audience, in a collective rather than private esthetic situation. And in the changed situation of performance art, the artist—like his work—is no longer separated by a conceptual and physical gulf from the viewer, but is directly vulnerable to the reaction of the viewer. In performance art, temporality insures that the very experience of perceiving the work is central. Thus, the psychology of the viewer is a major element in the unfolding character of the performance. Thus, performance art abandons the self-criticism of classic modernist art. The role of the viewer becomes a critical role, in contrast to modernism, which, to quote Clement Greenberg,

> Modernism criticizes from the inside [....] The task of self-criticism became to eliminate from the effects of each art any and every effect that that might conceivably be borrowed from or by the medium of any other art. [....] "Purity" meant

> self-definition, and the enterprise of self-criticism in the arts became one of self-definition [. . .][21]

Performance art, by flouting self-definition and favoring elements shared with other arts, rejects purity and, by implication, rejects the ideology of the autonomy of the artwork and the self-sufficiency of the artist. Counter to this valuation of the artist's sheer individual will, which usually manifests itself stylistically in formalist abstraction, are more recent manifestations both in the art of painting (of a return to realist styles, to *shared* conceptions of the nature of appearances) and in three-dimensional art (of a direct acknowledgement of the existing situation in real time and real space which is shared by the work of art and the viewer).

Performance art reevaluates the role of the artist in the culture, submitting him to the transaction with the viewer. No matter how self-referring, apparently remote, or even autistic the preoccupations of the performance artist become, his fundamental, definitive act is his initiation of direct transaction. Performance is structurally, then, an exoteric mode—and social, cultural, and political values are prominent in the historical genesis of the mode. Performance points beyond the competence of a specialized professional artistic class, beyond modernist self-criticism, to an art of situation, in which competence is extended to the viewer, in which the audience becomes the critics.

A grammar of performance will be formulated from the temporal as well as spatial usages of the mode, and from its possible agents of activity as well as its embodying materials:

> The relation of the performance to the space it occupies is characterized by the nature of the location and the concomitant situating of the viewer.

---

21. Clement Greenberg, "Modernist Painting" [1960], reprinted in John O'Brian, ed., *Clement Greenberg: The Collected Essays and Criticism* (Chicago: University of Chicago Press, 1993), 4:85 and 4:86.

The location may be a consecrated esthetic space—a gallery or museum—or a secular space—an ordinary room, a street, a landscape. The location may be typological (a particular type of place) or specific (a particular place) or arbitrary (any place).

The relation of the viewer to the performance space may be irrelevant or important. He may be separated from, surrounding, or within its area.

The temporal characteristics of performance divide into external and internal relations. In its external relation, its situation in a stream of time which precedes it, the occasion of the performance may be necessary or arbitrary. It may need to take place at a particular time of the day, the season, the year, or the decade. Or it may be capable of execution at any time at all.

The performance may be intermittent, resumable at will, or unique and unrepeatable. Its internal treatment of time depends on its duration, which may be determined by internal necessity or may be arbitrary. If arbitrary, the length may be variable or predetermined.

The structure of the performance activity may be uninflected and undeveloping, or be systemic (with imposed design) or be relational (with a causal order of beginning, middle, and end).

The materials of performance possess no independent significance. Rather, it is their manipulation that creates meaning.

The agent of activity may be the artist, or another who becomes his surrogate, or the audience, or its surrogate.

> The performer may be rehearsed or simply directed during the performance, or he may improvise within a structure, or he may even not perform—not be aware of his role at all. The agent of performance may even be animal rather that human.

In little more than a decade, the performance has grown into a primary form, distinct from what was called "artists' theater," in which the temporal artwork was separable from the art object. Of the first generation of American performance-makers, the creators of Happenings, most members returned to the production of objects. Of those who continued to work in temporal forms, many turned to mixed-media works, thus moving away from performance, which is, however transformed, an art essentially of the human figure.

The investigation of the properties of media is a divergence from figurative traditions. Recent dance, which has absorbed most of the innovations of mixed-media art, is not performance; nor is recent drama (even the most anti-illusionistic) because both, although arts of the human figure, are collaborative. Their esthetic totalities are shaped by more than one artist: at least one author (choreographer, director, writer) in active collaboration with performing artists. The performance piece, however is not collaborative, any more than a painting is collaborative. In performance the authorship is singular, and if the agent is other than the author or his surrogate, he is usually treated as material or medium rather than independent and equal partner.

Almost all performance tends to the primary use of the artist's self. An important exception to this tendency is the work of Allan Kaprow, the major figure from the generation of Happenings who did not turn to mixed-media art or return to object-making. Kaprow seeks to move beyond individualist authorship, centrality of self, by establishing new relations between the work, the performer, and the viewer. He seeks to synthesize them into a collective whole. Instead of specialized collaborators, Kaprow's performers are participants in monumental works whose boundary between shaping and witnessing is tenuous. Kaprow's is an art of the human figure in groups, in a new kind of community.

After Kaprow, pure performance turns almost entirely to the use of the artist's own self —his body, his psyche, his history. Most recent performances have constituted "self-portraits." The use of the artist's own self, as agent and material, comes to signify the art-making process itself—one of the major themes of both modern literature and painting, from Romanticism to Abstract Expressionism.

Performance is often a visual metaphor for the previously private act of creation; it offers the public exhibition of artistic activity as such. The artist's life-role becomes the overt theme, his presence its medium. His personality becomes exemplary. The master of such self-works at this time is the European Joseph Beuys, a member of the same generation of performance artists as Kaprow, who emerged from the movement of event-makers that called itself Fluxus.

Like Kaprow, Beuys exposes a radical esthetic connected with revolutionary, utopian politics. His performances present apparently arbitrary but deeply symbolic activities that center around the artist's manipulations of illogically combined materials and things. His half-comic, half-tortured presence is at the core of the performance.

In what might be called the second generation of performance artists, the theme is almost always narrowly restricted to the self. From a liberal point of view, this is a conservative direction because it maintains the now traditional relation of artist and viewer—the artist apart and above—a relation to which Kaprow seeks alternatives. And certainly, from the point of view of esthetic innovation, the individualism of the self-centered performance is in strong tension with the drive of performance to go beyond modernist self-criticism toward re-emphasized relations with the viewer.

The obsessive exposure of the self in public has been perhaps that of Vito Acconci, whose earlier activities—the fulfilling of neutral tasks—have given way to expressionistically charged works involving mashing cockroaches on his chest, burning himself, alleged public masturbation, and disturbing strangers by standing too close to them. Such themes seem intended to exploit as well as extend the distance between artist and viewer.

This distance is emphasized, too, but in an entirely different tone, by the English artists Gilbert & George. Their witty *Singing Sculpture* replaces neurosis with vaudeville, though retaining the flavor of compulsiveness, as it turns the couple into simulated gold-faced mannequins endlessly revolving and repeatedly miming a 1920 song written and sung by two other pairs of collaborators, mirroring ironically the doubleness of the performance artists.

Of the current group of young performance artists, only one has sought to go beyond such self-directed, if exemplary, activity. His major achievement in performance has been an introduction of representational style, of mimetic and figurative elements—both in mobile objects and in the form of living tableaux. Within non-illusionist contexts, he presents quasi-fictional, even narrative content. His are the most theatricalist of current performance, often actually taking place on proscenium stages in a manner suggesting their related visual art components: the pedestal and the frame.

To a degree precedented only by Warhol's reinvention of narrative films out of his multiple-image paintings and his static-image films, the representational performances of this young American artist approach conceptions of art broader than those of either the self-defining formalist object or the self-referring performance.

His living tableaux and his object pieces form two recent series of works in different materials but with overlapping preoccupations—with the human figure, with dream states, with social relationships, with sexuality, and with art—both with the decorative or applied arts and with fine art.

The object-pieces expose the roots of performance in earlier modern styles—assemblage, kinetic sculpture, environments, found objects, and event and conceptual art. But in these object-pieces, temporality—that is to say, theatricalism—is often explicitly introduced.

II. Scott Burton's Works

Sculpture/Theater. The name reveals the subject: the juxtaposition of the category of sculpture and the medium of theater. Sculpture is represented by a common plaster cast of a female nude, and theater by the elevations, framing, and spot-lighting of proscenium staging, and—more importantly—by the silent action of the object, which slowly revolves.

Three-dimensionality itself is the main subject, but preference for figurative art is heralded.

Not a moving statue, but a form of assemblage, is this *Three-Minute Sculpture.* It has 15 objects on 400 or so feet of rope, each object visible for the 20 seconds it takes to be pulled across a stage by off-stage agents. Each of the objects has its cross, like a parade of changing characters. The objects include easily identifiable things (like a large picture frame) to objects too small for the viewer to see from his seat (like a small carved African mask). This variability of scale causes palpable constraint between the fixedness of the theater audience and the freedom of mobility of viewer of visual and plastic art. A tension between sculpture and theater is created in this sequential assemblage.

An environment strongly suggesting another meaning of the word "theatrical" (that is, unreal-looking) is this piece called *Furniture Landscape.* The artist transformed the contents of an ordinary household of furniture into the formal rooms of a wooded landscape. The representational element is so strong in its evocation of domestic space transformed that the work almost suggests a form of surreal theater set.

Furniture Pieces continue the theme of applied art objects such as furniture, but [here they are] presented sequentially on a proscenium stage, with opening and shutting curtains to suppress the changing of the pieces. Each begins to seem anthropomorphic. The variation and contrast within sequence creates drama of objects irresistibly humanized and personalized:

latent figuration in vertical stool
& chair
contrasting pair
matching pair like twins

Changes introduces an actual human but as a subordinate element in another sequential assemblage, [here of] several changes of clothes. The performer repeatedly changed her clothes behind a screen in a performance whose activity consisted in the successive exhibition of a number of garments. Revealing, like the furniture pieces, [the artist's] interest in applied arts, such as clothing assemblage, [this work] also reveals a descendancy from the Surrealist use of mannequins. The woman is dehumanized into a support for clothing.

Disguise Piece. Another clothing piece: use garment not as an element of assemblage but as a costume or disguise. An apparent woman is seen, then an apparent man. However, the woman is a man and the man is a woman. Secondary sexual characteristics illuminate the transforming role of clothing in art. The emphasis is still on the objects here (the clothing) and not the actions of the figures.

Another living assemblage, *Animal Piece*, exhibited as sculpture: a brown rabbit and a green canary in a white, stage-like cage, The work suggests the puzzling combines of Surrealism, but a new emphasis on the work's action (in the form of mutual reactions of two species) becomes the main theme. The action is framed in the cubic construction of the miniature surrogate picture-stage.

A work advancing by a leap to an entirely new form of figurative narration is the artist's first *Slide Novella*, the ultimate conversion of sculpture to theater, of object to performance. The object: 40 color transparencies projected for 10 seconds each. Fully narrative and illusionist, the work—in a short-story-like structure—follows a young woman through a day. But for all its strong psychological content, it also remains a sequence of objects exhibited to the viewer. The regularity of timing acts on the performance like a picture plane in painting: it restrains the work's illusionism. The emotional theme is distanced by the schematic modular regularity of the sequence of 40 slides at 10 seconds each.[22]

This work is the culmination of the artist's object-pieces. His other recent series, the *Living Tableaux*, make equally far-reaching explorations into representational performance.

His living tableaux also approach the agent of the performance as an object to be subjected to time, but they introduce

---

22. Burton replaced a more extensive description of Slide Novella that was, in an earlier state of the lecture, presented after *Ten Tableaux* and *Allegorical Tableau*. He wrote of *Slide Novella:* "A pure narrative of almost cinematic story, whose form is the projections for an audience, of a group of 40 color transparencies for 10 seconds each. The first part is of a woman looking out a window. The work is called *Slide Novella* and follows her through her day in a short-story-like series of undramatic episodes that project a strong melancholy. She makes a phone call but reaches no one. She takes a walk to the waterfront but sees no one; she returns home and goes to bed; asleep, she dreams that she had found a pink scarf on her earlier walk. She also dreams that she is lying nude in a red room with a broken telephone beside her. Then she wakes up & the story ends with no other people appearing.This wholly narrative piece about being alone presents an illusion broken only by the slow and equal pacing of the images—each is shown for ten seconds, resulting in a regularity that acts in performance like the picture plane in painting. That is, it serves to restrain the illusionist aspect of the work and with non-relational, non-expressive divisions, for all its representative psychological content. Burton's slide novella is finally a collection of 40 objects exhibited in sequence to the viewer. The narrative thus provides the variations within the containing grid-like overall structure of the performance."

the object of the human body. The performers are denied dramatic or choreographic collaboration and are used instead as if they were acting neutrally and automatically, like statues—effigies of themselves. They herald a large-scale art of the human figure, referring constantly to heroic narrative figure compositions in frozen or slowly mobile tableaux.

This series started by still using people as if they were abstract entities, in purely schematic designs, in a work called *Thirty Compositions*, in which three women took 20-second poses separated out by blackouts so that no motion was even visible to the viewer. Though the design is systemic—15 symmetrical compositions performed at varying degrees of closeness and upright, leaning, kneeling, and sitting and lying, and 15 asymmetrical ones involving the same set of variables in an asymmetrical set—the 30 compositions resemble [each other] in scheme but not in form.

Bathers. An equally schematic and modular performance introduced an iconic element, however, with images of women posing as sunbathers. The performers entered at regular intervals to join the accumulating group, transforming the stage into the image of a live horizontal landscape. Still, the work introduced a quasi-narrative content indirectly suggesting a gathering in a landscape—a representational figure composition. The urge to make living pictures on a large scale produced the performance.

Ten Tableaux. A group of tableaux with 12 stationary performers on a revolving stage.[23] This form marks another instance of the artist's dependence on progressively revealed three-dimensionality to introduce the element of theater into sculpture. But in this piece, an overtly theatrical subject is introduced. First, the performers imitate statues: in a pediment or in small groups in a statue park, even using actual

23. Burton found that the theater space he had been provided for his performance at the University of Iowa was equipped with a revolving stage. He expanded the *Ten Tableaux* piece in reaction.

pedestals. Or, they imitate ordinary life actions like walking, dancing, and sleeping. Explicit narrative content ultimately breaks out in these slowly revolving tableaux in one piece that illustrates a specific moment in time—a moment in which all the performers are interrupted by something unseen to the viewer, something they all turn to regard. In such a theatricalist tableau, the performance reaches a full illusionism— as it does in one depicting a similarly critical and even more tense moment. A tableau of rape, displaying the group of women on one side and men on the opposite side, with one of each meeting in frozen violence in the center. These tableaux are as narrative as possible in content, but their unfolding in time is still abstract and schematic. They merely revolve.

But they are later followed by a very different piece, an entirely motionless tableau, whose lack of development in time, whose frontal frozenness, serves to accentuate the work's literary, near narrative content. It is in fact an allegorical tableau vivant. Its performers are again de-individualized by disguises: one woman wears a white dress and bears a lit candle, another wears black and has the mask of a grotesque. A man kneels, looking up, his arms bound in chains, a youth lies naked face down as if sleeping or dead, holding a seashell. The meaning of the allegory, although not available to the viewer, nevertheless still seems to exist—and to exist as the primary if dream-like force of this performance.

Poses. Also approaching the narrative performance ever closer was a performance in which a young woman assumed pose after pose, all of them drawn from a popular sexual iconography. [This piece] presented an oblique portrait of an isolated figure, a pregnant theme of his work.

In his most ambitious performance using living tableaux so far, he has made the order and length purely thematic—abandoning the last link with Minimalist and systemic structure. A work called *Behavior Tableaux*,[24] in which emotionally charged material (this time of social transaction rather than isolation) is also present and also distanced. This time [there are not] evenly spaced episodes. The episodes or tableaux are determined in length and in order by purely internal, narrative or thematic, demands. The displacement was accomplished in this performance by literally distancing the viewer 50 feet from the performers' space and by the extremely slowed-down and simplified—always neutral, never expressive—style of movement used by all the performers.[25] The performers also resembled each other in body type (tall and thin) and in style of dress. With these factors and with their facial features erased by the distance, the performers were thus de-individualized. (The institutional aspect of the furniture also contributes.) The meaning of each tableau is conveyed tentatively by the groupings, completely still or slow-moving, of the performers.

The initial theme of this performance piece is the behavior of concord—of equals existing in mutual acceptance. They group equidistantly and turn toward one another, or they slowly join together in an intimate group.

A second theme, however, reverses the first and introduces tensions, divisions, and disharmonies among the group. The [performers] separate into sub-groups or become isolated from each other. Or, they turn away from each other, as in a sequence in which one turns his face slowly away from another who has just entered. He continues across the stage-room to be treated identically by two other previous occupants of the space and finally to settles alone in an unaccompanied spot. A second

24. This is the 1972 work presented at the Whitney Museum of American Art. It is generally referred to as *Group Behavior Tableaux*.

25. Enforcing a great distance between viewers' seats and the *Behavior Tableaux* became a key tactic in Burton's presentation of these works. For some, he reached 70 to 80 feet. For instance, when *Pair Behavior Tableaux* was performed in the auditorium of the Guggenheim Museum in 1976, Burton limited the attendance to 30 people and had folding chairs set up for them behind the built-in rows of seating, all of which he insisted remain empty. See Michael Feingold, "Mr. Burton Makes Music With Bodies," *Village Voice* (March 8, 1976): 93.

intruder into the space causes a second head-aversion by one of the occupants, and ultimately even the performer who was previously shunned by the seated performers averts in turn his face from the performer approaching him. This theme includes confrontations between members of the group, which oppose similar tableaux of the earlier theme of the harmony of equals.

A third theme of these *Behavior Tableaux* is that of authoritarianism. The group divides into a one-to-four relation, with the individual dominant over the group. Whether he stands before them or they before him, the psycho-social interpretation of their spatial relationship must reveal his dominance.

The reverse of this theme is provided in a fourth theme that retains the one-to-four dispersal of the group but makes the individual into a sub-dominant class of one—very different from a sub-dominant class of four. Isolation, it is implied, depicts the position of low status as an intolerable and crushing one, in contrast to the self-assertiveness of the individual who is dominant.

The later themes are stated more dramatically or theatrically, as if to compensate for the intensity. This piece produces strong distribution of the sense of experiential time in the viewer. Its series of 70 long and slow tableaux deal with some of the most fundamental aspects of human social behavior. The achievement of this piece is to have found the exact location where human psychology and visual art meet: in the non-verbal language of the body. [The *Behavior Tableaux*'s] placement, posture, and gesture and its observations and violations of personal-space and body-surrounding territories reveal the unconscious attitudes literally shaping and deploying [body language]. This series of intense themes in a highly remote style extends—as surely as it is rooted in—a modern sculptural revival offered by inanimate Surrealist tableaux by Duchamp and Dali, and later Segal and Kienholz, and a tradition of monumental, three-dimensional figure compositions that, of earlier modernists, only Rodin attempted.

To such an ambition, the revival of an heroic figure art, have these performances aspired, evolving far from an earlier, intimate-scale series of performances called "Self-Works."[26] A series of four pieces, they used the artist's own body and psyche directly and literally, as did many other artists in the late 1960s. His self was the figure in a figure/ground relation with the performance locations—city streets occupied at the same time by other outdoor urban performances—as context with unique characteristics. Though close to a number of other artists who were also involved in using themselves directly as subject or medium, these performances using the self foreshadow some of the themes of his later, post-Conceptual performances.

Ear piece. One of these [*Self-Works*] was a piece in which he attempted to block temporarily his sense of hearing, his intention was to incorporate body processes into the work of art. But the piece is perhaps more interesting as it prefigures the theme of the isolated individual of the earlier tableaux and narrative performances.

Disguise. Likewise, the artist's intent in clothing as a variety of applied assemblage is prefigured in an early street disguise piece in which his intention was to create an invisible performance by going unrecognized among a group of people to whom he was previously known. He appears in the very unobtrusive guise of a woman shopper.

Dream. Another of this series of *Self-Works* initiated his incorporation of dream states into his performances in a piece in which he slept through a public art opening, creating a

---

26. *Self-Works* is the category Burton gave to all of his performances involving his own person. These include his contributions to the *Street Works* events in 1969, but the category also extends to his other interventions into public spaces. The executed *Street Works/Self-Works* come mainly from 1969, though he discussed further examples in 1970 in his lecture at the University of Iowa (see "Literalist Theater" in this volume). At this point in the lecture, Burton broke with his otherwise chronological account of his work, returning to the earlier *Self-Works* to set up the introduction of his alter ego at the conclusion of the lecture.

photo-tableau. He had furthermore directed himself to dream of himself doing a new outdoor performance.

Nude. In a literalist foreshadowing of his turn to narrative performance, he later acted out his dream. It had been of himself walking naked in the street. This performance also introduces the theme of the extreme, bizarre, or alienated behavior later developed in the narrative pieces and tableaux.

The name of the artist is Scott Burton. Burton's style is generally characterized by a dual Surrealist and minimal or purist combination of oneiric or fantastic intensity and formal distancing devices. Its formal characteristics are posedness and deliberate artificiality, slowness, and material austerity. These play against the frequently disturbing themes that may be stated either comically or tragically. The frontality of imagery and the preoccupations with clothing, costume, furniture, and settings [both] support what must be the most radical theatricalist position of any artist working in performance modes. Whether this mimetic and representational direction represents a return, in a new form, of earlier performance's valuing of widespread social accessibility—or whether such a conjunction is impossible in an unviolated modernist innovative sculptural context—is a question that Burton's future performances will help to answer.

At this point, he seems still to be held back by appeals to the sensibility of a highly initiated audience but seems also to predict a new large-scale, three-dimensional figurative art treating accessibly the life experience of the viewer and by extension, the preoccupations of larger culture.[27]

---

27. The manuscript ends here, with the final slide listed being Burton's own signature. The Oberlin lecture was followed by a blackout during which time Burton removed the suit and short wig he had been wearing and re-appeared on stage (with his own long hair) in a pair of decorated overalls out of which a dildo protruded prominently. This was the "Tragic Priapic Artist" alter ego that was Burton's most recent work and, fittingly, the final reveal of the lecture. His intentionally parodic mimesis of the stereotype of the "modern American artist" with this character was meant to acknowledge and to mock the "sensibility of a highly initiated audience." I discuss this character and the performance at length in my forthcoming book.

Make a Political Statement (1974)

In Joshua Cohn, Walter Robinson, and Edit deAk, eds., "We Asked a Number of Artists to Respond to This: Make a Political Statement," *Art-Rite* 6 (1974): 24–25.

E.N.: *Burton's statement was the longest of fifteen responses to the* Art-Rite *editors' imperative—other respondents included Ray Johnson, Adrian Piper, May Stevens, Howardena Pindell, and Lawrence Weiner.*

"Make a political statement." Or at least, a statement about politics. The art class is a conservative and stagnant class. It cannot hope to become a politically active class in its group social behavior (viz., the May 1970 Emergency Art Government). It can only hope to become politically alive if it becomes culturally alive; this it can do by redirecting its real energy, which lies *in its works.* But so far artists have not produced new styles or kinds of art that relate to more than a small part of the rest of the people or that have any vital relation to the energies—expressed or frustrated—of the whole culture. Only if we do so can we serve the better of those people and energies. There have been a few exceptions so far: (1) Tatlin was right when he designed/invented a new stove, a set of clothing, an orniopter, and a media megatower. (He also wrote, in 1932, "Work in the field of furniture and other articles of use is only just beginning: the emergence of new cultural institutions, vital in our daily lives, institutions in which the working masses are to live, think and develop their aptitudes, demands from the artist not only a feeling for the superficially decorative but above all for things which fit the new existence and its dialectic.") (2) Joseph Beuys is right when he says that the creativity of all men is our responsibility. (3) Robert Smithson was right when he prophetically started working on a land reclamation project, addressing the industrial desolation that every other modern artist has found picturesque. (4) Andy Warhol is right (in another way: the semantic rather than the pragmatic) when he makes an accessible or popular narrative film, *Frankenstein*, designed for broad audiences but keeps his subversive attitudes—Artaud speaking through *The Addams Family*. And a partial exception is the Women's Movement in art, which has not produced any new conceptions of art itself. (However, in what it has done to institutions and habits of taste, it is far advanced in comparison to the Gay Movement.) No other important instances from the area of "good" or "real" art occur to me. But these few could be inspiring.

Odd Years (1975)

Statement included in the xerox catalogue for the exhibition *Lives: Artists Who Deal With Peoples' Lives (Including Their Own) As the Subject And/Or Medium of Their Work,* curated by Jeffrey Deitch and held at the Fine Arts Building, New York, 1975.

E.N.: *Burton created this accompanying text-based work for the xerox catalogue to the* Lives *exhibition held at the Fine Arts Building in New York from November 29 to December 20, 1975. (He showed the 1975 work* Dream Sex *in the exhibition.) For the catalogue work, he chose only the odd-numbered years since he began making art in 1969, recounting the works in which he had used himself as the medium. The narrative begins with the* Self-Works, *but the development of his* Lecture on Self *takes prominence.*

1969 Appears in public as a woman.
Drugs self to sleep at public art opening.
Runs naked in streets.
1971 Appears as art critic lecturing on own art.
1973 Expands critical lecture on self.
Appears as tragic Priapic artist.
1975 Narrates wet dream.

ACKNOWLEDGEMENTS

David J. Getsy

This book owes a great deal to Julia Klein of Soberscove Press, who first approached me about a Burton archives project and was receptive to the idea of an ambitious collection such as this. I am very grateful for our discussions and her many contributions to its final form. I would also like to thank Kristi McGuire and Rita Lascaro for their hard work during the editing and design process. I could not have completed work on this book without the help of my research assistant, Beth Capper. In addition to her acumen and attention to detail, many conversations with her about Burton's writings were instrumental in my thinking about the project. My research on Burton has deepened through conversations and interviews with his friends, and I would like to thank Eduardo Costa, Mac McGinnes, Jane Kaufman, Michael Harwood, and Robert Pincus-Witten for their insights. Further conversations with Athena Tacha, James Rondeau, and David Raskin were crucial in working out other details. I am very grateful to the archivists at the Museum of Modern Art—in particular, Jonathan Lill and Michelle Harvey—for their help on my many visits to the archive. As holder of Burton's estate and copyright, the Museum of Modern Art allowed for the publication of archival materials and, indeed, made the project a reality. Much work was also done in the Archives of American Art at the Smithsonian Institution, and I would like to especially thank Marissa Bourgoin for her assistance. The staff at the Flaxman Library of the School of the Art Institute of Chicago and the Ryerson and Burnham Libraries of the Art Institute of Chicago provided frequent support of the project. Artists Rights Society (ARS) of New

York facilitated the publication of the texts and images. There are many to thank for their assistance with permissions for images and texts: Vito Acconci and Bernadette Mayer; Chris Baczek and Steven Eichner at the Utah Museum of Fine Art; Helen Cowdrey at Matthew Marks Gallery; Anne Bast Davis at the San Francisco Museum of Modern Art; Jessica Duffet and Tom Long at Castelli Gallery; Katherine Gile at Alexander and Bonin Gallery; Amanda Granek at *ARTnews*; Pascale Keller at the Kunsthalle Bern; Melanie Kress at American Federation of Arts; Katie Langjahr, Fernanda Meza and Chelsea Radigan at ARS; Janet Mackenzie Spens and Manuel Benavides at *Studio International*; Alvin Novak; Annie Ochmanek at *Artforum*; Tricia Smith at Art Resource; and Brian Washburn at Washburn Gallery. And finally, I am indebted to Jude Hansen for reminding me about the vitality of theater and so many other things.

INDEX